EMPIRES

EMPIRES

A Historical and Political Sociology

Krishan Kumar

polity

First published in 2021 by Polity Press

Polity Press
65 Bridge Street
Cambridge CB2 1UR, UK

Polity Press
101 Station Landing
Suite 300
Medford, MA 02155, USA

ISBN-13: 978-1-5095-2834-9
ISBN-13: 978-1-5095-2835-6 (pb)

A catalogue record for this book is available from the British Library.

Typeset in 10.5 on 12 pt Adobe Sabon by
Servis Filmsetting Ltd, Stockport, Cheshire
Printed and bound in Great Britain by TJ Books Limited

For further information on Polity, visit our website:
politybooks.com

To the students, staff, and faculty at the University of Virginia

Contents

Preface

Empires have been the commonest form – the "default" form, it has been said – of political organization for most of recorded history. They appeared at the dawn of human civilization and lasted – at least – until the second half of the twentieth century. They have been the subject of speculation by some of the greatest thinkers and writers, such as Herodotus, Ibn Khaldun, and Edward Gibbon. Novelists such as Joseph Conrad, Joseph Roth, Robert Musil, and V. S. Naipaul have made of them a searching inquiry. Artists such as Titian, David, and Delacroix painted them. Critics of empire such as Frantz Fanon and Edward Said have written of their lasting and, to them, deeply injurious effects.

After a period of almost ostentatious indifference in the European societies that once governed vast empires, empires have once more become the object of interest and of intense scrutiny there. Historians, sociologists, and political and literary theorists have turned their attention to them. There have been several television treatments of them, often resulting in popular books, such as those of Niall Ferguson and Jeremy Paxton on the British Empire. Opinion surveys record the return of a certain pride in empire among European populations. Nor is it only there. In Turkey, a television series – *The Magnificent Century* – on the life of the great sixteenth-century Ottoman emperor Suleyman the Magnificent has been immensely popular, and commentators have observed the spread of something like "Ottomania" there. China, too, has begun to re-assess its imperial past, no longer – as in the early days of communism – dismissing it as irredeemably "feudal" and obscurantist.

Unlike an earlier generation, and in distinction from more popular treatments, scholars today have tended to be cautious about making large-scale generalizations about empires. They have chosen to focus on restricted sets of empires, in particular regions and periods. There has been a particular interest in the modern European overseas empires that rose with the Portuguese and the Spanish in the sixteenth century, and continued with the Dutch, the French, and the English/British in the seventeenth and eighteenth centuries. The contemporaneous land empires of the Ottomans, the Russians, and the Habsburgs have usually been treated separately. Similarly, non-Western empires, such as the Chinese Empire and the Muslim empires of the Arabs, the Mughals, and the Safavids, also come mainly under the scrutiny of specialists in their cultures and history. For their part, the pre-Columbian empires of South America – the Incas, the Aztecs – are the preserve of experts in New World civilizations, seen as based on very different principles from those of Eurasia.

Particularly marked in this literature is the separation of "ancient" and "modern" empires. The early Mesopotamian and Egyptian empires, the Persian Empire and that of Alexander the Great, the Hellenistic empires down to the Roman Empire, have all been intensively studied. But they tend to be regarded as radically different from the empires that came later – above all, the overseas empires of the Europeans. This is seen as partly a matter of technology – difficulties of communication, etc. – but it is also seen as a difference of principle, in what the empires meant to the people concerned and what they strove to achieve.

This book is aware of differences, between Western and non-Western empires, and between earlier and later empires. For the first, the importance of Rome, and of Christianity, in the Western case, is as clear as that of other "world religions" and ideologies, such as Islam and Confucianism, in non-Western empires. Similarly, I stress temporality in empire – the awareness of past predecessors, and how different epochs give rise to different types of empire. The book discusses, in particular, two important "breaks" or dividing lines: the one marked by the "Axial Age" of world religions in the first millennium BCE; the other by the phase of conquest and colonization that began with the fifteenth- and sixteenth-century European "voyages of discovery." The second, I argue, marks a fundamental divide in the history of empires, with far-reaching consequences for the subsequent development of the world.

But I am equally concerned to stress the commonalities of empire, the shared things that, across time and space, allow us to speak of "empires" as a distinct species at all. Even societies that, like China, came late to using the language of empire to describe their long-lasting political system, were concerned to show how similar their empires were to others of the type, especially in the West. By the late nineteenth century, a common understanding of empire had come to link the various expressions of it in many different areas of the world, and at different times in world history. Not surprisingly, given their prominence in the world at that time, the European empires often supplied the model of empire, the idea of what it took to be an empire.

But the European empires themselves had a long history, and drew on traditions of empire that went back to the Romans, and, behind them, the empire of Alexander the Great. Alexander himself had continued, in many respects, the great Persian Empire of the Achaemenids that he had conquered, while the Achaemenids were indebted in their turn to the longstanding imperial tradition – Assyrian, Babylonian – in Mesopotamia, of which they were the inheritors and successors. Empires were linked in a variety of ways, allowing for the frequent movement of ideas and institutions across space and time. The concept of the *translatio imperii*, the handing over or passing on of empire, was one linking device that can be applied to many empires other than the Western ones for which it was originally invented.

That concept, and the idea of a "tradition of empire" to which it gave rise, are among the things explored in this book. Others include the relation between rulers and ruled in empires, where I argue for a symbiotic rather than a purely oppositional relationship; the connections between empires and nation-states, normally seen as antithetical principles but which can be shown to be intimately related and to exhibit in practice many similarities, even though ultimately diverging in their consequences; the reasons for the fall of empires; the question of whether, even after the formal end of the epoch of empires, they still persist in some form, while, in any case, leaving long-lasting legacies. Throughout, I draw upon the whole range of empires, East and West, and upon the whole history of empires since earliest times. Clearly, in a short work of this kind, this has to be selective; the pre-Columbian empires of South America, in particular, get short shrift, as do African empires. But China, as perhaps the most important non-Western empire, gets considerable attention, as, to a lesser extent, do the Muslim empires of the Arabs, the Mughals, the Safavids, and the Ottomans. I also consider the case of the "American Empire," often seen as an outlier.

This is one of the several ways in which this book differs from my recent *Visions of Empire: How Five Imperial Regimes Shaped the World* (2017). That book was mainly about the modern European empires. This book ranges more widely, in time and space, which allows me to deal with questions not considered in that earlier study.

Empire, this book stresses, has been a worldwide experience. This is what makes it so instructive an object of inquiry. It also suggests that the story of so widespread and long-lasting a form is not likely to be over.

Acknowledgments

I am grateful to the many students at the University of Virginia who have, over the years, taken my courses on empires and world civilizations. This book is really for them; it has been shaped by many of the questions that we have discussed, and their contributions have been invaluable. Aspects of it have also been presented in lectures at the University of Hong Kong; the University of New South Wales, Australia; Zhejiang University, China; the Higher School of Economics, St. Petersburg; the University of Copenhagen; University College, Dublin; the University of Basel; the Washington History Seminar; the University of Texas at Austin; and the University of Chicago. David Palmer, Saliha Belmessous, Dingxin Zhao, Alexander Semyonov, Peter Fibiger Bang, Siniša Malešević, Matthias Leanza, Dane Kennedy, Wm. Roger Louis, and Steven Pincus, respectively, were responsible for these visits, and I thank them as well as the participants at the lectures. Others who have continued to be companionable fellow students of empires, and from whom I have learned much, include John A. Hall, Chris Hann, Sankar Muthu, and Jennifer Pitts. A conference organized by Larry Wolff at the Remarque Institute of New York University on "The Decline and Fall of Empires" was both very enjoyable and highly stimulating. I also want to thank Nigel Biggar for inviting me to participate in his ongoing series of conferences on "Ethics and Empire" at Christ Church, Oxford, which brings together distinguished scholars of empires of every place and period. And grateful thanks, as always, go to the dedicated staff at the Alderman Library of the University of Virginia, especially its ILL/LEO section.

At Polity, I want to thank Jonathan Skerrett for commissioning this book, and for his help in giving it its final shape. Thanks also go to

Karina Jákupsdóttir for her great efficiency in seeing the manuscript through the production process. Thanks also to Leigh Mueller for her attentive and scrupulous copy-editing. I'm grateful to both for their patience in the face of many deadlines not met. Finally, I want to thank – again – Katya Makarova, my most attentive reader and one whose keen and discerning eye has saved me from many awkward phrases and unclear passages. We have a common interest in empires, and conversations with her have helped me immeasurably in clarifying my thoughts and sharpening my perceptions.

Krishan Kumar
Charlottesville, Virginia

I
Empires in Time and Space

The Problem of Definition: A Family of Meanings

"Definition," the great sociologist Max Weber once said, "can be attempted, *if at all*, only at the conclusion of the study" (1978: I, 399; my emphasis). Weber, as a great admirer, would also have been sympathetic to Friedrich Nietzsche's parallel observation that "only that which has no history can be defined" (1956: 212). Since all human ideas and practices have a history, that more or less rules out attempts at definition in the human (or social) sciences. In any case, both Weber and Nietzsche caution us against the efficacy – if not the impossibility – of defining phenomena in human society. Whether we are speaking of concepts or institutions, their protean character makes it extremely difficult to pin them down, like butterflies in neat glass cabinets.

Empires come in many shapes and sizes. They also evolve historically, both within themselves, as particular empires, and also collectively, as types of rule. That means that Weber's and Nietzsche's cautions apply to any and all attempts to define them. The danger is, at one level, an all-encompassing vacuity, a cover-all definition that is so general and abstract as to be virtually useless when considering particular cases; at another level, it leads to elaborate attempts to classify empires by type, or to distinguish them by historical periods or geographical regions, such that comparisons become awkward and difficult, if not impossible.

The approach in this book is not to attempt a precise definition of empire at the outset. That would lead to just the sort of straitjacket feared by Weber (for a famous example, look at the problems encountered by Durkheim in basing his *Elementary Forms of the Religious Life* on a strict definition of religion at the very beginning). If some sort of definition appears, then it will do so largely by emergence, as one goes through the material and discusses specific cases and issues. At the end of the book, perhaps, not just the reader but the author might have a better sense of the nature of the entity under consideration. At the very least, we might begin to see the "family resemblances," Wittgenstein-style, between different uses and meanings of the term "empire" (cf. Cooper 2005: 26–7).

That, at any rate, is the hope. Of course, even if they don't have precise definitions, words must have meanings (though, again, often a range), and so we must give some sort of meaning to the word "empire." At its most basic, and consistent with its origin in Latin *imperium*, it means absolute or sovereign rule over a people or territory, without the right of appeal to any earthly outside power (though not necessarily excluding appeal to a divine or supramundane authority). This was the earliest use of the term, during the Roman Republic. As the Republic became an Empire, the term was extended to mean rule over a multiplicity of peoples and lands, as in the *Imperium Romanum* (hence the usual connotation of empire with large or extensive political entities) (Koebner 1961: 4–5, 11–16).

Both meanings continue up to and including the present, though certainly in many current uses it is the second feature – rule over many peoples and lands, or of a "core" over various "peripheries" – that has tended to predominate (e.g. Howe 2002: 14–15; Osterhammel 2014: 428; Streets-Salter and Getz 2016: 3–4). Together, they allow us to distinguish empires, however broadly or imprecisely, from other political entities such as nation-states, though in practice, as we shall see, there can be considerable overlaps between empires and nation-states. For instance, "core" and "periphery" can be found in many large nation-states – e.g. Britain, France and Spain – as well as empires (hence the concept of "internal colonialism" – see further below). More helpful is the distinction between "metropole" or "mother country" and "colonies," though for obvious reasons that applies mostly to overseas empires and can be problematic with land empires, which often do not have anything that can clearly be designated colonies. Equally vexing is the attempt to distinguish between nation-states as having "citizens" and empires as having "subjects," since, until as late as 1948, the inhabitants of the United Kingdom – not generally thought of as an empire – were subjects of the British crown, not citizens.

Two other terms need to be noted. "Imperialism" is an

etymologically logical extension of empire (*imperium*), but, surprisingly, it does not seem to have been used until the mid nineteenth century, when it was popularized to describe the rule of Napoleon III and his Second Empire in France. The British adopted the term, at first disparagingly, as a synonym for Bonapartism, and later more approvingly, to describe their own rule in the British Empire. But the term nearly always carried a whiff of disapproval, a feature that became even more pronounced under the scrutiny of anti-imperial liberals and socialists. The liberal J. A. Hobson's *Imperialism* (1902) began the process, which, under Hobson's influence, was carried further by Marxists such as Lenin, Rosa Luxemburg, and Rudolf Hilferding, who analyzed – and denounced – imperialism as the desperate last measure of an embattled capitalism (Koebner and Schmidt 1964: chs. 4–8; Kiernan 1974: 1–68).

But, by the mid twentieth century, "imperialism" had largely been displaced by "colonialism," reflecting the view more from the colonies, or ex-colonies – the anti-colonial "Third World" – than from the metropole.[1] While imperialism could be, and was, defended by some thinkers, colonialism was, almost by definition, in the post First-World War environment of Wilsonian "self-determination" and nationalism, described as an evil (Manela 2009). Increasingly, in the large literature on empire produced by left-wing writers, European and non-European, both imperialism and colonialism carried connotations of oppression and exploitation. It was mainly this that led "empire" to become a dirty word by the second half of the twentieth century: to speak up for empire, as for instance the British statesman Winston Churchill did in the 1950s, was to show oneself incorrigibly reactionary and outdated.

A late refinement of "colonialism" has been the concept of "internal colonialism." This refers to the idea that many so-called nation-states have in fact been formed by an internal process of incorporation, whereby a core people or nation have conquered or swallowed up their neighbors. Examples would include Great Britain or the United Kingdom, in which the English conquered the Welsh and the Irish, and forced the Scots into a "parliamentary union," to form a composite state of four nationalities: an internal "English empire" (Hechter 1999; Davies 2000). France too – present-day France of the "Hexagon" – has also been said to have been created by an imperial process, in which the French kings based on the Île-de-France gradually expanded their power to take in adjoining lands and principalities – Burgundy, Brittany, Provence, etc. – thereby creating a centralized and culturally homogenized France (Weber 1976: 485; Goldstone and Haldon 2010: 18).

The concept of internal colonialism has many attractions, not least in undermining many of the spurious claims made by and on behalf of nation-states (Kumar 2010). It has found favor with a wide range of scholars, who have applied it to such matters as apartheid in South Africa, the relation of the black minority to the white majority in the United States, and Stalin's forced collectivization of the peasantry in the Soviet Union. Its very versatility and adaptability, covering so many different types of situations, has been seen as one of its weaknesses as a theoretical concept. The fact that it works mainly by an "artificial analogy" with conventional colonialism has also been seen as a serious methodological problem. Nevertheless, even its critics have acknowledged its usefulness in many spheres – in showing, for instance, the interaction of external and internal factors in the development of societies, as when perceptions and policies toward native peoples in the colonies are brought back home and govern the treatment of groups within the metropolitan society (Hind 1984: 553, 564).

One further usage should be mentioned. Some writers, following an influential article by two prominent imperial historians, John Gallagher and Ronald Robinson (1953), have wished to speak of "informal" as well as "formal" empire. Informal empire refers to a situation, such as obtained in the relation between Britain and parts of Latin America in the nineteenth century, where a state does not formally exercise sovereignty over another territory or people but displays a high degree of control, especially over its economic operations. While such situations undoubtedly existed and continue to do so (one source of the widespread talk of a twentieth-century "American Empire"), the notion of informal empire covers such a large number of cases and is so imprecise in its meaning – where does "control" begin and end? – that many have found it best to avoid it in their studies of empire. That sound advice will generally be followed in this book. However, in view of the importance of the case, and the fact that it has been the source of much interest and attention, we will, in the last chapter of this book, consider the question of how far America – the USA – can be thought of and studied as an empire.

In general, while the use of particular terms and concepts is unavoidable, we must always be aware of the range of meanings they convey, the sometimes conflicting elements they display, and above all the historical and cultural contexts in which they are employed. As an especially important example, consider that *imperium* is a Western term, in a Western language (Latin). It has given rise to most of the modern European equivalents (English "empire," French *empire*, Italian *impero*, Spanish *imperio*; Germans use *Reich* for the political form, but also have, more figuratively, *imperium* and also *imperialismus*, imperialism). In other words, when we use "empire" or any other European equivalent, we must be aware that we are dealing with a term that has a Western history and that applies in the first place to Western experience. That makes problematic its application to non-Western forms, ancient and modern, even when we wish – as we often do – to speak of the "Chinese Empire," the "Mughal Empire," the "Safavid Empire." Even more difficulties arise with the ancient "Egyptian Empire," the "Inca Empire," or the "Aztec Empire" – not to mention the "Commanche Empire." In most of these cases, there are no words in their languages that translate as "empire," as understood in the West. What, we might wonder, do they have in common? Why call them all "empires?" Why not simply use indigenous terms and explore their local and particular meanings?

This need not make us despair of finding any similarities or common meanings ("family resemblances"). For one thing, Western political vocabulary has been spreading across the world, with ever-intensifying force, since the 1789 French Revolution. The movement was given added impetus by the worldwide spread of the European empires, especially from the nineteenth century onward. So, vol-untarily or involuntarily, European social and political terms and thought – the state, the nation, empire, Marxism – had become the property of the entire world by the twentieth century. Moreover, even before that, what we can agree to call empires – e.g. Rome and China – interacted with each other in various ways. Merchants and missionaries criss-crossed the world, carrying ideas as well as goods and people. Certain figures, such as Alexander the Great, became emblems of empire throughout Eurasia. Whatever the differ-ent terms used for what we call empires, therefore, they might carry a similar resonance, stress certain common ideas and values. That makes comparison possible.

In the chapters that follow, we shall be tracing that movement of vocabulary and those interactions – by no means all one-way – that allow us to speak of empire in a generic way, always with an eye on specific differences. But first we must make a map of empire. We must lay out our examples, show the range of empires across space and time. We will only be able to deal with a handful of them, though they will be among the most significant. But it will be helpful, at the start, to get a sense of the totality of the imperial story.

Empires Ancient, Classical and Modern: Two Watersheds in the History of Empires

John Darwin, in his masterly account of "global empires," *After Tamerlane*, has said that "empire (where different ethnic communities fall under a common ruler) has been the default mode of political organization throughout most of history. Imperial power has usually been the rule of the road" (2008: 23; see also Howe 2002: 1; Goldstone and Haldon 2010: 19). Darwin is perfectly aware that there have been other political forms: tribes, chiefdoms, city-states, nation-states, leagues, and federations. But he is right to stress the ubiquity and longevity of empires – the fact that so much of recorded human history has been imperial history.[2] The earliest human civilizations, starting around 4000 BCE, soon took imperial form: Egypt, Mesopotamia, India, China. They were later, in the first millennium CE, joined by empires in what the Europeans came to call the "New World" across the Atlantic: the Toltec, the Aztec, and the Inca empires. The Mediterranean region threw up the Alexandrian and Roman empires. The Near and Middle East saw Hittite, Arab, and Persian empires. There were the steppe empires of Chinggis Khan and Tamerlane. Coming fairly late on the scene, from the sixteenth century CE onwards, there were the overseas empires of the Atlantic European powers, Portugal, Spain, the Netherlands, France, Britain. At about the same time, the Russians, Habsburgs, and Ottomans constructed great land empires stretching deep into Eurasia.[3]

Some empires, like the Egyptian and Chinese, lasted for thousands of years; others, like the European ones, lasted for hundreds of years. But, whether for shorter or longer periods, empires left an indelible mark on the world. The empire of Alexander the Great lasted no more than his short reign of 13 years (336–323 BCE), but it transformed Eurasia and left a lasting legacy.

With this profusion of empires, in space and time, for any analysis it becomes necessary to establish some sort of intellectual order. In this case, distinctions of space are less important than distinctions of time. At any one time, empires across the world – certainly the Eurasian world – were mostly aware of one another, and in many cases in active interaction with each other (the principal exception is the empires of the pre-Columbian New World). They can be compared as occupying similar tracts of space–time. The Chinese and Roman empires in the first century CE share many characteristics, as do the Mughal and Habsburg empires of the early-modern period, or the Japanese and French empires of the twentieth century.

What is more important is change over time. The later empires learned from earlier ones, striving to avoid their fates even as they strove to imitate them in key respects. At the same time, they benefitted – though this could also threaten them – from the economic and technological changes that took place in the world. This became a particularly marked feature after 1600 CE, as first merchant, and later industrial, capitalism began its transformation of the world. Empires that could not adapt to, or incorporate, the changes faced extinction or absorption by others.

We can in fact distinguish two watersheds in the history of empires. The first is suggested by the German philosopher Karl Jaspers, elaborating on his very influential idea of an "Axial Age" in his book *The Origin and Goal of History*. In a relatively short but intensely creative period, Jaspers argued, between *c*.800 BCE and *c*.200 BCE, there took place a revolution in human thought, such that all the great world religions and foundational philosophies came into being at this time. This was the time when Confucius and Lao-Tse were living and teaching in China; when India produced the great Hindu scriptures, the Upanishads, and also Prince Siddhartha Gautama, "the Buddha"; when Zoroaster in Iran taught a challenging view of the world as a struggle between good and evil, light and dark; when the Jewish prophets – Elijah, Isaiah, Jeremiah, and others – made their appearance in Palestine (leading eventually to offshoots in Christianity and Islam); and when Greek philosophers, from Thales to Plato, radically changed human thinking in ethics and politics. "In this age," claimed Jaspers, "were born the fundamental categories within which we still think today, and the beginnings of the world religions, by which human beings still live, were created. The step into universality was taken in every sense" (2010: 2).[4]

Jaspers confessed that he could find no overarching cause linking these intellectual developments, nor could he explain why they occurred in only three regions of the world: the West (divided into "occidental" and "oriental" parts), India, and China. But he noted two significant things about them. One was that they occurred in the areas where the earliest civilizations, and the earliest empires, had arisen: Egypt, Mesopotamia, the Indus Valley, and China. Secondly, although most of the principal thinkers themselves flourished in a period of small competing states, the Axial Age concluded with the birth of a number of "world empires," in all three regions, in which their philosophies figured prominently. Not only does this suggest some sort of connection between the Axial

Age philosophies and these new empires; it also, Jaspers thought, allowed us to distinguish between empires that preceded the Axial Age – "ancient" empires – and those that succeeded it – "modern" or "world" empires.

By convention, the earliest known empire – the Akkadian Empire – was that of Sargon of Agade (r. 2334–2279 BCE), in southern Mesopotamia. The Akkadian Empire was formed by the conquest of the neighboring city-states of Sumeria, which, c.4300–2334 BCE, had laid the foundations of the region's civilization, the earliest in the world (Farrington 2002: 14–15; Haywood 2005: 26–7). At the beginning of the second millennium BCE, power shifted to other Mesopotamian powers: Assyria in the north and Babylon in the south. The Assyrian and Babylonian empires dominated the region for the next 1500 years – particularly powerful were the Assyrian Empire of 911–612 BCE and the succeeding Babylonian Empire of 625–539 BCE. All these empires drew upon the cultural, scientific, and technological achievements of the Sumerian city-states – for instance, Sumerian cuneiform. At the same time, they created something fundamentally new, in the political and partly cultural unification of the large areas of the Middle East that they governed for hundreds of years. Their rulers formed the club of "Great Kings" that dominated the region in the second millennium BCE (Haywood 2005: 46–9; Mieroop 2009; Bedford 2010: 49).

The Assyrian and Babylonian empires at various times covered not just Iraq and Syria but also Palestine and parts of Egypt and Anatolia. In Anatolia, they came up against the formidable power of the Hittite Empire (seventeenth–twelfth centuries BCE). In 1595 BCE, the Hittites invaded and sacked Babylon, thus ending the first Babylonian Empire. Babylonia rose again in the sixth century BCE until its conquest by the Persian ruler Cyrus the Great in 539 BCE. With this, the Persian Empire was born, "ending the 400-year-long dominance of Mesopotamian states in Middle Eastern history" (Mieroop 2009: 82).

Parallel to the growth of Mesopotamia, though apparently independently, was that of Egyptian civilization from around 3100 BCE. But it was not until the time of the New Kingdom (1539–1069 BCE) that Egypt became a true empire, conquering Nubia to the south, much of Palestine and Syria in the north, and extending to Libya in the west and the Red Sea in the east. Egyptian pharaohs of the New Kingdom claimed the title of "King of Kings," "Ruler of Rulers," "Lord of all that the sun encircles." Their empire, it was boasted, spanned "the four corner-poles of the sky" (Kemp 1978: 10; Morkot 2001: 227; Manley 2009: 30).[5]

Egypt's northward expansion was halted by the Hittites at the great battle of Qadesh (1285 BCE), and it was forced out of Nubia in the eleventh century, though "Egyptianization" had proceeded sufficiently there for Egyptian civilization to persist in the region – as the Kushite Empire – for several centuries beyond the New Kingdom (Kemp 1978: 33–9; Adams 1984: 59–60; Morkot 2001: 244–51; Haywood 2005: 64–7). The Empire's decline in the last 500 years of the first millennium BCE was slow but steady. First, the Persians in 525 BCE, then, more decisively, Alexander the Great in 332 BCE, occupied Egypt, though it was not until the Roman conquest – following the defeat of Antony and Cleopatra at the battle of Actium in 31 BCE – that the Egyptian Empire was formally extinguished. Altogether, in one form or another, it had lasted 2,000 years – "history's first, and most enduring, colonial empire" (Adams 1984: 63).

The Persian Empire, the empire of the Achaemenids (550–330 BCE), was the first Axial Age empire, the first "world empire," based on a "world religion" – in this case, Zoroastrianism. It exceeded in size all the earlier Middle Eastern empires – as well as those of East Asia – extending from the eastern Mediterranean to the Indus, and including not just Persian, Assyrian, and Babylonian territories, but Ionian Greece and several Greek states on the Greek mainland (Macedonia was for a while a tributary state). For the Greek historian Herodotus, it was the greatest empire the world had known hitherto, its boundaries "God's own sky, so that the sun will not look down upon any land beyond its boundaries" (Herodotus 2003: 417). The Persian king was hailed as "king of the four rims of the earth," "King of Kings" (*shahanshah* in modern Persian), a title adopted in a host of later empires in Eurasia (Kuhrt 2001: 105).

The *pax Achaemenidica* proclaimed by Darius I celebrated "the God-given and universal state of peace that was guaranteed by the kings and desired by their subjects" (Wiesehöfer 2010: 67). The Persian word *data* – "law," "order" – spread into all the Near Eastern languages, illustrating acceptance of the authority of the Persian "Great Kings," and admitting the state of beneficence that was said to have been conferred by them on all. Similar in showing the widespread impact of Persian rule was the adoption of Aramaic as the *lingua franca* of the empire, which then went on to influence many Near Eastern languages and scripts, such as Hebrew, Syriac, and Arabic. An empire-wide, Persian, ruling-class culture informed the attitudes and style of life of the many indigenous elites, reaching down also to their peoples: "No inhabitant of the empire was forced to choose between an 'imperial' and a 'local' identity . . . but at the same time he was invited to regard himself as – and to be proud of being – a member of the most successful and prosperous entity of his own time, the Persian Empire" (Wiesehöfer 2010: 89–90; cf. Mann 1986: 240–1).

It was Herodotus who seems to have been the first to promote the influential idea of the *translatio imperii*, the handing on of empire, in which the Achaemenids were seen as successors to the empires of the Assyrians and Medes (in the Bible, Babylonia is substituted for Assyria) (Wiesehöfer 2003; Llewellyn-Jones 2009: 104). In Hellenistic times, this allowed the empire of Alexander the Great, carrier of Hellenic (Greek) civilization across a vast swathe of Eurasia, to be seen as successor to the Persian Empire. Later, as Roman writers elaborated this tradition, came a fifth empire, the Roman Empire (27 BCE – 476 CE), and its continuation, the Byzantine Empire (which lasted until 1453 CE). Rome and Byzantium did not just continue and further Hellenic civilization, as Graeco-Roman civilization; they also gave birth to the world religion of Christianity, and were instrumental in its establishment and diffusion.

At about the same time, the Qin and the Han dynasties formed the first Chinese Empire (221 BCE – 220 CE). These promoted the Axial Age philosophies and religions of Confucianism and Daoism, and were also responsible for the great growth of Buddhism in China. Buddhism was also central to the Mauryan Empire (321–185 BCE) in India, while later the empire of the Guptas (319–530 CE) displaced Buddhism and re-asserted the primacy of Hinduism as the dominant religion in India.[6]

It was Jasper's contention that the "classical" or Axial Age empires represented something new, something that separated them decisively from the empires of the ancient civilizations. The ancient civilizations and their empires "appear in some manner unawakened . . . Measured against the lucid humanity of the Axial Period, a strange veil seems to lie over the most ancient cultures preceding it, as though man had not yet really come to himself" (Jaspers 2010: 6–7). Jaspers stresses the lack of "a spiritual movement" in the ancient civilizations. Despite their great accomplishments, which furnish the material for the later Axial Age civilizations, they experience no "spiritual revolution" comparable to that of the Axial Age. Hence they exist in "pre-history," as opposed to the "history" opened up by the Axial Age. In these ancient civilizations, "living expresses and is patterned upon unproblematic acceptance of things as they are. The fundamental human problems are embedded in sacred knowledge of a magical character, not broken open in the restlessness of search" (Jaspers 2010: 12, 44, 48).

Others, in something of the same terms, have also seen the Axial Age as marking a fundamental divide between the ancient and the classical civilizations, and the empires founded upon them. Eric Voegelin saw the new "world empires" of the Axial Age as "accompanied by an opening of spiritual and intellectual horizons which raised humanity to a new level of consciousness." The new thinking is not the cause of the rise of the world empires, but there is an "ontological connection," a "meaningful configuration," linking them: "An affinity of meaning subtly connects a creation of empire which claims to represent mankind with a spiritual efflorescence which claims representative humanity." There is an "association" between the Achaemenid Empire and Zoroastrianism; the empire of Alexander and Hellenism; Asoka's Mauryan Empire and Buddhism; the Chinese Empire and Confucianism, Daoism, and Buddhism; the Roman Empire and the mission to spread, first, Graeco-Roman civilization, then Christianity. These associations are seen to distinguish these empires from the older "cosmological empires" of the Mesopotamian and Egyptian type, which simply seek to integrate humanity within an eternal order of both men and gods, rather than requiring humanity to live up to the demands of a "world-transcendent God" (Voegelin 1962: 171–2, 178; see also Mann 1986: 341–71; Pollock 2004).

A further way of distinguishing the empires of the age of "classical civilizations" – civilizations based on Axial Age philosophies and religions – from those of "ancient civilizations" is to note the enormous speeding up and intensification of exchanges and interactions between empires in the classical age (Bentley 1996: 760–3). Here, the fifth-century Persian Achaemenid Empire led the way, as it did in many other respects. The vast empire linked East and West in ways unparalleled by any previous empires. An extensive system of roads joined its various parts, allowing for swift communication and even a postal service, the first in the world. Ideas, people, and goods moved freely across the large expanse of empire.

The empire of Alexander the Great, which succeeded the Achaemenid Empire, was indebted to it for many of its innovations and practices, not least its respect for the traditions and cultures of the various regions (Briant 2002: 875–6; Wiesehöfer 2010: 86, 92). Alexander's marriage to a Bactrian princess, Roxane, his later marriage to two Persian princesses, as well as the marriages arranged between his Greek Companions and Persian princesses, symbolized the East–West cosmopolitanism that Alexander – disdaining the teaching of his tutor, Aristotle – wished to promote. Zoroastrianism in the Persian case, and Hellenism in that of Alexander, were indeed the guiding ideologies of their empires, but their influence was the greater for not being forcibly imposed on the empire's subjects (a lesson learned by many later empires).[7]

Later, via both the terrestrial and the maritime "Silk Roads," China and Rome were able to inhabit the same Eurasian space, adding to the density of interactions between the western and eastern portions of Eurasia. Africa too was brought into the picture, giving meaning to the emergence of "Afro-Eurasia." Increasingly, empires were neither Western ("European") nor Eastern ("Asian"), but Eurasian (Bang and Kołodziejczyk 2015).

In all ways, in the growth in scale as well as in the intensity of interaction, empires of the Axial and post-Axial Age "stepped into universality," to use Jasper's phrase. Empires were no longer relatively isolated entities, each striving to expand its territory at the expense of others but lacking universalist ideologies with which to justify their conquest. Speaking of Egypt, Bill Manley says that, with the possible exception of relations with Nubia, "no ideology spurred the New Kingdom into conquering lands beyond the Nile." What mattered was simply "political self-interest," with economic gain always a by-product of territorial acquisition, and often the driving force behind it (Manley 2009: 30). That seems true of most of the other ancient empires – Assyrian, Babylonian, Hittite. At most, they claimed to bring peace and order to a chaotic and disorderly world, to re-establish the equilibrium of the cosmos and to put in order its disparate parts.[8] Other than that, these ancient empires have rightly been seen as "empires of domination," largely held together by compulsion and lacking the universalist ideologies that gave the classical empires their greater impact and generally longer life (Mann 1986: 130–78; Goldstone and Haldon 2010: 24). There was nothing like the "Romanization" that in the Roman Empire brought into being Romanized local elites, Romanized towns, and a common Roman culture across the whole expanse of the empire – the Roman "civilizing mission," as we might call it (Kumar 2017: 44–59).

It is obvious that we cannot hold too rigidly to the idea of an "Axial Age watershed" in the history of empires. Some earlier empires, in certain phases – e.g. Egypt in its "Egyptianization" of Nubia, or the "neo-Assyrian Empire" of Ashurbanipal, with its spread of the worship of Assur – certainly contained elements of a unifying ideology. More generally, there was the spread of Akkadian as the official language of the whole Near Eastern region, for its convenience in trade and diplomacy. Elements of "transcendence," putting the empires under standards higher than those of mere order and security, existed alongside the dominant "immanent" ideologies that justified rule by kings and elites (Adams 1984: 59–60; Mann 1986: 152, 160–1; Bedford 2010: 47–59). Empires, of whatever kind – almost by their nature – must legitimate themselves by appealing to some large idea, some promise of doing good in the world.

But most of these ancient empires remained firmly tributary, content to accept loyalty oaths and to collect tributes from client states rather than to incorporate them in the regular system of imperial administration or assimilate them into the dominant culture of the imperial rulers. Nor did they feel the need to spread religious ideas in the population at large, content to restrict them largely to the ruling groups whose integration was all that mattered. These empires were not there to proselytize or to spread a universal truth. They were empires of conquest, and they endured so long as their coercive power was sufficient to keep their subject populations in check.

Second Watershed: European Imperialism

There are perhaps fewer qualifications necessary in discussing the second great watershed in the history of empires, that marked by the rise of the overseas European empires in the sixteenth century CE. That is because, from a relatively early date, they were quickly seen as expressions of a major turning point in world history. They arose as the result of the great European "voyages of discovery" of the late fifteenth and sixteenth centuries, and the subsequent conquest and colonization of the New World – itself the prelude to a wider, world-wide, diffusion of European power.

"The discovery of America," wrote Adam Smith in *The Wealth of Nations*, "and that of a passage to the East Indies by the Cape of Good Hope, are the two greatest and most important events recorded in the history of mankind" ([1776] 1910, II: 121). Smith stressed, as a principal result of these voyages, the "uniting, in some measure, [of] the most distant parts of the world," with effects on commerce and communication that he considered on the whole "beneficial," though he noted that the natives of the non-European world might think differently. But he had no doubt that, for good or bad, the events were of world-historical importance.

Karl Marx and Friedrich Engels concurred with this general assessment, though looking to an eventual outcome of this historic development – in a socialist revolution – that Smith probably would not have approved of. For them, as for Smith, "the discovery of America, the rounding of the Cape," revolutionized commerce and manufacturing. "The East Indian and Chinese markets, the colonization of America, trade with the colonies, the increase in the means of exchange and in commodities generally, gave to commerce, to navigation, to industry, an impulse never before known . . . Modern industry has established the world market, for which the discovery of America paved the way" (Marx and Engels [1848] 1977: 222–3). This development, they claimed, has "called forth a new phase of historical development"; it has "produced world history for the first time, in so far as it has made all civilized nations and every individual member of them dependent for the satisfaction of their wants on the whole world" (Marx and Engels 1963: 52, 57). For Marx and Engels, the fact that commerce and industry were now increasingly global gave them, and the world in which they operated, an entirely new character. Capitalism, as it developed, would be increasingly global, using – where necessary – nation-states as its tools, but never contained by them.

World historians today have been in general agreement with this view of the impact and significance of European exploration and colonization in the sixteenth and seventeenth centuries. C. R. Boxer declares that "it was the Portuguese pioneers and the Castilian conquistadores from the western rim of Christendom who linked up, for better or worse, the sundered branches of the great human family. It was they who first made humanity conscious . . . of its essential unity" (Boxer 1977: 2). This gave a new prominence, and a new role, to Europe. Europe, in the Middle Ages, might, as compared with Chinese, Indian, and Islamic civilizations, have been relatively backward; but from the sixteenth century onward it steadily grew in strength, until finally it came to dominate the world. William McNeill, the doyen of world historians, calls the period from 1500 CE to his own time "the era of Western dominance," and says "the year 1500 A.D. aptly symbolizes the advent of the modern era." The voyages of Columbus, Vasco da Gama, and Magellan, to name only the most famous, began a process that changed the balance of power in the world. China and Japan, and a few other places, were for a while able to ignore "the extraordinary revolution in world relationships" that this wrought. But by the nineteenth century, they too saw that they had to come to terms with European power, on pain of succumbing to it (McNeill 1991: 565–6).[9]

The European empires that arose in this period were at once an expression and a principal agent of this world-transforming process. They differed from both the "ancient" empires of the second millennium BCE – Assyria, Babylon, Egypt – and the "classical," Axial Age, empires – Persia, Macedonia, Rome – that succeeded them. The new thing was the construction of globe-encircling overseas empires.

Both of the earlier kinds of empires were essentially land empires, even if, as with the Achaemenid and the Alexandrian, they spanned a vast section of the Eurasian landmass. They might contain some overseas territories, as with North Africa and Britain in the Roman Empire. But these tended to be in the "near abroad," not too distant from the heartlands. As a result, it was armies, rather than navies, that mattered – Rome, again, partly excepted.

There were indeed in this era some empires that were mostly maritime. The best known are the Athenian Empire – the "Delian League" and its successor – and the Phoenician Empire, one of whose colonies, Carthage, itself built up a maritime empire in the western Mediterranean. But if these were empires, they were of a decidedly loose-knit kind, mostly for protecting trade routes or organizing for common defense. They were very different from both the land empires of the ancient world and the later overseas empires of the Europeans.

Doubt has been cast on whether it is right to think of the Athenian Empire as an empire at all.[10] Athens had "allies," rather than colonies or territories over which it claimed possession, and it made little effort to establish anything that one might call an imperial administration. Moreover, it was relatively short-lived. The Delian League, founded in 478 BCE as a mutual-protection federation of allies under Athenian leadership, was dissolved in 404 BCE, following Athens's defeat by the Spartan League in the Peloponnesian War. The second "Athenian Confederacy" of 377–338 BCE was even shorter-lived – it was effectively over by 358 – and even less an empire, before it succumbed to Philip of Macedon at Chaeronea in 338 BCE (Griffiths 1978; Blanshard 2009: 145–6).

The Phoenician Empire – if it can be so called – was, even more than the Athenian, a loose association of states in which the mother country, Tyre, exercised little direct control over its colonies. Not much more did Carthage, its principal colony, which, after the overthrow of Tyre by the Babylonians in 573 BCE, assumed the leadership of the Phoenician colonies in the western Mediterranean. Carthage did, in the third century, build up a substantial land empire, in North Africa; but its overseas "empire" in the fifth and fourth centuries – the Phoenician colonies in Sicily, Sardinia, Spain, and Corsica – existed mainly as an association for the protection of long-distance trade, on which Carthaginian fortunes depended. Carthage might in that respect certainly be accounted as a "hegemon," but there seems to have been no intention to exercise anything that we might call imperial rule. The Phoenician colonies often acted independently of Carthage, looking to it sometimes for assistance and leadership in conflicts with other powers, but neither seeking nor expecting to be subjected to its authority. Carthage, on its side, was more interested in securing trading relationships than in exercising political control. Only with the loss of Sicily and Sardinia – and hence of valuable trade – to Rome in the First Punic War (264–41 BCE) did Carthage turn for compensation to a land empire in Africa (Whittaker 1978; Haywood 2005: 68; Quinn 2017).

The European overseas empires, by comparison with these maritime empires, as well as most of the land empires of the ancient world, were not just bigger, but culturally and ethnically far more diverse. Alexander's Macedonians were, it is true, astonished when they confronted the elephants of King Poros on the Hydaspes in northern India in 326 BCE; and Bactrians and Sogdians, along with Persians and Indians, contributed a decidedly cosmopolitan character to his empire (as they had to the Persian Empire that preceded and, in a sense, prepared the way for it). Romans too encountered "barbarous" cultures among the Celtic tribes that they encountered and conquered in Gaul and Britain and, adding these to the peoples of the eastern Mediterranean and North Africa, their empire was marked by a real degree of ethnic diversity.

But it is probably true to say, firstly, that most of the peoples and cultures absorbed in these empires were already in some way known to the Greeks and Romans; and, secondly, that – racially and ethnically – they were not so far removed from the ruling peoples, Greeks and Romans. This, as we will see in greater detail later, is a common feature of land empires, as opposed to overseas empires.

What none of these empires experienced was what the Spanish experienced when confronted with the Caribs of the "West Indies," or the "Indians" of the old civilizations of the Aztecs and Incas. Here was an encounter with a New World, and new peoples, that was unprecedented in world history. Europeans struggled to make sense of the meaning of the encounter. They had to decipher new languages, of a non-Eurasian kind; new religions different from all the "world religions" of Eurasia; new peoples who alternately saw the Europeans as gods and devils; new crops, and new animals, that would transform the ecology of many parts of the Old World. This was the "Columbian exchange" (Crosby 1972), and reflections on it preoccupied some of the finest minds in Europe, from Montaigne to Shakespeare.[11]

In strictly historical terms, it was the Portuguese in the fifteenth century who began the armed expeditions and voyages that led to the first European overseas empires.[12] The taking of Ceuta, on the North African coast, in 1415 – best seen as part of the Iberian *Reconquista* against the "Moors" – marked the beginning of

Portuguese involvement in Africa (Beazley 1910). Explorations down the West African coast in the mid fifteenth century led to foundations at Guinea and Angola, which became important Portuguese bases for the Atlantic slave trade. At the same time, Portugal took possession of the east Atlantic islands of Madeira (1433), the Azores (1439), and the Cape Verde Islands (1460). There it pioneered the slave-based plantation – sugar in the first place – that became so prominent a feature of the colonial economy of the Americas.

In 1487–8, Bartolomeu Dias rounded the Cape of Good Hope at the tip of Africa, and in 1497–9, Vasco da Gama completed the voyage to India, returning with prized spices – pepper and cinnamon – but stirring up strong anti-Portuguese feeling on India's west coast. Later voyages to the Malabar coast by Pedro Alvares Cabral and da Gama led to serious conflicts with Indian rulers, in one of which the Portuguese garrison at Calicut was overwhelmed and its inhabitants massacred. In forceful response, Alfonso de Albuquerque took Goa in 1510 and, continuing east, Melaka (Malacca) in 1511. Melaka opened the way to China and Japan. In 1555, the Portuguese first established their settlement at Macau in the Pearl River delta of Guandong province. Besides creating a long-lasting foothold in mainland China, Macau served as a staging post for the important trade that, from 1571, for more than six decades, flowed between Nagasaki – built up by the Portuguese – and Goa, and thence to Europe.

Albuquerque was the true architect of the *Estado da India* – the "State of India," the Portuguese Empire in India (Newitt 2005: 81–8). But, as with the British later, "India" meant more than just India. The *Estado da India* embraced the entire Portuguese Empire east of the Cape of Good Hope, from the East African littoral to settlements in China, Japan, and the East Indies. The Portuguese viceroyalty of Goa, its headquarters, covered not just the settlements on the Malabar coast and in Sri Lanka (added in 1594), but Mozambique and other East African captaincies such as Mombasa and Malindi, the vital south-east Asian port of Melaka, other Portuguese possessions in south-east and east Asia – such as Macau in China, and Timor in the Indonesian islands – and Hurmuz and Muscat on the Persian Gulf. Administration of this vast area was necessarily decentralized in practice – "captains," deputizing for the viceroy, controlled much of the local trade and administration – but the very concept of the *Estado da India* signaled Portugal's ambition to be the dominating European presence in the East, just as Spain dominated the West. For many centuries, the Portuguese crown continued to claim the title first assumed by King Manuel I (1495–1521), as "Lord of the conquest, navigation, and commerce of Ethiopia, India, Arabia, and Persia" (Boxer 1977: 48).

The division between Spain and Portugal of the whole non-European world had been formalized by the famous Treaty of Tordesillas of 1494, sanctioned by successive popes. It became for both Spain and Portugal, well into the eighteenth century, the "basic charter of empire," legitimating their conquests, respectively, in the western and the eastern hemispheres (Disney 2009, II: 48). The treaty did apportion part of the western hemisphere to Portugal, so that when, in 1500, Pedro Alvares Cabral, en route to India, discovered Brazil, he was able to claim it for Portugal. Not much was done there for several decades. But in 1548, the crown, encouraged by the success of sugar plantations in some of the early captaincies, and hopeful of finding – as had the Spanish recently in upper Peru – large deposits of silver, appointed a governor-general and promoted more vigorous economic development. By the end of the sixteenth century, Brazil had become the world's largest producer of sugar (Dias 2007: 80; Disney 2009, II: 213–16).

Many promising initiatives took place under the governor-general Mem de Sá (1558–72). These included the founding of São Paulo (1553) and Rio de Janeiro (1567), and the expansion of the Pernambuco and Bahia regions as bases for development in the north. Immigration from Portugal was also encouraged, and by 1600 there were around 50,000 Europeans in Brazil. The discovery of gold, and later diamonds, at Minas Gerais in 1695 brought a further rush of immigrants from Portugal, so that, by the end of the eighteenth century, there were over half a million Portuguese in Brazil. No other Portuguese settlement, in either Africa or Asia, ever achieved such numbers (Dias 2007: 80, 82).

Other Europeans also saw possibilities in Brazil, and from 1630 to 1654 the Dutch, as part of their attack on the Portuguese colonies, occupied and settled a large region of northern Brazil. Following a Luso-Brazilian rising in Pernambuco in 1645, and war between a recently restored Portugal and the Netherlands, the Dutch were finally evicted in 1654. This allowed for the further development of the sugar industry, which by the early seventeenth century had already made Brazil the world's largest exporter of sugar (Boxer 1977: 112–13).

Sugar meant slaves, a conjunction already announced by the Portuguese in their sugar plantations on Madeira and São Tomé. Following the crown prohibition in 1570 on the enslavement of native Amerindians, Brazil turned increasingly to Africa, mainly to Portuguese Angola and Guinea. By the seventeenth century, Brazil had become the largest importer of African slaves in the Americas. Ultimately, by the time of the abolition of slavery there in 1888, Brazil had imported nearly 4 million African slaves, about 42 percent of the total Atlantic slave trade, and slaves made up about a third of the population of the country (Disney 2009, II: 239, 247; Stearns et al. 2015: 538). Such numbers, of course, meant that Afro-Brazilians and their culture, even more than African-Americans in North America, would become a key component of Brazilian society (Dias 2007: 82).

Many years ago, the scholar C. R. Beazley protested against the general tendency to ignore the Portuguese Empire when considering "that overseas expansion which marks the opening of the modern world" (1910: 11). Spain generally gets most of the attention, followed by the Dutch, the French, and the British.[13] But Beazley rightly pointed out that it was Portugal, nearly a century before Spain, that was the true pioneer, in worldwide exploration, discovery, and settlement, leading to European dominance. He gives much of the credit – more than most scholars would today – to the inspiration of Prince Henry "the Navigator" for "that colonial, commercial, and crusading expansion" that marked Europe in the fifteenth and sixteenth centuries: "The Portuguese Infant makes his nation the pioneer of Europe in its final conquest, by maritime paths, of the outer world" (Beazley 1910: 12; cf. Boxer 1977: 17–24; Disney 2009, II: 27–33).

But even if Henry's role is exaggerated, there is no doubting the adventurous and daring quality that, before anyone else, drove the sailors of the little country of Portugal to push out into the unknown, to go beyond Africa to India and the Far East, to settle the Brazilian wilderness in the New World: "By the 1540s, one of the smallest, most remote and poorest nations of Europe had created a mercantile empire more than five times her size, stretching around the globe" (Dias 2007: 68). At the opening of his great epic poem *The Lusíads*, about Portugal and the Portuguese, Luis de Camões wrote: "Boast no more about the subtle Greek or the long odyssey of Trojan Aeneas; Enough of the oriental conquests of great Alexander and of Trajan; I sing of the famous Portuguese To whom both Mars and Neptune bowed" (Camões [1572] 1997: 3). It is a fitting tribute to the world's first truly global empire.

The Spanish were, indeed, next to the Portuguese, the other great pioneers.[14] But "Spain" in this context is misleading, for what we are really dealing with is not just Spain but the vast Spanish Habsburg Empire. In the sixteenth century, under the Holy Roman Emperor Charles V and his son Phillip II, the Habsburg lands comprised not just Spain but also Burgundy, the Netherlands, and the Italian territories of Naples, Sicily, Sardinia, and Milan. As Holy Roman Emperor,

Charles could also call upon the German lands. Charles and Philip also exercised rights over the junior branch of the Habsburgs that ruled Austria, Hungary, Bohemia, and Croatia. It was this Europe-wide Habsburg land empire – though undoubtedly the Spanish part, based in Seville and Madrid, took the leading role – that created the great overseas empire in the New World.

Unlike the Portuguese, the Spanish overseas empire from the very start received the rapt attention of contemporaries, and has done so ever since. Hernán Cortés's conquest of the Aztecs of Mexico (1519–21), and Francisco Pizzaro's conquest of the Incas of Peru (1531–3), aroused the wonder and stirred the imagination of sixteenth-century Europeans, whether in admiration or condemnation. The Spanish did not stop there. They went on to conquer areas of South America further south and east – modern Chile and Argentina – eventually dividing the continent between themselves and the Portuguese. Moreover, the Pacific also beckoned. Backed by a modification to the Treaty of Tordesillas, the Spanish colonized the Philippines, thus giving themselves an invaluable base for the much-prized trade with China and the East Indies. For over 200 years, Spanish galleons, laden with Spanish silver, made the annual voyage from Acapulco to Manila, returning with Chinese tea, porcelain, silks, and the spices of the Indies (Parry 1990: 131–3; Kamen 2003: 197–216).

The distinctive thing about the Spanish Empire was that – unlike the Portuguese Empire – it combined a land and an overseas empire. Its Europe-wide holdings, in the reigns of Charles V and Phillip II, supplied the men and materials for its worldwide conquests in the Americas and the Pacific. A pan-European presence was joined to a pan-global presence beyond European shores. Such a combination was not unique – the French and British empires, as we shall see, had elements of it – but no empire, past or present, has had this on such a grand scale. When, from 1580 to 1640, Portugal was united with Spain under the Spanish crown, Spain's overseas empire was further augmented by the addition of the Portuguese colonies. The result was a colossus of unprecedented size and geographical reach. The English Elizabethan chronicler William Camden remarked that the realms of Phillip II "extended so farre and wide, above all emperors before him, that he might truly say, *Sol mihi semper lucet*, the sunne always shineth upon me" (in Kamen 2003: 93). C. R. Boxer confirms this: "The Iberian colonial empire which lasted from 1580 to 1640, and which stretched from Macao in China to Potosi in Peru, was . . . the first world-empire on which the sun never set" (Boxer 1977: 108; see also Muldoon 1999: 114–18).

There was a further difference from the Portuguese Empire, which perhaps helps explain the prominence of the Spanish case in the discourse on empire. The Portuguese Empire was largely made up of a string of fortresses and *feitorias* – "factories," trading posts, often fortified – in coastal cities across the world, from Madeira to the Moluccas. Their purpose, as explained in 1519 by a Portuguese governor to the Queen of Quilon on the Malabar coast, was not to conquer territories but merely to protect Portuguese merchandise on the seashore (Boxer 1990: 209). This may have been just diplomatic smooth talk, but it was true that, as Jane Burbank and Frederick Cooper put it, the Portuguese Empire was largely an "enclave, seaborne empire" – an empire of trade, akin perhaps to the Phoenician Empire of the ancient world, but on a global scale (Burbank and Cooper 2010: 154–8). It was not, with the exception of Brazil, a settlement empire. Partly because of Portugal's small population, the Portuguese kings found it very hard to get Portuguese to settle in its overseas colonies. When they did, the vast majority were male. They lived with or married local women, creating the large Eurasian populations that were so characteristic of Portuguese settlements, from Mozambique and Goa to Melaka and Macau (Dias 2007: 78–9).

This did not prevent the spread of the Portuguese religion (Catholicism), language, and culture. Indeed, these were vigorously promoted, and have remained remarkably resilient in the former Portuguese regions of the world – not just in Brazil, but also in Africa and Asia. C. R. Boxer comments that the Portuguese chronicler João de Barros "was not far wrong" when he wrote, prophetically, in 1540: "The Portuguese arms and pillars placed in Africa and Asia, and in countless isles beyond the bounds of three continents, are material things, and time may destroy them. But time will not destroy the religion, customs, and language which the Portuguese have implanted in those lands" (Boxer 1969: 93; see also Boxer 1977: 125–7; Dias 2007: 68).

But the thinness of the Portuguese settlements meant that, when the Dutch, following the union of Spain and Portugal in 1580, began to pick off the Portuguese colonies one by one, they met less resistance than when they attempted to do the same with Spain's colonies. Portugal's maritime colonies were much more vulnerable to attacks by the powerful Dutch navy than the land-based Spanish viceroyalties of Mexico and Peru, which could not be reduced by seaborne attacks alone. (It was noticeable that the one Portuguese colony that most successfully – after a period of Dutch occupation – resisted the Dutch was the land-based colony of Brazil.) Hence, while Portugal lost many of its major colonies in the face of the Dutch onslaught of the seventeenth century, Spain emerged relatively unscathed.

Thus, of the two pioneer overseas empires, it was Spain that kept the main body of its empire intact for the longest, and so attracted the attention of commentators for many centuries. The Portuguese Empire entered the eighteenth century seriously weakened, and, despite the reforms of the Marquis of Pombal in the second half of the century, was never able to recover its former prominence. In the eyes of most commentators, it sank into insignificance. Similarly, while both Portugal and Spain lost their American empires in the Wars of Independence of the 1810s and 1820s, Spain continued to hold on to important possessions in the Caribbean and the Pacific – Cuba, Puerto Rico, the Philippines – only losing them after the Spanish–American War of 1898.

It does, though, perhaps tell us something about Portuguese – as opposed to Spanish – rule that, in the end, it was the Portuguese who held on to the remaining portions of their empire for the longest – longer in fact than any other European empire. Most of the European empires were gone by the 1960s. Though Goa was taken from Portugal by a newly independent India in 1961, it was only after the Portuguese Revolution of 1974 that Portugal gave up Guiné-Bissau, Angola, and Mozambique; and it was only in 1999 – two years after the handover of British Hong Kong to China – that it returned Macau to China. The Portuguese were the first to create a world-spanning empire; they were the last to renounce it.

After the Portuguese and Spanish, and hard on their heels, came the Dutch, the French, and the British overseas empires. Later came the Germans, the Belgians, and the Italians. These, the overseas empires, were the newer things. Alongside them, and to some extent showing continuities with the older forms of empire, were the land empires of the Russians, the Scandinavians, the Austrian Habsburgs, the Ottomans. By the time of the First World War, Europe, mainly through its empires (including former colonies in the Americas, but excluding the non-European parts of the Ottoman Empire), controlled over 84 percent of the world's land surface (Hoffman 2015: 2). Truly was Europe making a world in its own image, one that would henceforth bear its marks in all its main lineaments.

But what of China, Japan, and Iran? They too had empires, and while they were heavily influenced by Europe, they resisted European domination. What too of former non-European empires, such as that of the Arabs in the Middle East and North Africa, or the Mughals in India? Though they gave way to European successors, their legacies also lived on. They are part of the story of empires.

Moreover, though empires are often treated as isolated and independent entities, their history is one as much of interconnectedness and interaction as of independence. Europe may in the end have predominated, but even then it may be seen to have shared in a Eurasian *oecumene* that was the common home of all empires, Eastern as well as Western. Empires had much to communicate to each other, much to learn from each other. To some extent they were engaged in a common enterprise, even as they saw each other as rivals and enemies.

We must, that is, consider the extent to which there is a tradition of empire, a sense of succession as the torch of empire passed from one empire to the next. We must also consider commonalities: what do empires – all empires – share, as empires? We have argued that concepts of empire must have a shared meaning, even as they display differences common to members of the same family. But can we say more about that shared meaning, in terms of common ideals and practices? Are there themes and tropes of empire that help to distinguish them as a distinct species of rule? To answer that, we have to venture into new territory. We have so far mainly concentrated on the Western experience of empire since the Axial Age. We need now to bring other Axial Age empires into the picture, so that we can consider empire in the round, as a global experience.

2
Traditions of Empire, East and West

Translatio Imperii: "Eternal Rome"

Empires are many, or so we are accustomed to think. We can classify and typologize them – ancient and modern, Eastern and Western, land and overseas empires – but that is merely to put them into some sort of order. Most modern studies of empire see in them a fundamental diversity and plurality. "Empires," rather than "empire," feature in their titles as much as in their analyses.

But an earlier tradition of use and reflection tended to see empire as a singular and unitary enterprise. For most Western Europeans, until about the eighteenth century, there was only one empire, the Holy Roman Empire, inaugurated by Charlemagne in 800 CE (Koebner 1961: 19). It might, from the fifteenth century onward, come to be called "The Holy Roman Empire of the German People," but, ruled as it was by the multinational Habsburgs for much of the time, that did not, in the eyes of most people, confine it to the Germanic states. It stood for all Europe, all Christendom. Its "Roman" title pronounced its universality as much as its association with the German states indicated the political power that was the "carrier" of the imperial idea (Koebner 1961: 31–3; Wilson 2016: 1–3).[1] When Napoleon abolished it in 1806, that was in order to replace it with his own empire, the Napoleonic Empire, which also strove to be pan-European, if not global. German or French, there could only be one empire in existence at any one time. The element of continuity, despite the rupture, was proclaimed first by having Napoleon's coronation as emperor in 1804 blessed by the pope, as had been Charlemagne's; and also by Napoleon's marriage to Marie-Louise, the daughter of the last Holy Roman Emperor, the Habsburg emperor Francis II (Heer 2002: 276).[2]

That was one reason why European kings and queens, such as those of France and Britain, who often ruled over large realms – later called empires – were for long reluctant to call themselves "emperors" or to call their realms "empires." They preferred to call themselves monarchs, leaving the imperial title to the Holy Roman Emperors (Koebner 1961: 55–6; Muldoon 1999: 9, 114).[3] If they used the term "empire," that was generally in the old sense of "sovereignty" or "absolute authority." When Henry VIII famously declared, in the Act in Restraint of Appeals of 1533, that "this realm of England is an empire," he meant by this that the king of England acknowledged no superiors in his realm – that his rule was absolute and allowed of no appeal to a higher power, such as the pope (Ullmann 1979). He did not mean that England was a particularly extensive state, or that it ruled over a multiplicity of states and peoples, as the idea of empire had come to imply in addition to its original meaning of absolute sovereignty. He certainly meant no challenge to the Holy Roman Empire (though, as he had shown by putting himself up for election in 1519, like a number of other rulers he was not averse to the idea of offering himself as a candidate for the office of Holy Roman Emperor) (Scarisbrick 1970: 97–105).

The Holy Roman Empire self-consciously and self-professedly saw itself as a direct descendant of the original Roman Empire, the more so as that empire from the time of Constantine had already declared itself a Christian empire. The Holy Roman Empire was a *renovatio imperii*, a renewal of empire; and empire meant Rome. The way the West declared the unique, unitary, and universal nature of empire was by privileging a tradition that pivoted on the Roman Empire. It was acknowledged that the earlier empire of Alexander the Great – none other was seen as relevant – had been important. But, it was argued, that was relatively short-lived, and its Hellenizing mission had in any case been taken over and put on a firmer and more permanent footing by Rome. Rome, in its own self-understanding, was coterminous with civilization itself, with the whole *oecumene* of the known world. "The world and the city of Rome occupy the same place," declared the poet Ovid. Rather like the Chinese with their idea of their empire being "the Middle Kingdom" (*Zhongguo*), beyond which was simply barbarism, the Romans looked on the world beyond their empire as filled with uncouth tribes and kingdoms. Later, when in the fourth century the Roman Empire adopted Christianity as the state religion, to the barbarism of the tribes could be added their paganism. Rome's "civilizing mission" could take on, in addition, its Christianizing mission.

There was and could be only one empire, the Roman Empire. As the great classicist Theodor Mommsen put it, it was "a familiar concept to the Romans that they were not only the first power on earth, they were also, in a sense, the only one" (in Pagden 1995: 23). What is more, as proclaimed by a host of contemporary – echoed by later – commentators, it was indispensable to the peace and prosperity of the world (Kumar 2017: 47–59). The "fall of the Roman Empire" – its break-up in the West in 476 CE – did little to shake this conviction, nor the belief that there could be only one empire.

For one thing, the Roman Empire as a whole did not fall – only its Western part. It continued in the East for another thousand years, in the form of the Byzantine Empire, whose citizens always called themselves Romans: *Rhomaioi*. Then there was the renewal of the Roman Empire with the inauguration of the Holy Roman Empire by Charlemagne – blessed by Pope Leo III – on Christmas Day 800 CE. The justification of the move, at least in part, was that, with the deposition of the Byzantine Emperor Constantine VI in 796 by his mother Irene and her assumption of power, the throne of Byzantium was technically vacant, since it was argued that a woman could not rule. "To its supporters, the [Holy Roman] Empire was not an inferior, new creation, but a direct continuation of the ancient Roman one with the title simply being 'translated' (transferred) by Leo from Byzantium to Charlemagne and his successors" (Wilson 2016: 27).

The idea of the "translation of empire" – *translatio imperii* – allowed for the persistence of the Roman Empire in various guises, from Constantine's Rome to Byzantium, to Charlemagne's Holy Roman Empire. Since the Holy Roman Empire lasted for a thousand years, to 1806, there was a Roman Empire in existence for a very long time. If we accept, as the Catholic Church claimed, that it was the true successor and continuation of the Roman Empire, the Roman Empire is with us still.

But later empires could also claim to be continuing the Roman inheritance, even if not necessarily giving themselves the Roman title. Richard Koebner has shown that, in opposing the claims of the Holy Roman Empire to rule all of Italy, the Italian humanists of the fifteenth century revived the classical meaning of *imperium* as relating to extensive states in general, not necessarily tied only to the Roman title (Koebner 1961: 50–60). This meant that, in time, other states could challenge the Holy Roman Empire's claim to be the only empire, the only one inheriting the dignity and mission of Rome. By the eighteenth century, the Ottomans, the Spanish, the British, the

French, and the Russians could claim to have empires every bit as grand as, if not grander than, the Roman Empire. In the Russian case, there was indeed the declaration that Moscow was the "third Rome," following on the fall of the Byzantine Empire to the Ottomans in 1453. But the Ottomans, British, and French did not feel the need to call themselves Romans. "Romans are dead out, English are come in," declared Thomas Carlyle triumphantly in 1840 (in Kumar 2017: 14).[4]

But whether or not they called themselves Roman, all the Western empires felt that they, more than an increasingly weak and disorganized Holy Roman Empire, had taken on the mantle of Rome, in promoting the imperial mission of civilization in the world. Still, there should be ideally only one empire. Dante had expressed that idea with classic force in his *De Monarchia* (*c*.1314).

> Mankind is the son of heaven, which is quite perfect in all its working ... Therefore mankind is in its ideal state when it follows in the footsteps of heaven, insofar as its nature allows. And since the whole sphere of heaven is guided by a single movement (i.e. that of the Primum Mobile), and by a single source of motion (who is God), in all its parts, movements and causes of movement ... then if our argument is sound, mankind is in its ideal state when it is guided by a single ruler (as by a single source of motion) and in accordance with a single law (as by a single movement) in its own causes of movement and in its own movements. Hence it is clear that monarchy (or that undivided rule which is called "empire") is necessary to the well-being of the world. (Dante [1314] 1996: 13–14)

In his plea for universal monarchy or empire, Dante singled out the Roman Empire as the providentially ordained agency for bringing peace, justice, and righteousness to the whole world: "The Roman people were ordained by nature, carrying out God's purpose, to rule; therefore the Roman people by conquering the world came to empire by right" (Dante 1996: 47). But the Italian humanists raised the possibility that others than the Romans might now have the right and duty to carry out that God-given task. In the nineteenth century, many British were convinced that, as Lord George Curzon put it in 1894, the British Empire was "under Providence, the greatest instrument for good the world has ever seen" (in Porter 2004a: 138).

It was Herodotus, as we have seen (chapter 1), who seems to have been the first to introduce the idea of the transference of empire – the *translatio imperii*. For him, the succession went from the Assyrians to the Medes to the Persians. It was easy, then, for Hellenistic writers later to see the Macedonian Empire, the empire of Alexander the

Great, as successor to the Persian, and easier still for Romans later on to see their empire as the successor to the Macedonian.

But another – and, for the medieval West in particular, a more telling – source was the Old Testament of the Christian Bible. In the Book of Daniel (2:31–45), Daniel interprets the dream of Nebuchadnezzar, the Babylonian emperor, as foretelling a succession of four "world monarchies" or empires. The first monarchy, symbolized by gold, is that of the Babylonians. After its fall, there will follow a succession of monarchies – not named – of inferior metals: silver, bronze, and iron mixed with clay. Daniel prophesies a fifth monarchy, that of "the God of heaven," that "shall stand forever."

In the fourth century CE, the Christian Father St. Jerome reinterpreted both Herodotus and Daniel and authoritatively named Daniel's four "world monarchies" as those of Babylon, Persia, Macedonia, and Rome. He added two influential features: that the concept of "empire" was singular and exclusive, and that the Roman Empire had to be the last empire, that it had to endure until the coming of God's fifth monarchy: "Empires could not co-exist, but followed each other in a strict sequence that was epochal, involving the transfer of divinely ordained power and responsibility for humanity, rather than merely changes of ruler or dynasty. The Roman empire had to continue, since the appearance of a fifth [earthly] monarchy would invalidate Daniel's prophecy and contradict God's plan" (Wilson 2016: 38).

The European Middle Ages, taking their cue from St. Jerome's exegesis of Daniel (especially as popularized by Orosius in his fourth-century *Historiae contra paganos*), adopted the concept of *translatio imperii* and coupled it with a parallel transfer, the *translatio studii* – the transfer of knowledge and culture, of civilization (Le Goff 1990: 171–2). In this modification, not only was there but one world empire, the Holy Roman Empire, there was only one world civilization, European Christian civilization, whose health and flourishing was the God-appointed mission of the empire. Successive empires had given rise to successive civilizations, in a westward movement that began with the Indians, Egyptians, Assyrians, Babylonians, and Persians, passed through Greece and Rome, and culminated in Western Europe. "All human power or learning had its origin in the east, but is coming to an end in the west," wrote Bishop Otto of Freising in the twelfth century (in Le Goff 1990: 172). The concept of "the rise of the West" was born.

Later European empires found it easy to fit themselves into this tradition. The Habsburgs, ruling in Spain and Austria, and virtually hereditary Holy Roman Emperors, were best able to present themselves as the legatees of Rome. More surprising are the Muslim Ottomans, conquerors of the Byzantine Empire, who also – at least initially – saw themselves as Rome's successors, presenting themselves as descendants of the Trojans who, according to legend, founded Rome. The Russians, on the other hand, claimed that it was their empire, standard-bearer of Christian Orthodoxy, that was the true "third Rome," and "there will be no fourth."

In the eighteenth and nineteenth centuries, the British and the French vied with each other as to whose empire best represented the "civilizing mission" in the world, as of Rome of old. Comparisons with Rome were frequent and inevitable, given the importance of Rome in the self-understanding of both empires. Then, in the twentieth century, the American and the Soviet empires took up the competition, on an equally global scale and with the same stark message that the choice was between one or the other – American-style capitalism or Soviet-style communism. With the fall of the Soviet Union in 1991, America seemed to stand alone, the world's "lonely superpower." In the eyes of many of its supporters, it came to be seen as the new Rome, its mission to spread liberal capitalism throughout the world. The Roman model of empire stood once more vindicated (the more persuasively as Britain could be portrayed as playing Greece to America's Rome).[5]

All these – even, for practical purposes, the Ottomans – were, of course, Western powers. The West might come to think of itself as the superior civilization, and its empire, or empires, as the most powerful and influential in the world, successors to the ancient empires. But not all the other empires had gone. The Assyrians and the Babylonians, the Egyptians and the Macedonians, the Greeks and the Romans, may have had their day. The Indians too, after a brief period of imperial glory, might also seem to have succumbed to other powers, and other civilizations. But what about the Chinese and their empire, still flourishing in the European Middle Ages, and beyond? What of the Muslim empires that had grown and spread with such astonishing speed since the birth of Islam in the seventh century, and that only too obviously competed with the Christian empires for power and control? What, too, to make of the Aztec and Inca empires, still thriving when the Europeans made contact with them in the "New World" in the sixteenth century? What did they think of themselves? Did they also think of themselves as the "only" empire? Did they also have a tradition of empire, a sense of the succession and continuity of the imperial idea and ideal? We need to turn to non-Western ideas of empire, to get a fuller and more comprehensive view of the imperial phenomenon.

The Chinese Empire: The "Middle Kingdom"

Of all the non-Western empires, the Chinese Empire is the oldest and longest-lasting. It was formally inaugurated in 221 BCE, and it did not end until 1912 CE. Its continuity, over more than two millennia, has sometimes been questioned. Certainly, there were significant periods of foreign rule, most notably the Mongol Yuan dynasty (1279–1368) and the Manchu Qing dynasty (1644–1911). But most scholars agree that non-Chinese (or non-Han) rulers were quick to adopt Chinese ways and the basic forms of Chinese culture, including its language. In that sense, a high degree of continuity can be rightly claimed, making the Chinese Empire equaled only by the Egyptian in the sheer length of its survival (see, e.g., Keay 2009: 79; Zhao 2015).

As with all the non-Western empires, the Chinese case is bedeviled by the problem of names. What to call it? Is it actually an empire? Is it right to speak of a "Chinese Empire," in the way we speak of the Roman or British empires? In most of the Western languages, the word for "empire" derives from the Latin *imperium*. Hence, there is a broadly shared vocabulary of meanings. There are, at the very least, "family resemblances" among all the Western empires.

No such commonalities, deriving from some original shared parent, exist for the non-Western cases. When we speak of the Chinese, or the Mauryan, or the Mogul, or Safavid empires – as we can and should – we do so because, at some point, observers and commentators began to designate them as such, usually by analogy with Western empires. Even more important is the fact that natives of the state or country in question also began to call their states empires, and to compare them with other empires – again, usually Western ones.

We can see how this might happen from a very recent example. Until the early 1990s, few Russians spoke of the "Soviet Empire." Even in the West, it was mainly those hostile to the Soviet Union who called it an empire – the "Evil Empire," as US President Ronald Reagan termed it – wishing to attribute to it the qualities of expansionism, and perhaps oppression, generally associated with imperialism. But after the fall of the Soviet Union in 1991, not only did many more in the West come to speak of the Soviet Empire – Russians and other inhabitants of the former Soviet Union also began freely to refer to it as such (Khalid 2007: 113). It became common to compare the Soviet Empire with other empires, including the old tsarist Russian Empire. Scholars from both Eastern Europe and the West wrote books and organized conferences around the theme (see, e.g., Barkey and von

Hagen 1997). It is now widely accepted that, despite its own denial, the Soviet Union was an empire in all but name. Now that it has been given that name, the way is open for wide-ranging comparisons with other empires (Beissinger 2006).

Sometimes, perhaps, it takes the fall of empire for the name to be applied, and to stick. Many of America's enemies, and even some of its friends, have been prepared to talk of the "American Empire." In some cases, this has been out of a well-meaning wish to get America to wake up to its responsibilities, and to its role in the world (e.g. Ferguson 2005). Others have hoped that, whether or not is it right to call America an empire, by treating America as an empire it will be possible to make helpful comparisons with other large and powerful states that have held hegemonic power in the past (e.g. Maier 2007). But it has proved impossible to get general agreement on this question. Perhaps only when – and if – America falls substantially from its current position as world hegemon will talk of "the American Empire" gain widespread currency. Currently, if America is an empire, it is an empire that dare not speak its name (see further on the American Empire, chapter 6 below).

It is interesting that it was only when China began to decline, in the late nineteenth century, that it came to be called an empire and to accept that designation, in more or less Western terms. At the time, however, this did not necessarily amount to an admission of weakness – more a desire to show that China was or had been the equivalent of the great Western powers that styled themselves as empires. Only later, with the fall of the empire in 1911, did "empire" acquire negative connotations in China, as a sign of China's backwardness and inability to keep up with the West. Misunderstanding Western developments – the European overseas empires were at their height after the First World War and showed no indications of wishing to give up on empire – Chinese reformers began to argue that only by becoming a "nation-state" would China throw off its ancient heritage of "feudalism" and Confucian traditionalism. To be modern, they argued, was to be a nation-state, Western-style, not an old-fashioned dynastic empire saddled with a Confucian heritage (Schwarz 1984; Duara 1995: 85–113; Rowe 2012: 253–4; Wang 2014: 59–60).

The history of the term "empire" in relation to China, as used by Europeans and the Chinese themselves, is complex (and apparently understudied).[6] By the mid seventeenth century, Europeans, who had previously referred to China as a "kingdom," began to speak of "the Chinese Empire," on the analogy of the European empires (Brook 2016: 962). By the eighteenth century, this designation had become common. In his widely read *The Spirit of the Laws* (1748),

Montesquieu had much to say about the "vast Empire of China," some of it favorable, some not ("China is a despotic state, whose principal is fear") (Montesquieu [1748] 1962, I: 122, 125).

To label China an empire was not – *pace* some scholars – to accuse it of backwardness or obscurantism: all the leading powers in Europe were empires, and those that were not aspired to become so. It was, on the contrary, a recognition of China's importance on the world stage, its power and distinctiveness. It was to break into this world, with its cultural and material wealth, that the West put such pressure on China in the nineteenth century, beginning with the British Opium Wars of the 1840s. A consequence of these European incursions, renewed in the 1860s and again following the Boxer Rebellion of 1900, was, indeed, fatally to weaken Chinese power. But neither for the Europeans, nor for the Chinese themselves until the end of empire, was the designation of empire meant to suggest an archaic and "premodern" form of rule.[7]

For the Chinese themselves, in relation to their own lands, the term "empire" (*diguo*) carried ambiguous and changing meanings. The ancient texts refer to "empire" and "emperor" (*huang*), but largely in the sense of an "empire of virtue," a state governed by virtuous rulers – such as the mythical "Five Emperors" – who, rather like Plato's Guardians, reject force as the means to exercise power, relying instead on wisdom and justice (Wang 2014: 31–2). For much of the time, the term most commonly used to describe the territorial state, qualified by its dynastic name, was the "Great State" (*daguo*), as in *Da Song guo*, the Song Great State, or *Da Qing guo*, the Qing Great State (Brook 2016: 959–62). Often coupled with this was the recognition of the Chinese ruler as the "Son of Heaven," endowed with the "Mandate of Heaven" (*tian ming*) to rule "All under Heaven" (*tien-hsia*). By *tien-hsia* was meant the whole known civilized world, usually identified with *Zhongguo* (the Middle or Central Kingdom) – that is, China itself – though, like empire, only in the nineteenth century did *Zhongguo* become the common term – as it is today – to refer to the country that others called "China." Principally, it seems, the Chinese referred to their own country simply by using the name of the ruling dynasty. One lived, not in *Zhongguo*, but under, or in the time of, the Qin, the Han, the Tang, the Song, the Yuan, the Ming, or the Qing dynasties.

It might seem from this that the step from "Great State" to "empire," from *daguo* to *diguo*, is not so great. In fact, however, it marked a profound transformation in Chinese thought, reflecting a new sense of China's changed place in the world. China had once seen itself as the center of world civilization, and its wealth and power indeed gave it a commanding position in the world economy for many centuries (Frank 1998). Starting with the Opium Wars of the 1840s, China entered on what it came to call its "Century of Humiliation," which ended only with the communist victory of 1949. The realization of China's terrible weakness, brought home in the nineteenth century in repeated defeats by Western powers and an inability to stop Western encroachments on Chinese sovereignty, forced Chinese intellectuals to rethink the whole classical heritage of Confucianism that had legitimated rule in China ever since the foundation of the unified Chinese state under the Qin and Han (221 BCE – 220 CE). The result was the more or less wholesale rejection of traditional Confucianism, and the social system it was thought to support ("feudalism"). In its place came a new "dominant ideology," heavily inflected with Western thought. The "Heavenly Principle," based on Confucian thought, was replaced by the "Universal Principle," derived from Western positivism (Wang 2014: 61–100). It was within the context of this new thinking that the term "empire" was given a new meaning. Empire was still *diguo*, but *diguo* now acquired new connotations – ones that made it possible to compare China with the Western empires, while at the same time allowing it to conceive much of its past in terms of empire.

As with much of the influence of Western thought that entered China in the late nineteenth century, Japan here provided the gateway. Following the Meiji Restoration of 1868, Japan had sent out hundreds of intellectuals, scientists, and businessmen on extended tours of the West. The resulting accumulation of knowledge was the springboard for a vast program of modernization and industrialization, whose first fruits were the crushing defeat of China (1894) and Russia (1904) in wars that clearly announced Japan's arrival on the world stage. Chinese intellectuals could not fail to be impressed by the difference between Japanese and Chinese fates when confronted by Western powers. To defeat the West, it was clear, you had first to join it, or at least to become like it.

When the Meiji emperor overthrew the Tokugawa shogunate in 1868, he named his state the "Empire of Great Japan" (*Dai Nippon teikoku*). Typically, this reflected dual influences, old and new. It drew upon the ancient Chinese categories of "Heavenly Emperor" and *diguo*, as the empire of virtue (the Sinitic characters for Japanese *teikoku* and Chinese *diguo* are identical). At the same time, it was very conscious of the contemporary British and other European empires. In calling itself an empire Japan was proclaiming its similarity to the other great empires that were currently taking over and reshaping the world. Over the next half-century, until its defeat in the

Second World War, Japan showed that it was fully capable of playing its part in that global enterprise.

The term "empire," as something equivalent to the Japanese and European cases, entered China in the late nineteenth century. It helped, of course, that historically there were such close relations between Japanese and Chinese thought. The new use was consciously modeled on the Japanese example, and in so doing it gave the word *diguo* a meaning that it had conspicuously lacked in in its traditional uses (Wang 2014: 33–5; see also Rowe 2012: 265–6). But, now that it was decided that China was an empire like other empires, it was possible retrospectively to apply the term to much of China's earlier history – to show, in fact, that China had had one of the most powerful and longest-lasting empires in the world.

When, in 221 BCE, the first emperor of the Qin (Qin Shi Huang) conquered the six rival kingdoms and established a unified state, he gave himself the title "First Emperor" (*Shi Huangdi*). Succeeding rulers continued the title, mostly to distinguish themselves from the earlier Zhou concept of "king" and the system of decentralized feudalism with which it was associated. To be an emperor in this sense did not necessarily mean that one ruled an empire, *diguo* – there were other more common terms for the Chinese realms – but it established that one was the "Son of Heaven," charged with carrying out the will of Heaven. It also gave one supreme military authority, and the task of maintaining justice and order in the newly centralized state.

All this was sufficient for the new meaning of *diguo* to be applied retrospectively to the rule of the Qin and Han, as well as succeeding dynasties (Lewis 2007: 2). China, it was decided in the late nineteenth century, was and always had been an empire, in the sense that Rome and Byzantium and other Western states had been or were empires. Of course, it had its peculiarities, but so did all empires. For all the filiation and sense of continuity, Rome was different in many respects from the Spanish or British empires (for one thing, not being an overseas empire). But that, nevertheless, does not prevent comparisons, which are always based on some sense of commonalities. There was, in all those cases, the same belief in universality and uniqueness, the same conviction that one had a God-given mission to rule mankind in its own interest, the same hopes and fears concerning the fate of the empire (Fairbank and Goldman 2006: 44).

China had all of this. Its very name, *Zhongguo*, the "Middle Kingdom" – the kingdom at the center of the earth – proclaimed this.[8] Chinese civilization, anchored by its Confucian philosophy, was the greatest there was or had ever been. The Chinese Empire had a duty to spread this civilization as far as possible, so that all should enjoy its benefits. The rule of "All under Heaven" could extend beyond the Han heartland, to take in Khitans, Jurchens, Mongols, Manchus, Uighurs, Tibetans, Japanese, Vietnamese, Koreans, and others.

At various times, such as under the early Ming and Qing, China was expansive, potentially even constructing an overseas empire. The seven far-ranging voyages of the admiral Zheng He (1405–31) to India and Africa (and perhaps beyond) suggested that China had overseas ambitions and aspirations. It had "the ships, the men, and the money too. . . . China looked poised to command the seas and engross that trade on which, within a century, European states would construct empires and claim world dominion" (Keay 2009: 380-1; see also Dreyer 2007; Brook 2013: 93–4). A fascinating "counterfactual" question is: what if China had built up an overseas empire nearly a century before the Europeans? How different might subsequent world history have been? But, for reasons much discussed – though still unclear – the Ming emperor abruptly cut short the sea-going voyages and destroyed the great treasure fleet. The more urgent thing, it appeared, was to concentrate on internal problems, especially the threat of barbarian invasions from the north. At any rate, no later emperor re-commenced these long-distance sea-going ventures. China was not to have an overseas empire.

But this did not necessarily mean giving up on other forms of expansion. There has been a strong tendency to see the Chinese Empire as "self-limiting," content simply to secure its frontier regions – occasionally and reluctantly forced to annex troublesome areas to strengthen that security, but with no great interest in expansion. This is tied to conventional Western stereotypes of the Chinese as traditionally isolationist and inward-looking, hiding behind their Great Wall, despising and distrusting "foreigners." Hence, it is argued, the strong opposition at the Ming court to Admiral Zheng He's expeditions, and their successful suppression. China, it is felt, is different from other empires, certainly of the Western kind, for whom expansion was a quasi-natural tendency, whether or not deliberately or actively sought.

The Chinese today seem to wish to encourage this view of their past empire, partly because they are currently being accused, in Xi Jinping's "Belt and Road Initiative," of seeking to construct a global empire, and so displace American ascendancy (Miller 2017). But whatever one's view of that, one has to see that the idea of a self-limiting empire in the past is something of a myth. As with all empires, there were fluctuations in the ebb and flow, periods of expansion and periods of retrenchment, enthusiasm alternating with a foreboding sense of imperial overreach and possible decline. But, again like all empires, China seized the opportunity when it saw it, especially when it felt there was a need to expand and take in new territories.

The Growth of the Chinese Empire

The Chinese Empire expanded from its core region in the north around the Yellow River (Huang He).[9] Early consolidation by the Zhou (1045–771 BCE) was followed by a period of fragmentation and division – the "Spring and Autumn" and "Warring States" era (722–221 BCE) – which was, however, culturally and intellectually highly creative, giving rise to the "Hundred Schools of Thought." These included the formation of Confucian thought, as well as the writing of Sun Wu's influential *The Art of Warfare*. Confucius (551–479 BCE) looked back to early Zhou rule as a model of a just and harmonious society, especially as practiced by the Duke of Zhou (the younger brother of the first king, and regent to his son). Taking their cue from Confucius, harking back to the days of the "good old Duke of Zhou" became a rallying-call for many subsequent reformers (Keay 2009: 51–7, 219). To the Duke was also attributed the idea of the ruler as endowed with "the Mandate of Heaven," which, however, could be removed if he behaved unjustly. In partial opposition to the Confucianists were the Legalists (*fa-chia*, fourth–third centuries BCE), who stressed Machiavellian *realpolitik* and the pursuit of stable and peaceful rule by any means necessary, however harsh. Punitive law and a strong and efficient bureaucracy were the chief means to that end (Schwartz 1985: 321–49; Mote 1989: 101–14; Zhao 2015: 52–5, 184–7).

The short-lived Qin dynasty (221–206 BCE), starting with Qin Shi Huangdi, the "First Emperor," brought about reunification, and introduced standardization in many areas, including that of the written language. It built the first of the Great Walls, joining up the northern walls of earlier Chinese states. It also saw the beginnings of the bureaucratic state, overriding the traditional authority of the family or clan and basing itself on Legalist principles. Feudal fiefs, characteristic of Zhou *rule, were replaced by political units* known as commanderies (*chun*), jointly governed by civil and military governors. Strict bureaucratic rules governed all social relations (Schwartz 1985: 345–9; Fairbank and Goldman 2006: 55–7; Lewis 2007: 260–1; Zhao 2015: 195–8, 254–67). It is conventional to date the beginning of the "Chinese Empire" proper with the Qin; there are good reasons for this, despite the brevity and violence – leading finally to rebellion – of their rule.[10] Their legacy was long-lasting (Mote 1989: 100–3; 2003: 4; Jenner 2009: 258–63).

The 400-year reign of the Han (202 BCE – 220 CE), briefly broken by the Xin (8 –23 CE), continued many Qin policies while establishing the empire on a firmer basis. The Qin's authoritarian Legalism was softened, and Confucianism made more central to the empire's ideology – an amalgam of Confucianism and Legalism that Fairbank and Goldman call "Imperial Confucianism" (2006: 62; see also Jenner 2009: 274–5). The Han institutionalized the examination system for the selection of civil servants schooled in the Confucian classics. There was also territorial expansion. Under the emperor Han Wudi (141–87 CE), the empire incorporated large sections of southern China, and even parts of northern Vietnam (Annam). The "Gansu Corridor" to the west, containing the exit route to the Silk Roads through Dunhuang, became a Chinese protectorate. The border regions of southern Manchuria and northern Korea were pacified. By the end of Han rule, the empire had established the borders that were to remain substantially in place until the Qing expansion of the eighteenth century.

The Han also established tributary relations with the steppe nomads (chief among them, the Xiongnu) of the north and northwest, a pattern of fundamental importance for much of the empire's history. For their armies, the Chinese needed the strong horses bred so abundantly by the nomadic peoples; the nomads needed Chinese tea, silk, and silver, among other items. After frequent but largely futile attempts to conquer the nomads, "trade and tribute," or trade as tribute, became the preferred Chinese method of dealing with the "barbarians" (Mote 2003: 185; Perdue 2005: 34-6; Fairbank and Goldman 2006: 61–2; Lewis 2007: 132–3; Jenner 2009: 263–6). Not until the Qing – themselves, as Manchus, of "barbarian" origin – did a different, bolder, strategy emerge.

A prolonged period of "warlordism" – a characteristic feature of Chinese imperial history – followed the fall of the Han in 220 CE. A century later, China divided into Northern and Southern dynasties (317–589 CE). The short-lived Sui (581–618), like the Qin before them, effected a military reunification, which was followed by a more lasting political and cultural integration under the Tang (618–907). As with the Qin (and Zhou), both the Sui and Tang hailed from border regions – again, a characteristic feature of Chinese history, where partly Chinese or non-Chinese peoples have played a major role in the development and consolidation of the empire (Mote 2003: 5; Fairbank and Goldman 2006: 77). "From 420 C. E.," says Peter Davidson, "there were two Chinas: dynasties of Han Chinese in the south with their boats, and steppe dynasties in the north with their horses" (Davidson 2011: 105).

"Most Chinese regard the Tang dynasty (618–907) as the high-point of imperial China, both politically and culturally" (Lewis 2009: 1; cf. Farrington 2002: 56–9). Poetry, porcelain, painting, and sculpture – strongly influenced by the Buddhism promoted by the Empress Wu – reached new heights. Territorially, the Tang were more ambitious than the Han. Tibet, Nepal, and Kashmir were made tributaries. Northern Vietnam was recaptured. Extensive Sinicization of Japan and Korea took place, with tributes paid to the Tang. The Tang pushed westward into Central Asia, across the Tarim Basin and Dzumgaria, before being stopped by the Arabs at the Talas River (Ferghana) in 751 CE. Eventually, Islamicization of the western territories forced the Tang back, so that the empire's borders at the end of the Tang were similar to those at the end of the Han. Central Asia from now on would be a region of Islam, not, as had been the case up to then, one where Buddhism and Chinese culture had flourished (Lewis 2009: 145–7, 158–9).

There were, however, significant movements of population that created a new internal geopolitical structure. A steady movement of ethnic Chinese to the economically prosperous south eventually created a long-lasting pattern in which "a wealthy but relatively demilitarized south materially and fiscally sustained a capital located for strategic reasons in the north" (Lewis 2009: 13; cf. Mote 2003: 6, 19). This reinforced the sense of "two Chinas": a politically dominant north ruling an economically richer but subordinate south.

The Tangs' territorial ambitions in the west were eventually thwarted, but this did not prevent extensive and regular contacts with the nomads to the north, helped by the Tang's own partly Turkic origins in the northwestern border region (Lewis 2009: 147–53). The ancient Silk Roads flourished in this period, linking the Tang capital to the "Western Regions" of China, to India (homeland of Buddhism, which spread widely in China under the early Tang), and to regions even farther west, bringing China into contact with Zoroastrian, Manichaean, Islamic, Jewish, and Nestorian Christian communities. The Tang capital Chang'an – the world's largest at the time with a million inhabitants – was open to the world. Alongside the Daoist and Buddhist places of worship were Islamic mosques, Christian churches, Jewish synagogues, and Zoroastrian temples. Mark Lewis calls Tang China "the cosmopolitan empire": "it was the most open, cosmopolitan period of Chinese history . . . For at least two centuries the Tang dynasty's embrace of foreign peoples and cultures was a defining moment of Chinese civilization" (Lewis

2009: 145, 147; cf. Mote 2003: 5–6; Fairbank and Goldman 2006: 78).

Tang rule was disrupted by two massive rebellions – the first led by the general An Lushan (755–63); the second by the bandit chief Huang Chao (878–84). These devastated the country and severely weakened Tang power, leading to its overthrow by a former rebel commander, Zhu Wen, in 907. Thus was inaugurated the period of the "Five Dynasties and Ten Kingdoms" (907–60), during which China broke up – again – into warring states. But, as with the earlier era of warring states, fundamental changes were taking place beneath the political disorder. One such was the more or less permanent shift of China's political center from west to east (Mote 2003: 17–18). Chang'an and its surrounding region in the Wei valley of southern Shaanxi, long the historic center of the empire, declined in importance, weakened by repeated sackings and pillagings in the late Tang. Zhu Wen, unburdened by historic sentiments, moved the capital east, first to Luoyang and then, even farther east, to Kaifeng. The Sui-Tang canal system was strengthened, linking the economically prosperous region of the Yangzi River basin more firmly to the north-east and the Yellow River near the capital at Kaifeng. This also brought trade routes closer to the coast, so connecting them to trade with Korea and Japan and the Khitan empire to the north. The stage was set for the vast expansion of commerce in the Song era.

A further change during the late Tang and the Five Dynasties period was the erosion of the power of the great clans or lineages that had dominated political life for centuries (Fairbank and Goldman 2006: 83–5). Many of their leading members were killed in the political disorder of these years, and their clan lands broken up. Their successors were to be the new elite selected "on merit" in the civil service examinations. This too was a development sealed under the Song. Like many later empires – the Russian, the Ottoman – but well before them, the Chinese Empire was to have a service aristocracy, not – in principle at least – a hereditary one, as was common with all feudal monarchies.

In 960, Zhao Kuangyin, a commander of the palace guard under the last of the Five Dynasties in North China, was acclaimed by his troops as a new emperor. This inaugurated the Song dynasty, divided into Northern Song (960–1126) and, following the conquest of the Song capital Kaifeng by the Jurchens, Southern Song (1126–1279), with its capital at Hangzhou.

The period of the Song dynasty has always been acclaimed as one of the most creative in all of Chinese history: "China's greatest age," say Fairbank and Goldman (2006: 88; cf. Elvin 1973: 179–99; Mote

2003: 119–67, 323–50; Keay 2009: 343–4). Cities grew – Kaifeng and Hangzhou, with over a million inhabitants each, were the largest cities in the world at the time; the economy flourished; there were great technological innovations; printing and paper money were put to extensive use; a reformed civil service examination and a reshaped Confucianism – "neo-Confucianism" – were established as the long-lasting foundations of the Chinese state. The reconstituted scholar-bureaucrat elite – those who "lived by the brush" – led the way in calligraphy, painting, poetry, and scholarship, setting a standard that became the benchmark for all later strivings in those fields (Mote 2003: 152, 321).

This was also an age in which China's international trade – hitherto a small part of its commerce – increased sharply, driven partly by the spice trade with the East Indies stimulated by the growing demand in the capital cities. Large ships, making use of the new compartmented hull and guided by the stern post rudder, made long voyages to the East Indies, India, and even east Africa. In the early Ming, the admiral Zheng He made similar, more celebrated voyages, and the speculation made about those can equally be applied to these earlier voyages. As Fairbank and Goldman put it: "Any modern-minded expansionist looking back on all this growth and creativity can imagine how Song China, left to itself, could have taken over the maritime world and reversed history by invading and colonizing Europe from Asia" (2006: 93). Neither in the Song nor the Ming did this happen, and one can give many reasons – not least, in both cases, the need to attend to threats from the "barbarian" north. But the very fact that the question can be raised tells us something about the power and potentiality of the Chinese Empire – and also, given the outcome, something about its character.

Many have seen it as paradoxical that, at the height of its prosperity and creativity, China under the Song should succumb to the Inner Asian steppe peoples, leading eventually to Mongol rule, in the Yuan dynasty (1279–1368), over the whole of China. One principal reason seems to have been a failure to maintain the relatively stable relationship with the steppe peoples based on the "trade–tribute" system. In this, the steppe peoples paid homage to the Chinese emperor in return for lavish gifts, usually of silk, which in turn usually led to trading relationships between the two parties. The Zhou, the Qin, the Sui, and the Tang, all of whom derived from or intermarried with steppe families, had for much of the time co-existed with the steppe peoples on this basis. The system could even allow for rule over parts of China by steppe peoples. This took place with the two-centuries-long Liao Empire (916–1125) of the Khitans that followed the breakdown of Tang rule. The Khitans ruled their empire in North China as a dual state, keeping steppe traditions and practices in the larger northern part and adopting Chinese ways, with the help of Chinese administrators, in the southern part. It was, says Frederick Mote, a remarkably successful and long-lasting system, a flexible and "well-balanced combination of Chinese and tribal elements" (Mote 2003: 90; see also Fairbank and Goldman 2006: 112–15).

The Song, rashly attempting costly and ineffective military ventures against the Liao, proved unable to work the system. Their weakness led them to be forced to pay tribute to both the Khitans and another northern people, the Tanguts of the Xixia state (Mote 2003: 112–18; Keay 2009: 305–14). When, in 1125, yet another steppe people, the Manchurian Jurchens (Ruzhen), took over the Liao Empire and established the Jin dynasty (1115–1234), the Song were unable to resist their advance and retreated to the south, creating the Southern Song dynasty. The Jin did not just absorb the Liao Empire and the Song's northern territories; they swept down south all the way to the Yangzi basin, and even besieged the Southern Song capital, Hangzhou. The Song were forced to pay tribute to the Jin, as they had previously to the Khitans, and to acknowledge formally their vassal status.

Though, like the Khitans, the Jin retained something of the steppe military structure, they more fully absorbed and practiced Han-type administration and cultivated Chinese culture (Mote 2003: 222–48). They adopted Chinese court rituals and etiquette. Their leaders spoke Chinese and were educated in the Confucian classics. They thus made stronger claims to be the Song's legitimate successors, holders of the Celestial Mandate. Symbolically, they moved their main capital from the northern city of Harbin in Manchuria to their southern capital, Yanjing, the future Beijing (later, pressed by the Mongols, they moved the capital again, farther south to the North Song capital Kaifeng).

Beijing ("Northern Capital") is, in a sense, China's northern, steppe, capital, on the borderlands with the steppe people, just as Hangzhou and Nanjing ("Southern Capital") are its southern capitals. The Great Wall is a stone's throw away from Beijing. But the Wall, just like the Roman *limes*, was always porous, with "barbarians" on both sides, and Sinicization as much a feature in the Chinese case as Romanization in that of Rome. The Jin Jurchen are a clear example of this. Their later Manchurian successors, the Manchu Qing, would be even more so. In both cases, this did not mean giving up their own ethnic identities, but involved creating a "supra-ethnic," "universal" empire, based on Confucian principles, in which both Chinese and nomadic peoples could find a place. In the "neo-Confucian" synthesis formulated under the Southern Song, room was made for rule by non-Chinese dynasties, provided they adhered to "universal" Confucian principles. "Steppe and sown" – nomadic "barbarians" and sedentary Chinese – thus can be seen as having made joint contributions to Chinese civilization (Fairbank and Goldman 2006: 117–18; cf. Mote 2003: 145).

Such an understanding could be applied also to the Mongols, to whose formidable force, under the leadership initially of Chinggis Khan ("Universal Ruler") himself, the Jin in their turn succumbed. In 1215, the Mongols took Beijing. The Song seized the opportunity to ally themselves with the Mongols against their common enemy, bringing Jin rule to an end in 1234. Their reward was for them to be conquered in turn by the Mongols in 1279. The Mongols instituted the Yuan dynasty (1279–1368), the first foreign dynasty to rule the whole of historic China, and the first dynasty since the end of the Tang to unify China under one ruler. They were also the first to rule the whole of China from what, under the Mings, would be called Beijing, but which the Yuan emperor Khubilai Khan, reconstructing the old Khitan Liao and Jurchen Jin capital, called Dadu ("Great Capital"), and which he had laid out along rectilinear lines that would define the classic Chinese imperial capital.

The Yuan and their successors – Ming (1368–1644) and Manchu Qing (1644–1911) – will concern us later, as will various aspects of Chinese imperial rule. Here, the main thing has been to give a brief outline of the foundations of the most important of the non-Western empires. Any general account of empire has to include a consideration of the 2,000-year-old Chinese Empire. And yet the question persists: Was China truly an empire – an empire in the sense that Rome's successors in the West were empires? We have seen how late it was for China to call itself an empire in those terms, in language borrowed – via Japan – from the West. Does this assumed language conceal a different reality, one that makes "the Chinese Empire" very different from Western – and perhaps even other non-Western – empires?

Frederick Mote is one who argues this case. For him, "empire" in the West "has usually meant a kingdom expanded by conquest to rule over additional territories whose people were distinct in history, language, and culture." The "Chinese Empire" did not do this: "the Chinese emperors, with but few exceptions, did not attempt to extend their direct rule over peoples beyond the pale of their culture and language." He even questions whether the term "emperor" is the right one to use in the Chinese case. He prefers to call the first Qin ruler the "First August Supreme Ruler" (*Shih huang ti*), not, as it is usually translated, "First Emperor"; and he argues that "August Supreme Ruler" (*huang ti*), not "emperor," is the term we should use for all succeeding rulers down to the end of the empire in 1911. If we wish to use the term "imperial" in relation to the Qin and succeeding dynasties – and Mote seems to have no problems with that – we should understand it to mean "a new era in the structure and the manner of domestic politics," a new and higher degree of centralized control and administration than to be found in any of the preceding kingdoms; "it has no particular implications for China's relations with non-Chinese peoples beyond her borders" (Mote 1989: 111–12; see also Mote 2003: 183, 983 n.7).

We have already remarked on the limitations of such a view. Mote himself agrees that Chinese expansion under the Qing is an "exception" – a very large exception, considering that the Qing ruled from 1644 to 1911, one of the longest-lasting dynasties in Chinese history. We shall see that there are, indeed, peculiarities of the Chinese Empire, but perhaps no greater than those to be found in other empires.

There is a related question. Mote accepts the standard view of the cultural unity and continuity of Chinese civilization over the 2,000-year period of the empire. Chinese civilization was "essentially an intramural civilization. It consistently generated within itself the essential elements of any new cultural and institutional mix that might develop" (Mote 1989: 101). The linguistic unity brought about by the standardized written script, together with such other "cultural tests" as "their own awareness of their 'Chinese' distinctiveness and cultural centrality as a community in the world," made the Chinese "one people" (Mote 1989: 112). That was indeed, for Mote, an accomplishment that preceded the empire; the empire did nothing new in that respect – it simply continued and consolidated it.

But for many others, this assumption of cultural homogeneity and continuity is problematic, the result of centuries of official Han propaganda (Keay 2009: 294–6). It ignores the frequent irruptions of non-Chinese peoples and regional cultures – Mongols, Manchus, Uighurs, Tibetans – into the Chinese heartlands, and the additions and modifications they made to Chinese culture. It neglects the enormous role played by foreign religions such as Buddhism, even if Buddhism was to some extent sinicized and politically marginalized. It plays down the massive discontinuities in political rule, such as the "Warring States" period that preceded Qin unification, the "Period of Disunion" following the fall of the Han, and the "Five Dynasties and Ten Kingdoms" period that followed the demise of the Tang. These are seen merely as temporary interruptions to the "normal" state of affairs, which is orderly dynastic rule. Following the practice of the official historians, this view artificially stretches the reigns of the principal dynasties, ignoring the fact that, for a good deal of the time – late Tang, late Song, late Qing – the putative rulers had lost control over much of the country. It also refuses to acknowledge that some of the most creative developments in Chinese culture – beginning with "the hundred schools of philosophy" that arose during the Warring States era – occurred precisely during these periods of "breakdown." "Warlordism," loosely understood, can be seen to have been as regular a feature of Chinese history as dynastic order. It cannot simply be swept aside as an aberration. Perhaps, as Prasenjit Duara suggests, it can even be considered an alternative history, a history of "provincialism," offering alternative possibilities for Chinese development (Duara 1995: 177–204).

Once more, in other words, China and the Chinese Empire may not be unique. There are discontinuities and diversities, crises and renewals, of the kind that can be found in all empires. This can co-exist with a good measure of continuity, provided by overarching ideologies and common practices over long periods of time. We will need to consider both aspects when we come back to the Chinese Empire. But we can now glance at some other instances of non-Western empires, in concluding this brief discussion of non-Western traditions of empire.

Empires of Islam

In the desert region at the edges of the great Byzantine and Sasanian (Persian) empires were a variety of tribal groups, the Bedouin Arabs. They were in contact with wealthy and cosmopolitan market towns such as Mecca near the Red Sea. Here, Zoroastrian, Jewish, and Christian monotheistic ideas flourished. Around 613 CE, Muhammad (c.570–632), a merchant from Mecca, had a revelation in which he announced a new religion, Islam, which derived many of its ideas from the great monotheistic religions in the region. On the basis of Islam ("submission"), Muhammad fused a number of the warring Arabic tribes into a new community of believers (*umma*) whose members were *Muslims* ("those who submit"). The *umma*, with its universalism and its doctrine of the equality of all believers, sought to replace blood (kinship) with religion as the basis of social organization (Lewis 1958: 43–4). It was clearly and defiantly opposed to tribal practices and beliefs, thus stirring up bitter opposition to Muhammad in Mecca. Forced to flee to Medina, he returned to prevail in Mecca and to spread Islam across much of the Arabian peninsula.

Under Muhammad's successors ("Caliphs"), the Arabs created a vast empire, overwhelming the Persian Sasanians and making deep inroads into the Byzantine Empire.[11] In the century after Muhammad's death, first under Umar (634–44), then the Umayyads (661–750), Islam exploded across the Middle East, Central Asia, North Africa, and the Iberian peninsula. The Arabs conquered Syria, Iraq, Persia, Egypt, Spain. They reached to the borderlands of India. Crossing the Pyrenees, the Arabs were eventually stopped by the Frankish king Charles Martel at Tours in 732: a great and celebrated event for the Christians, but not apparently one that Muslims regarded as particularly significant. They had enough on their hands: by the end of the eighth century, the Arabs had an empire stretching from the Atlantic to the Indian Ocean. Only Alexander had mover farther and faster.

The far-flung Arab Empire was cemented by the Umayyads' successors, the Abbasids (749–1258 CE). Moving the capital from Damascus to Baghdad, they created an Islamic civilization that has always been regarded as one of the highpoints of world civilization (Kennedy 2006). In 751, the Abbasids defeated the Chinese at the Talas River, deep in Central Asia. Not only did this stem Tang ambitions, it brought paper and Chinese papermakers to the Arab lands. The cheapness and utility of paper – replacing papyrus – helped to stimulate a massive program of writing, translating, and publishing. The Greek classics – Plato and Aristotle, as well as countless texts in mathematics, mechanics, astronomy, and medicine – were translated into Arabic (reaching the West via Islamic Spain). Indian mathematics was combined with Greek geometry to produce algebra. A stream of technical innovations produced pumps, water clocks, and ingenious mechanical toys, such as singing birds. Under the famed caliph Harun al-Rashid (786–809), Baghdad was, by the consent of many scholars, "the intellectual center of the world" (Farrington 2002: 68).

The Abbasid caliphate fell to the Mongols in 1258; Baghdad was looted, thousands died. But that was far from the end of the Islamic empires. New ones were created by the Ottomans in the thirteenth century, and by the Mughals and the Safavids in the sixteenth century. For all of them, the Abbasid caliphate provided something of an inspiration, a model to be imitated. Its combination of Arabic, Hellenistic, and Persian elements was to be a powerful influence in all the later Islamic empires. It is that that allows us to consider these empires, for all their variety, as examples of a generic type of Islamic empire.

There is a further point. The Islamic empires were defined by religion to a degree that went beyond that of most other empires. Their states were never highly defined, their boundaries remained porous. They were a civilization more than a bounded polity. The *umma*, the community of the faithful, was not a territory but a moral community, whose growth was a moral obligation on all Islamic rulers. That is one reason for the expansiveness of the Islamic empires, their striving (*jihad*) to spread the *dar al-Islam*, the realm of Islam, throughout the world. That also made them, like most empires, universalist: they had found the truth of the world, and the world should live under – "submit to" – the rule of that God-revealed truth. Again, as with most empires, that belief was qualified by the pragmatics of imperial rule, the need to acknowledge the diversity of their subjects' faiths. The Arab, Ottoman, and Mughal empires were all aware of that, which partly accounts for their success, as we shall see. But none forgot that their primary purpose was to preserve and spread the religion of Islam to all the corners of the world – to create a world-wide *umma*. Or if they did, there were others who arose to remind them, giving Islamic empires a higher degree of precariousness and instability than was to be found in most empires. The *umma* was in a sense a rival to empire, or to any other consolidated state. It was, says Bernard Lewis (1958: 44), "a theocracy." Its urgent call could in certain circumstances undermine the legitimacy of any Islamic polity, including one headed by a caliph.[12] Islam, says Barbara Robertson, "was not the captive of any government, nor dependent for survival upon the state, nor could it be predictably manipulated by centralized authority" (in Ferguson and Mansbach 1996: 322). The same, of course, could probably be said of all the world religions; but Islam seems to have developed this indifference, even hostility, to politics to an exceptional degree.

Splits and breakdowns indeed strongly mark the history of the Islamic empires. After about the early tenth century, there was no single state that represented all Muslims. Even before the Mongol conquest of the Abbasids in 1258, a number of powerful rivals had already arisen, all claiming the caliphate. A branch of the Umayyads had taken power in Spain and in the tenth century declared themselves caliphs. So too did the Ishmaili Fatimids (909–1171) in Egypt. The Ishmailis were Shi'ites, and the Sunni–Shi'ite split gave rise to several other dynasties – e.g. the Idrisids of Morocco – challenging the Abbasids, even if they did not all claim the caliphate. In the sixteenth century, the Sunni Ottomans claimed the caliphate, but even then there was not general agreement, the powerful Shi'ite dynasty of the Safavids (1501–1732) of Iran opposing them (Hourani 1992: 38–43, 81–6). It was not until the revival of the caliphate in the Ottoman Empire in the nineteenth century that there was more or less general acceptance of its legitimacy among Muslims; and it was less than a century later that, in 1924, the caliphate was abolished by Mustapha

Kemal Ataturk. During the whole of this time, what seemed to have mattered most was not the existence of the caliphate – a largely political matter – but the strength and power of the religion of Islam. Different leaders, not necessarily claiming to be caliphs, could put themselves forward as the greater champions of Islam.

Despite the divisions and rivalries, a number of powerful Islamic empires arose to succeed that of the Abbasids. One was in India. Islam had made converts in India from the earliest years of the new religion, mainly through Arab traders there. Moreover, right from the start, from the first Muslim conquest of Sind in 712, Hindus had been declared *mushabin ahl-i kitab* ("those resembling the 'People of the Book'"), thus according to Hindus the rights and protections that had been extended to Jews and Christians, as *dhimmis* ("protected people"), in other Muslim lands. Such a policy was, indeed, more or less a precondition of Muslim rule over the millions in the Hindu majority (Dale 2010: 24–6).

In the late tenth century, a Turkish slave dynasty, the Ghaznavids, established a Muslim state in north-west India, a prelude to the succession of Muslim dynasties in north India known as the Delhi Sultanate (1206–1526). The Delhi Sultanate has been called an empire but its authority was fragile, a regime of military feudalism based on an elite of cavalry officers who frequently warred with each other (Davidson 2011: 112–13; Rothermund 2013: 24–7). In 1398, it was fatally weakened by the great Turco-Mongol conqueror Timur, who sacked Delhi. The Sultanate endured for another century, but its authority was increasingly ignored (Dale 2010: 30–1).

In 1526, the Turco-Mongol leader Babur (1526–30), who could trace his descent from both Timur and Chinggis Khan, defeated the last Sultan of Delhi, Ibraham Lodi, and inaugurated the Mughal (Persian for "Mongol") Empire (1526–1858).[13] Under the "Great Mughals" Humayun (1530–56), Akbar (1556–1605), Jahangir (1605–27), Shah Jahan (1627–58), and Aurangzeb (1658–1707), the Mughal Empire expanded to take in much of present-day India, with the exception of sections of the south. Their power began to wane in the eighteenth century, under the assaults of the native Hindu Marathas and the encroaching European powers of France and Britain. Following Robert Clive's defeat of the Nawab of Bengal at Plassey in 1757, the British gradually took over the rule of India, ousting their main European rivals, the French. The Mughal emperors retained formal rule, but power was increasingly in the hands of the British East India Company. In 1857, following the Indian Mutiny, the British Crown took over direct rule of India and abolished the Mughal Empire.

Other powerful Islamic empires, in addition to the Mughals, included the Ottoman Empire (1260–1923) and the Persian Safavid Empire (1501–1732). In the seventeenth century, the Islamic empires, sharing many features and in constant contact with one another, controlled a vast region of Eurasia, stretching from Hungary and the Balkans to the Bay of Bengal. In one form or another, Islamic empires were a presence in the world for over a thousand years, from the earliest Arab empires of the 800s to the fall of the last Islamic empire, the Ottoman, and the abolition of the caliphate in 1924.

We will explore aspects of these empires, as well as the Chinese and some other non-Western empires, in subsequent chapters. But we should note also a number of other important non-Western empires that space forbids more than a mention of in this book. There are the pre-Islamic Indian empires of the Mauryans (321–185 BCE) and the Guptas (320–550 CE). There are the short-lived steppe empires of the Xiongnu, the Huns, the Gok-Turks, and the Mongols, of which the Mongol Empire of Chinggis Khan (1206–27 CE) was the largest and mightiest. There are the pre-Columbian empires of the Aztecs (1427–1521) and the Incas (1438–1532) in South America, successors of the great kingdoms such as those of the Toltecs, the Chavin, the Mayas, and Teotihuacan that preceded them. There are the empires of Ghana (940–1180 CE), Mali (1312–1468), and Songhay (1493–1591) in West Africa, the last two centered on the city of Timbuktu, with its great library. Any truly comprehensive treatment of empires (e.g. Davidson 2011) would need to discuss these, as well as those considered in this book. There are many differences between them, of course, and there persists the problem of applying the Western term "empire" to them when their own languages contain only approximations. But, acknowledging the difficulties, they can all be considered varieties of empire, thus indicating once more the pervasiveness of the empire form throughout history and across many lands.

In the end, from the sixteenth century onward, it was the European empires that slowly came to predominate and to take over the world. For the last 500 years, the history of empire has to center on the European empires, because even when they did not take actual possession their power was felt throughout the globe. But we should never forget or ignore the examples of other kinds of empires, in the non-European world, for their experience has contributed much to the rich repertoire that makes up the empire story. We shall have frequent occasion to refer to at least some of these, even if we are forced by reasons of space to leave many out.

3
Rulers and Ruled

Opposition and Accommodation

Empires are far-flung and diverse entities. They incorporate many lands and peoples. Historically, they have generally been ruled by dynasties – powerful families such as the Habsburgs, the Romanovs, the Ottomans. Most empires have been monarchies – rule by one person – though not all monarchies are empires (some, such as that of Louis XIV, indignantly repudiated the title, as something lesser than a great kingdom). But there have been some significant examples of empires that were republics. Rome acquired most of its empire while still a republic. The medieval Venetian Republic, under a popularly elected Doge, acquired a large maritime empire. So, too, did the Dutch after they broke away from Spain in the seventeenth century and founded the Dutch Republic. France rebuilt its empire, after losses to the British, under the Third Republic. The republican Soviet Union, too, might be considered an empire – as indeed might republican America.

The nature of rule – monarchical or republican – influenced the relationship between rulers and ruled in the empires. An emperor who was regarded as a god, or a monarch ruling by divine right, regarded their subjects, and were regarded by them, in a different way from that of popularly elected republican leaders. In both cases, there was a contractual and conditional element, though an entirely informal one. Monarchs were expected to provide justice and security. In addition, they might be expected to see to the welfare of their subjects.

Republican leaders were expected to provide these as well. But, in addition, they had to satisfy certain aspirations based on citizenship.

The metropolitan populations of republican empires were citizens, though not necessarily equal. The peoples of the colonies usually were not, at least in the early years. But the rulers in most cases held out the promise of citizenship, generally conditional on accepting certain terms, such as conforming to the practices of the ruling people and being judged by their legal authorities. So, for instance, Muslim Algerians in the French Empire could acquire citizenship by renouncing certain Muslim practices, such as those relating to the family and marriage, and accepting instead the regime of French law based on the practices of the metropolis (Kumar 2017: 441–2).

For all Western empires, thinking about citizenship – as in so many other matters – referred constantly to Rome. During the Republic, Rome had developed a complex but carefully worked-out procedure for granting citizenship, by stages, to its subjects. This had worked well with its allies in Italy. Under the empire, the system was extended to the many non-Italian peoples – Gauls, Iberians, Britons – that were incorporated in the empire. Eventually, in 212 CE, the emperor Caracalla extended Roman citizenship to practically all the free subjects of the empire – an act that has always been regarded as momentous as much for its symbolism as in its practical effects. At a stroke, subjects became citizens (Kumar 2017: 60–4).

For all the European empires, Rome's treatment of citizenship supplied the model. This applied not just to the republican empires, which owed their very form as republics to Rome, and which were premised on the concept of citizenship. It increasingly came to affect the monarchical empires as well, as their own metropolitan subjects came to demand the rights of citizenship. By the late nineteenth century, the British, the Russian, and the Habsburg empires were all facing pressures for further extensions of citizenship rights – including the right to select their representatives – to their metropolitan populations. It was inevitable that such movements and ideas would spill over into the colonies, the more so as many of the indigenous elites from the colonies were being educated in the heartlands of the metropolitan powers. Citizenship, as a right of membership in the empire, became a strident call in all the European empires, by then dominating the world.

Such calls were not so evident in the non-Western empires, such as the Chinese and the Ottoman. Their traditions did not include the idea of citizenship, at least in the form in which that had come down to the West through Rome. But that did not mean that they ignored questions of how and on what terms peoples who were not of the dominant majority should be included in the empire. The Islamic empires had clearly worked-out policies on this. The Chinese, too, were faced with this question when, especially in the eighteenth century, their empire came to incorporate a significant number of people who did not belong to the majority Han. They faced a different, but in a way analogous, question when their rulers – the Mongol Yuan and the Manchu Qing – were of a different origin from the majority Han. How were the Mongol and Manchu elites to treat the Han – not just the majority people but the admired source of the empire's culture? One way was to treat the Han Chinese as but one – even if the most numerous and important – of a diverse set of peoples over whom the emperor ruled. This became the favored way of the Qing dynasty, with the emperor wearing "many hats" – and many titles – in relation to Jurchens, Mongols, Tibetans, and Chinese (Di Cosmo 1998; Esherick 2006: 231; Rowe 2012: 17).

Rulers and ruled in empires – more so than in nation-states – have usually been seen in oppositional terms. That is because, unlike nation-states with their presumed ethnic homogeneity, empires have generally had a variegated membership. Their members come from different backgrounds, with different religions, languages, and histories. Sometimes they are physically – "racially" – distinguishable from each other. In nation-states, common ethnicity, whether actual or simply presumed, suggests a different relationship between rulers and ruled, a certain equality based on shared ethnicity and a common national identity. In empires, this equality seems denied not just in principle – empires are hierarchical, not egalitarian – but by the very fact of the co-existence of a multiplicity of cultures, many of which do not accept the others as equal or as deserving of recognition. Conflict and antagonism seem to be built into the very structure of empires.

Particularly important is what appears to be the necessary conflict between the ruling peoples of empire and the often large number of different peoples they rule. The asymmetries of power are compounded by the asymmetries of culture, and perhaps of race. Attitudes of superiority and inferiority seem natural accompaniments of this. The subject peoples must surely live in a state of more or less permanent opposition, more or less permanent hostility, to the ruling people and its representatives. This may be concealed for much of the time, and open expression of it in the form of protest or rebellion may be rare. But it must be presumed to be there, and investigation should reveal it. Opposition and antagonism between rulers and ruled in empires are structural; they must be taken to be essential features of all empires.

There is, no doubt, much evidence of this, and it is certainly the common coin of much commentary, both popular and scholarly, on empire (see, e.g., Moses 2010). But it is misleading to see it as the only or principal feature of the relations between rulers and ruled. In most empires, rulers and ruled lived with each other for centuries, if not millennia. A state of permanent opposition between them is unimaginable. No empire could have survived for long if that were the case. There are patterns of accommodation, as well as opposition. Subject groups could find niches within empires that gave them a space and an opportunity denied them elsewhere (the Jews in the Ottoman and Habsburg empires are a good example of this). In several cases, the very definition of the group, and its identity as such, was given to it by empire (most Balkan identities are a product of the Ottoman or Habsburg empires). Often empires found themselves mobilizing and stimulating groups previously passive or latent, giving them a presence and a strength that might later be turned against the empires (as we shall see more fully later, nationalism was often as much the child of empire as it was its antagonist).

A powerful approach, presented by the imperial historian Ronald Robinson, has stressed the extent to which European imperialism depended on collaboration between European rulers and indigenous elites. Without such collaboration, he argues, European rule would have been impossible. Europeans had neither the means nor the knowledge necessary to control the vast tracts of territories and the many groups incorporated in the European empires. They needed local agents as indispensable allies in their rule. The history of imperialism therefore consists of a shifting series of "bargains" between colonial administrators, on the ground or at home, and the various indigenous elites who controlled specific regions or represented specific ethnicities and other traditional groups. When these collaborationist arrangements broke down, when indigenous elites teamed up with anti-colonial nationalists, the end of the European empires was in sight (Robinson 1972, 1986).

In all these ways, rulers and ruled related to each other in a manner that went beyond the oppositional, and that could sometimes even appear as collusion. Their relationships were many-stranded, and only rarely can be reduced to opposition. Like all long-lasting societies, empires were organic entities, demanding a certain adjustment of parts and an accommodation between them. This is not to deny that there were rulers and ruled, authority and hierarchy – even, at times, force and oppression. Empires are not democratic or egalitarian. But nor are they irrevocably divided into two camps, permanently at war with each other. The subject groups are part of the empire; they find their place within it, and can at times even be among its most fervent supporters.

Metropole and Colony: Distance and Nearness in Land and Overseas Empires

Most studies of empire draw a distinction between the metropole, the empire's "headquarters" and main source of power and policy, and the colony or dependency, made up of possessions of the metropolitan power. A related more abstract usage, with similar meaning, is that of "core" and "periphery" as component parts of the empire. Power and influence are taken to flow from the metropole or core to the colony or periphery. A popular image of empire is that of the rimless wheel: the peripheries are linked to the core but not directly to each other, so that the core controls all communication between them (Motyl 2001: 4). But everyone agrees that the flow is never entirely one way and that peripheries can influence the core.

The distinction between land and overseas empires is a further helpful way of understanding relations between metropole and colony. This distinction is partly chronological as well as analytical. As we have seen, the overseas empire really came into its own only with the European empires of the sixteenth and seventeenth centuries. Earlier empires were mostly land empires, though sometimes including, as with the Romans, some overseas territories (North Africa, Britain). The European empires were new in the enormous extent of their overseas territories, often thousands of miles away from the metropolis.

Analytically, land and overseas empires seem to set up very different relationships between metropole and colony, core and periphery.[1] In the land empires, metropole and colony are usually geographically – and even culturally – close to each other. In the land empires of the Ottomans, the Austrian Habsburgs, and the Russian Romanovs, the colonial possessions were mostly adjacent to the metropole, radiating out in a series of concentric rings from the center. In most cases, the physical distance between metropole and colony was not so great. The Russian Empire was huge, but in a wide swathe from Moscow and St. Petersburg, east and west, the lands were linked to each other in a continuous thread. Russians spread out across the whole empire (like the westward movement of nineteenth-century Americans). There was nothing like the oceans that separated the metropole from the colonies in the British and French empires.[2]

There were cultural differences, of course. The Muslim Ottoman Empire had many Christian subjects; the Orthodox Christian Russian Empire had many Muslim and Catholic subjects; the Catholic Habsburg Empire had Protestant and Muslim subjects. All these empires also had substantial Jewish populations. But not only were many of these differences found within the metropolitan territory itself. In addition, all these minority religions shared with the dominant religion the property of being "protected people" – dhimmi in the Arabic term. They were all related, all "children of Abraham." It was precisely their nearness to each other that occasionally produced such violent and bloody conflicts between them. They were family conflicts, a case of "the narcissism of small differences," as Freud put it. Even with the far-flung Russian Empire, stretching from the Baltic to the Pacific, the range of cultural differences was never as great as that, say, separating Indian Hindus from British Protestants in the British Empire, or Indochinese Buddhists from French Catholics in the French Empire, let alone the religions of the Aztecs and the Incas from that of their Spanish conquerors.[3]

There was, therefore, a degree of nearness, even neighborliness, in the land empires not found in the overseas empires. The empires were formed out of a process of "internal" colonization, lapping up, one after the other, the territories adjacent to the core. Over time, the populations of both core and periphery might move and intermingle, thus blurring the distinction between them, and indeed that between the very idea of "core" and "periphery." Russians from Moscow might be different from Muslims in Kazan, but there was constant movement between them and many overlapping circles. In cosmopolitan imperial cities such as St. Petersburg, Vienna, and Istanbul, peoples from all parts of the empire lived and worked side by side. In such situations, core and periphery can slide into each other; determining which is which can sometimes be difficult. Was the core of the Habsburg Empire Austria, or Hungary, or indeed Bohemia? Was the core of the Ottoman Empire Anatolia – the "Turkish," Asian, part – or Rumelia, the "European" part?

It would be wrong, on the other hand, to exaggerate the difference between core and periphery in the overseas empires. There were many attempts at integration in both the British and French empires: schemes of imperial federation, policies of association and assimilation, more inclusionary policies of citizenship in the later years. Overseas empires, as much as land ones, strove to create a sense of belonging that would link all the peoples of the empire into something like an imperial community. Great imperial exhibitions, such as that at Wembley in 1924 and in Paris in 1931, tried to promote that "unity in difference" in a lavish display of the various cultures of the empire.

But, undoubtedly, the sense of difference between Europeans and Africans and Asians, the difficulties of communication across the long distances separating metropole from colony, the cultural differences between Western and non-Western civilizations, all served to make the distinction between metropole and colony much stronger in the overseas empires than in the land empires. This feeling could be intensified when the colonies were themselves inheritors of historic civilizations, as with India in the British Empire or Indochina in the French Empire. Here was introduced an element of the "clash of civilizations" largely lacking in most of the land empires (though, again, we should not exaggerate the differences: the Ottomans were perfectly conscious of the heritage of the great civilization of Byzantium – and, behind it, Rome – among their Christian subjects; Russians were similarly aware of the sophistication of the Muslim civilization to which many of their subjects belonged).

There was a contrary feature that, once more in the overseas empires, served to emphasize the difference between the ruling people of the metropole and the subject peoples. This was when the colonized peoples were seen not as the inheritors of historic civilizations, but, on the contrary, as "peoples without history" – savages or barbarians lacking all the elements of civilization. That was largely how the British viewed the "Indian" tribes they encountered in America, as well as many of the African tribes they conquered in Africa. The Spanish were more aware of the achievements of the Aztecs and Incas, but also chose to regard them as cruel and barbarous pagans whose cultures had to be erased. Land empires sometimes showed aspects of this attitude – as, for instance, in the way Russians regarded certain Siberian tribes – but, generally speaking, most of the peoples they absorbed only too clearly had their own historic traditions. If an empire chose to ignore this, as the Chinese tended to do with the nomadic societies of Central Eurasia that they ultimately conquered, this was because it had developed an unusual sense of its own uniqueness and importance. But even here, particularly under the Qing, the Chinese found it politic to show respect for the particular traditions of the non-Han societies they ruled (Di Cosmo 1998).

The different relationships of core and periphery had a number of important consequences for the two types of empire. In the land empires, the ruling peoples and their subjects were relatively close to each other in terms of race and ethnicity. The members of the Austrian Habsburg Empire were all basically European, mostly Christian, heirs of the classical Graeco-Roman civilization. The Chinese Empire was predominantly Han, though there were several ethnic minorities, including in time a significant number of Central Eurasian Muslims and Tibetan Buddhists. The Ottoman Empire included Christians and Muslims, as well as a Jewish minority, and the ruling elite had Turkic origins. But for most of its history it occupied the territory of the historic Roman and Byzantine empires, and both rulers and ruled drew upon a common cultural legacy which, for much of the time, allowed for a relative ease of interaction.

With the overseas empires, there were far greater differences between groups, especially between the ruling groups and their subjects. In the Spanish Empire, the ruling Spaniards oversaw an empire composed of American Indians, Caribbean tribes, and Filipinos. The Portuguese Empire included Africans and Asians, as well as American Indians. The same was true of the Dutch, the British, and the French empires. In all these cases, not only were there enormous differences of religion, tradition, and history. Increasingly, the differences came to be expressed in terms of race. By the late nineteenth century, racial ideologies had come to occupy a prominent place in the thinking of all the metropolitan powers. For the overseas empires, this could mean a stark opposition between white and black – or, at the very least, European and non-European (see, for Britain, Rich 1990: 12–26; Lorimer 2005; Schwarz 2013).[4]

This did not mean a lessening in the efforts at inclusivity, the creation of a sense of common imperial membership. But it clearly implied that there were significant obstacles to be overcome in achieving that goal. Racial stereotypes – primitive Africans, passive Hindus, murderous Malays – promoted a sense of radical difference that would have to be negotiated or overcome if all groups were to feel a sense of belonging. For the overseas empires, that posed a far greater challenge than was the case with the land empires, with their more homogeneous populations. "Oh, East is East, and West is West, and never the twain shall meet!" – Rudyard Kipling's frequently quoted line expressed a popular opinion that he was at pains to show was belied by actual experience. In his "The Ballad of East and West" (1889), from which this line comes, he depicts a moving episode of respect and recognition between an English soldier and an Indian rebel fighter. The poem concludes: "There is neither East nor West, Border, nor Breed, nor Birth / When two strong men stand face to face, tho' they come from the ends of the earth." But Kipling certainly pointed to what became a common anxiety in the overseas empires as they strove to make for greater integration. For some, such as the great imperial historian Sir John Seeley, the difference between Indian and European civilization was so great that he could see no future for India as part of the British Empire (Seeley [1883] 1971: 143–230). There was a further consequence of the differing relationships of metropole to colony in the two types of empire, when empire came to an end, as it did in most European countries in the 1950s and 1960s. In the overseas empires, the great geographical and cultural differences between the metropole and its colonies meant that the separation, in one sense, was more easily accomplished than in the land empires. The overseas colonies were able to draw upon historic identities, or newly constructed ones that stressed non-European roots and traditions, to form new states that sharply distinguished themselves from their former colonial rulers. India might continue for a time to use English as a *lingua franca*, and there was no doubting the impact of British institutions on the new state. But, equally, India had no doubts about its existence as an ancient culture and civilization that long preceded British rule. As, in a different way, Ghana or Zimbabwe both showed, the new states emerging from the British overseas empire were able with a good degree of plausibility to assert their own individual identities (though often by ignoring or papering over some glaring cracks).

This did not mean that there were not bitter struggles over independence, as the case of France in Algeria and Indochina shows, or the independence struggles in Portuguese Africa and the Dutch East Indies. But it meant that, once the independence of the colonies was achieved, it was easier for the metropolitan rulers to turn their backs on their former colonies. They might attempt to preserve links, as in the British Commonwealth of Nations or the French "francophone community," and economic, military, and cultural contacts of an important kind certainly persisted. But the ease with which these could be ignored was shown with brutal clarity when the British, without any consultation with their Commonwealth partners, broke many of the ties with them to join the European Community in 1974. Similar effects were felt in former French, Dutch, and Portuguese colonies as the now renamed European Union sought to achieve greater integration. The importance of this again became clear when the British voted to leave the European Union in 2016 ("Brexit"). Hoping to revive links with former colonies, as a compensation for the loss of European markets, the British were politely but firmly informed by Australians, New Zealanders, Canadians, and others that their former colonists had now established ties with many other parts of the world and saw little profit in renewing British contacts (Murphy 2018).

With the land empires, the end of empire brought no relatively easy separation of the kind possible in the overseas empires. The very closeness, culturally and geographically, between the metropole and colony, core and periphery, meant that unraveling the links was tortuous and immensely difficult. This is well illustrated in the case of the Russian and Soviet empires. When the Russian Empire dissolved in 1917, the problem of the relation between Russia and its erstwhile dependencies was resolved by bringing them all back in under the umbrella of the Soviet Union, a new Russian Empire. When the Soviet Union in its turn disintegrated in 1991, the problem of the relationship between core and peripheries once more resurfaced, so far without any resolution. Russia has found itself incapable of truly distinguishing itself from Ukrainians ("Little Russians") and Belorusians ("White Russians"). It has hundreds of thousands of ethnic Russians stranded in its "near abroad," in the Baltic countries of Estonia, Latvia, and Lithuania, as well as in the Central Asian republics of Kazakhstan, Kirghizstan, Uzbekistan, and Tajikistan. Russia has sought, sometimes by force, to reconnect with its former colonies, most notably in the annexation of the Ukrainian region of Crimea in 2014. What is clear is its difficulty in seeing itself as a "normal" nation and a normal nation-state, with its own identity separate from those territories and peoples over whom, for centuries, it exercised control.

Russia is not alone in this. It is a problem faced by all former rulers of land empires – the Ottoman Turks and Austrian Germans, as much as Russians. Separating themselves from their former colonies and dependencies has been a challenge to all, with varying degrees of success. At the other end of Eurasia, China faced the same challenge when its empire collapsed in 1911. Its response was similar to that of Russia in 1917–21, though in the Chinese case the process was longer and more painful. First under the Nationalist Republic, then under the communists from 1949, China restitched the parts of its former empire, so that the borders of China were more or less what they had been under the last imperial dynasty, the Qing. Unlike the Soviet Union – and undoubtedly learning from its example – the operation has so far been successful; the empire has been resurrected, its worldwide mission re-affirmed, most recently in its global "Belt and Road Initiative."

We will have more to say about all of this when we consider decolonization and the end of empires. Here, in concluding this general treatment of the differences between land and overseas empires, we need to enter a number of caveats. All point to the need to be cautious about drawing too hard and fast a line between the two types of empire (cf. Osterhammel 2014: 429–30).

The first thing to note is that some empires are simultaneously both land and overseas empires. This means that they partake of the characteristics of both, though in uneven proportions, depending on the scale and importance of the various parts. The sixteenth-century Spanish Empire of the Habsburgs included not just the conquests in the New World and the Philippines, but also large parts of Western Europe, in the Netherlands, Germany, and Italy. The Austrian Habsburgs gradually took over many of the European possessions of their Spanish cousins, the British and Dutch relieved them of several of their overseas colonies, and, most importantly, their South American colonies revolted in the early 1800s and seized their independence. But right up to the end of the nineteenth century, the Spanish Empire – now, since 1700, under the Bourbons – remained a composite of land and overseas empire. At this stage, its overseas empire remained central to its identity; only with the loss of most of its remaining overseas colonies – Cuba, Puerto Rico, the Philippines – in the Spanish–American War of 1898 was it thrown back on its metropolitan core, and the problems of coming to terms with its vastly reduced status in the world.

The British Empire included not just the overseas empire constructed by the British, but also the "English Empire," a land empire created by the English that, starting in the Middle Ages, came to include all the peoples of the United Kingdom: Irish, Welsh, and Scottish, as well as the ruling English people. The metropolis – in other words, the "United Kingdom of Great Britain and Ireland" – was itself a land empire, one that became the springboard for the creation of a much larger overseas empire, the "British Empire" as conventionally understood. We shall see later that this has in fact been a remarkably common process. So-called nation-states, generally regarded as the metropolitan core of the empire, are often themselves "mini-empires," built up by a process of internal colonialism that later disguises its origin in an imperial process and declares itself an always-existing nation-state.

Land and overseas empires also face some similar problems when empire is gone. It may be easier to manage separation between metropole and colonies in the case of the overseas empires. But, as in the land empires, the ruling peoples in the overseas empires also face a crisis of identity when they no longer rule far-flung empires. It is uncomfortable to be reduced to the dimensions of a nation-state when you have once been the center of a global empire. The Portuguese, the Spanish, the Dutch, the British, and the French, once proud rulers of world-spanning overseas empires, in a short space of time found themselves rulers only of their own home territories. The shock can be traumatic. It may, however, take a different form from that afflicting rulers of land empires, and its manner of attempting to resolve it will also be different – it cannot, for instance, think of re-attaching lost territories, as in the case of present-day Russia.

We will be examining this too in greater detail later. But it makes the point that both land and overseas empires share many features of the postcolonial or post-imperial condition. The contrast between past and present, between being a great empire and a "mere" nation-state, is unsettling in both cases. Life after empire is challenging for both. They may make attempts to forget their past, or to suppress uncomfortable aspects of it. But it returns in a myriad of forms to haunt them. Put another way, the question of the legacies of empire is an unavoidable one for both of them.

One last point. While it is often helpful to distinguish between land and overseas empires, we might feel that in the end they have more in common than they have dividing them. For the West, as we saw earlier, there is a common imperial tradition that stresses universal-ity, the imperial mission, the promise of citizenship, and the need to manage diversity. All Western empires, of whatever kind, operated within this tradition. Eastern empires, such as those of the Mughals and of China, also shared many of these features, adding themes of their own such as, in the Chinese case, an overriding concern with unity. All empires faced common problems, all felt the need to justify their existence as large and powerful states ruling over diverse popu-lations. Simply to designate an entity an empire implies fundamental commonalities.

Rulers, Settlers, and Natives

All empires have had to deal with the phenomenon of settlers from the home country. For the land empires, there were Greeks in Bactria (roughly, modern Afghanistan), left behind after Alexander's empire; Romans in Spain, Gaul, and Britain; Russians in the Baltic countries, on the Black Sea shores, in Central Asia and the Far East; Germans in Bohemia and Galicia; and Turks in the Balkans. They carried their languages and cultures with them. As representatives of the ruling peoples in the empire, they tended to have a disproportionate influ-ence in their regions. Though generally a relatively small minority, they were the carriers of the "superior" imperial culture. They were models for imitation, as one sees clearly with Romanized Gauls and Britons, or Russified Uzbeks and Kazakhs. Similarly, the Chinese took their culture with them as they expanded into Taiwan, Outer Mongolia, Tibet, and Xinjiang.

Conflicts with native elites, and resistance on the basis of local cultures, were inevitable. Vercingetorix in Roman Gaul and Boudicca in Roman Britain are celebrated examples, as is the longstanding resistance of the Caucasian tribes to Russian rule. But in the land empires, these conflicts were in many cases attenuated by two factors. One was the relative closeness of the local cultures to the ruling culture, as where empires ruled over mixed populations of Christians, Muslims, and Jews. The other was the empire's concern, in the interests of order and stability, to allow where possible the persistence of local customs and cultures. Aggressive assimilationist policies ran the risk of stirring up costly resentments and the need to put down resistance. In varying degrees, all land empires, from the Roman to the Russian, practiced accommodation with local elites and local cultures. Even the Chinese – of all the land empires, the most conscious of their cultural superiority – felt compelled to respect the local Buddhist culture of Tibet and the Muslim culture of the Xinjiang Uighurs.

These considerations applied in the overseas empires as well. But in their case, there were additional complicating factors. The most important had to do with the mass emigration of Europeans to the colonies. This began as a trickle in the sixteenth and early seventeenth centuries, as relatively small numbers of Portuguese, Spanish, Dutch, French, and British crossed the Atlantic to settle in the New World communities. Numbers increased in the later seventeenth and eighteenth centuries, with Asia now being added to the points of destination. But European migration was still relatively low and slow. As late as 1800, there were fewer than 5 million Europeans in North America, and less than 2 million – mostly of Spanish origin – in Spanish South America (Portuguese Brazil had just under a million Europeans out of a total population of 2.8 million). Australia had only 10,000 Europeans; New Zealand was still nearly 100 percent Maori.

In the nineteenth century, the stream of European settlers grew into a flood. Between 1820 and 1930, more than 50 million Europeans – about one-fifth of the entire population of Europe at the beginning of that period – migrated to other lands. Many went to the newly independent United States – but many also to the overseas European empires, now including Africa and the Middle East, as well as the Americas and larger swathes of Asia.

The British led the way, exporting over 20 million of its rapidly growing population in the nineteenth and early twentieth centuries. Between 1815 and 1924, over 4 million Britons moved to Canada, over 2 million to Australia and New Zealand, nearly a million to South Africa (13 million went to the USA). The metropolitan French had always been less willing to settle in their colonies, but by 1900 Europeans – French, Italian, Spanish, and others – numbered over a million in French Algeria, making up about a tenth of the total population.

No other subdivision of the human species has occupied so many parts of the earth as Europeans. The result has been the establishment of a large number of "neo-Europes" around the globe. Apart from Europe itself, people of European descent make up over 90 percent of the population of Australia and New Zealand, over 80 percent of the population of North America, and over three-quarters of the population of South America. There are, or were, also substantial communities of Europeans in North and South Africa, and smaller pockets in Asia. No other groups – African, Asian, Amerindian, Polynesian, or other – are to be found in so many places, in such numbers. A UN report of 1953 commented that "the great exodus from Europe has been the most important migratory movement of the modern era, and perhaps the largest in all human history" (in Cipolla 1974: 115).[5]

Such massive movements of Europeans around the world were bound to have enormous consequences for the indigenous populations of the lands in which they settled. Rarely were the migrations peaceful. In many cases – in North and South America, the Caribbean, Australia, and to a lesser extent New Zealand – the indigenous peoples were virtually extinguished (Wolfe 2006). If they were not physically eliminated, by conquest and the spread of European diseases, their numbers were radically reduced and their cultures marginalized or suppressed. Frequently, their remnants were removed to remote and unproductive regions of the country, sometimes in the form of reservations, as with the Amerindians of North America.

Diminished indigenous communities therefore formed one part of the structure of the colonial empires where large numbers of Europeans settled. A second layer was created by the need for labor when the European empires established large-scale plantations, for the production of sugar, tobacco, cotton, and coffee. In the Americas, this meant the importation of African slaves, amounting, between 1450 and 1850, to over 12 million shipped across the Atlantic (Stearns et al. 2015: 538). Even after the slaves were freed, between the 1830s and the 1880s, they formed a highly distinctive and discriminated-against part of the population. In addition, there were now significant numbers of indentured laborers, mostly Indian and Chinese, brought in to work the plantations in the place of freed

African slaves, most of whom shunned plantation work. They, too, shared second-class status with the freed slaves.

Together with the Europeans, the slaves (along with freed slaves and indentured laborers) and indigenous peoples formed the characteristic three-part structure of the colonial empires in the Americas. There were differences in the ways in which the Portuguese, the Spanish, the Dutch, the British, and the French dealt with the various populations. But there were certain fundamental similarities. One was in the tension between the metropolitan authorities and the white settler communities, most of whom had their own local assemblies and a considerable degree of autonomy. Typically, the settlers wished to extend their territories and increase their control over the indigenous peoples. The metropolitan authorities, hampered by geographical distance and difficulties of communication, generally sought to protect the indigenous peoples and to limit settler control over them.[6]

This conflict was one of the major causes leading to the secession, or attempted secession, of the settler colonies from the empires. It can be seen clearly in the actions of the settlers in the British North American colonies, once they had achieved their independence from Britain in 1776–83. Unconstrained by the former metropolitan power, the white settlers pushed steadily westwards into the Indian lands, displacing and dispossessing them and forcibly removing them to distant territories, often at the cost of great suffering and loss of life. In South America, the newly independent republics formed after throwing off Spanish and Portuguese rule in the 1810s and 1820s also felt free to act more coercively and uninhibitedly toward their slave and Indian populations. One can almost discern here the operation of a law: that the freer and more democratic the white settler communities, the harsher their behavior toward their non-European subjects. This is one aspect of the "dark side of democracy" (Mann 2005: 70–110).

There was a further feature that was common to the colonial empires. This was – following a failed revolutionary period (1780–1830), in which an attempt was made to equalize the conditions of metropolitan and colonial subjects of all colors – a constitutional arrangement based on the "rule of difference," a separation of laws and regulations applying to the metropolis and those applying to the colonies (Fradera 2018). Napoleon Bonaparte, in the French Constitution of 1799, had established the principle of *spécificité* ("specialness"), declaring that "the form of government of the colonies is determined by special laws" (in Fradera 2018: 86). There would be one regime for the metropolis, another for the colonies. This was a prelude to the re-imposition of slavery in the French colonies in 1802, following its abolition in the revolutionary Constitution of 1795. Nothing could have symbolized more starkly the difference between political conditions in the metropolis and those in the colonies.

Other empires in the nineteenth century followed the French in establishing regimes that distinguished metropolitan conditions from those in the colonies. In the metropolis, there was a steady process of democratization throughout the nineteenth and early twentieth centuries. In the colonies, rules governing citizenship were tightened up, making it less easy for non-Europeans to become citizens. Laws were enacted that increasingly showed a racial basis, separating whites from non-whites and limiting the rights of ex-slaves, indentured laborers, and indigenous peoples (in this respect, the USA, in the racial segregation and Indian reservation policies that followed the Civil War, showed a clearly "imperial" character). Liberal at home, authoritarian in the colonies: that was the policy of what Josep Fradera calls the nineteenth-century "imperial nation" – "the nation plus the empire ruled by special laws" (Fradera 2018: 237).

There is a considerable degree of truth in all of this; but we must be careful about applying the argument too rigidly, or too widely. For one thing, the British Empire does not really fit the picture (as Fradera admits). After the loss of the American colonies, and learning from that lesson, the British gradually conceded greater and greater degrees of autonomy to its colonies. The first to enjoy the fruits of the new attitude were the Canadians, following the Durham Report of 1839. Australia and New Zealand followed later, as did South Africa. By the early twentieth century, the so-called "dominions" were in good measure independent as far as domestic matters were concerned, a situation formally confirmed by the Statute of Westminster of 1931.

Of course, these were all "white dominions," and the rights and privileges granted disproportionately benefitted the white settler populations that – except in South Africa – made up the majorities in those territories. But, typically, the settlers thought of themselves as British, members of the "British world."[7] Though assertive in their claims for autonomy, they were also proud of their Britishness, and followed developments in the metropolis closely. Democratization there, and changing conceptions of citizenship, filtered through to the British colonies as well. This led to the dominions taking the lead in extending rights of franchise and representation to larger and larger sections of the population. "Difference" existed, and racial ideas were as strong there as in Europe. In South Africa (largely because of the passivity of the British as compared to the Boers, and the negligence of the metropolitan government), this would lead eventually to a vicious

regime of apartheid. But, elsewhere, what one observes is an increasingly liberal concern for the situation of the indigenous peoples, and
an attempt to protect them as well as to incorporate them in society.
The fact is that, despite the failure of the revolutionary period
to bring about equality of citizenship in the metropolis and colony,
the ideological forces unleashed by the revolutions of 1776 and
1789 could not be rolled back. The empires might try to re-assert
some form of duality and *spécificité*, but doctrines of the rights of
man and the revolutionary slogan of "liberty, equality, fraternity"
swept across the world in the nineteenth century (Bayly 2004: 86–7).
Newspapers, steamships, the electric telegraph, the mass movement
of peoples from Europe to the colonies, all played their part in this.
Slowly but steadily, these ideas forced elites – in both the metropolis
and the colonies – to open up public life to formerly excluded groups.

Unlike in Canada, Australia, and New Zealand, Europeans in
South Africa were not, of course, the majority. And this leads us to
introduce another note of caution about the alleged state of duality
between metropolis and colony. It seems to apply particularly to the
colonies where slavery had played an important part in colonial life,
and the relationship between slaves or ex-slaves and their European
masters was of especial significance. This would apply to the British,
French, and Spanish in the Caribbean, the Dutch in the East Indies,
and the Portuguese and Spanish in South America. By the time of
the full-scale colonization of Africa, in the "scramble for Africa" at
the end of the nineteenth century, slavery had been abolished almost
everywhere and so did not apply in the relations between colonizers
and colonized in Africa (which did not mean an end to enforcement
and exploitation).

In the colonies in which Europeans were a minority – though sometimes a large one – the pattern of relationship between metropolis,
settlers, and indigenous peoples was necessarily different from that
in which Europeans were a majority. This would apply to the French
in Algeria and Indochina, the British in India and elsewhere in Asia,
the Dutch in the East Indies, and all the European powers in Africa.
Here, we do not find the three-fold structure of the settler colonies.
Here, the indigenous people are the vast majority, slavery is not a
major feature, and the Europeans are a relatively thin stratum on top
of the native population. Here, therefore, one finds mainly a two-tier
structure of Europeans and indigenes.

Once again, there are considerable variations. In Asia and North
Africa, Europeans were conscious that the native populations were
part of ancient civilizations, stretching back in some cases for over
2,000 years. The British in India inherited a sophisticated Hindu and

Muslim culture whose magnificent monuments – Hindu temples, the Taj Mahal and other Muslim structures – were all around them. The French in North Africa found a rich Arab culture that had been built on a pre-existing Roman one. In Indochina, they observed a venerable civilization formed out of Buddhist and Confucian elements, together with a thriving commercial culture and a vibrant urban life.

Occasionally, the Europeans expressed indifference or even disdain toward these cultures, which they stigmatized as "backward" and obscurantist, left behind by the stream of history. This could be true even of educated observers, such as Sir John Seeley. Seeley was aware of the achievements of Indian civilization, but he thought that "India was all past and, I may almost say, no future." It was mired in "superstition, fatalism, polygamy, the most primitive priestcraft, the most primitive despotism" (Seeley [1883] 1971: 147). The historian and statesman Thomas Babington Macaulay also thought that Indians were very different from Europeans – "in race, colour, language, manners, morals, religion" – but he held out the hope that, through education, they might be brought to "an equal measure of freedom and civilization," indeed to full independence (in Hall 2005: 34).

But there were plenty of others – such as Lord Curzon, Viceroy of India – who had great admiration for the cultural achievements of ancient Indian civilization, and did much to promote the study of it and to preserve its monuments. Indeed, Curzon saw this as one of the duties of the imperial power, one that they were peculiarly well equipped to discharge: "A race, like our own, who are themselves foreigners, are in a sense better fitted to guard, with a dispassionate and impartial zeal, the relics of different ages, and of sometimes antagonistic beliefs, than might be the descendants of the warring races or the votaries of the rival creed." These relics are "part of the heritage which Providence has committed to the custody of the ruling power" (in Sengupta 2013: 180). Similar sentiments were expressed in relation to the Muslim culture of North Africa, and France's mission there, by Maréchal Louis Hubert Lyautey, Commissary-general of Morocco (Quinn 2002: 178–9). In the sixteenth century, Portuguese and Spaniards had not had the same attitude toward preservation and restoration, ruthlessly destroying all the monuments of Aztec and Inca culture (though one should not forget the defense of native rights by such passionate campaigners as Bartolomé de las Casas). By the nineteenth century, the European empires had begun to develop a different attitude, and to institute policies – insofar as they were compatible with imperial rule – designed to conserve native cultures, especially in their physical form (even if that might mean, as with Egyptian treasures or the

Elgin marbles from the Parthenon, carting them off to the metropolis for safekeeping) (Swenson 2013).

Relations between Europeans and natives in these Asian and North African colonies depended to some extent on the number of Europeans. Where these were relatively low, as with the British in India, a certain degree of social insulation could co-exist with constant interactions for commercial, legal, and administrative purposes. While the earlier intermixing between the races, characteristic of the eighteenth century, gave way to greater separation, especially in the wake of the Indian Mutiny of 1857, the rise of a substantial educated Indian middle class could lead to a considerable degree of social interaction and even political cooperation (Washbrook 2014). It is noticeable that the founder of the Indian National Congress in 1885 was a retired Imperial Civil Service (ICS) officer, the Englishman Allan Octavian Hume (another prominent figure was also an ICS officer, William Wedderburn). Later, a significant number of British sympathizers – Annie Besant was perhaps the best-known – were to be found in the independence movement led by Gandhi and Nehru. While novels such as E. M. Forster's *A Passage to India* (1924) stressed the difficulties of friendship and integration between British and Indians, others, such as Paul Scott's *The Raj Quartet* (1965–75), showed the possibilities of intimate relations between the races, and the enormous affection many British felt toward India and Indians (and vice versa).

For climatic and other reasons, the British found it difficult to settle in large numbers in India.[8] But, for the administrators, traders, missionaries, soldiers, policemen, doctors, engineers, and educators who lived for considerable periods of time there, India exercised a fascination that they found difficult to throw off once they returned home to the metropolis. Nostalgia for the Raj became a powerful theme in British postcolonial popular culture, as shown by the success of such television series as *The Far Pavilions* (1984), based on M. M. Kaye's novel of the same name, and focusing on a love affair between an English officer and an Indian princess at the time of the Indian Mutiny.

For the French and other Europeans in Algeria, things were different. There were over a million Europeans in the North African colony by 1900. They were a minority, but a large minority. For many of the *colons*, Algeria – not metropolitan France – was their home; Algeria was French, Algerians part of the French nation. Unlike the British in India, they did not see their residency as temporary. Many were born there and expected to die there. They accepted that they shared the colony with the Muslim majority, and were open to admitting

Muslims to French citizenship provided they accepted French norms. They were aware that the Arabs had created a powerful civilization in North Africa, and admired the cities they had built. But independence for Algeria was, for the *colons*, an impossibility, a betrayal.

One can see that even in the French Algerian writer Albert Camus, sympathetic to Muslim aspirations but equally aware of what Algeria meant to the French Algerian community. His posthumously published autobiographical novel, *The First Man* (1994), vividly evokes the life of that community, and its fervent attachment to the land. When, in the 1950s, conflict between French and Muslims in Algeria intensified, Camus was agonized, but still insisted that France could not and should not leave Algeria in the hands of the Muslim majority: "She cannot, because she could never agree to throw one million, two hundred thousand Frenchmen into the sea" (in Kumar 2017: 448). His death in 1960 meant that he did not live to see precisely that outcome.

The British in India and the French in Algeria – also, to some extent, in French Indochina, though there were far fewer French there – illustrate the varying possibilities where European minorities lived among majorities whose culture and civilization were old and respected. A different pattern, and a different set of attitudes, can be found in those colonial situations in which Europeans were still minorities, but where they regarded the culture of the majority as radically undeveloped, even barbaric. Typically, this was the case with European settlers in the sub-Saharan African colonies of the British, French, Germans, Portuguese, and Belgians. Africa for them was the "dark continent," unknown and perhaps unknowable. It represented humanity in its primitive beginnings. In Joseph Conrad's *Heart of Darkness*, Marlow, as he journeys up the river into the depths of the African jungle, reflects that "going up that river was like travelling back to the earliest beginnings of the world" (Conrad [1902] 1995: 59). People, climate, vegetation – all suggest humanity in a wild and untamed condition, before it became civilized.

It was in Africa, above all, that what Partha Chatterjee calls the "rule of colonial difference," the sense of a radical separation of the ruling people from the ruled, operated most clearly (Chatterjee 1993: 10). It would be wrong to suggest that this "rule" applied everywhere. Even in the overseas empires, where it was most likely to apply, it was qualified particularly in those Asian settings where a certain commonality – as in a shared "Aryanism" in India – was perceived to link rulers and ruled (Kumar 2017: 330–2). It applied even less in the land empires, as we shall see.

But Europeans were confronted in Africa with societies that they thought were fit subjects only for anthropologists studying "primitive cultures." They were societies without history, or, if they had a history, it was the "prehistory" of humanity, the story of its origins. The European idea of the Christianizing and civilizing mission found its apogee in Africa. Even Marlow's reminder to his English friends that Britain "also has been one of the dark places of the earth," that it needed to be colonized and civilized by the Romans, did not mean that it was not also Africa's fate so to be colonized and civilized by the Europeans (the Kurtzes of the imperial enterprise notwithstanding). There was no other possible future for it.

But that still left open the possibility that, at some indeterminate date, the African populations would have achieved the level of civilization that would allow them to live in a condition of equality with Europeans, and indeed to aspire to independence. Even the white settler communities in Africa, the ones most inclined to insist on the difference between Europeans and Africans, accepted that – some of them, at least (Lowry 2014: 143–4). In any case, the metropolitan authorities made it clear that they would not allow the settlers – a minority in all African societies – to set the terms of colonial life (Lonsdale 2014: 75–7). In Kenya, the established white community was forced to accept Kenyan independence in 1963; in Southern Rhodesia, an attempt by the settlers to go it alone was cut short by the British government, leading to African independence in the now renamed Zimbabwe. In both these cases, as with the white dominions when Britain joined the European Community in 1974, a sense of "betrayal" was inevitable. White Kenyans and white Rhodesians protested their Britishness to the end; when Southern Rhodesia declared independence in 1965, it mimicked the American Declaration of Independence in justifying its action by an appeal to essentially British rights, the rights of "true-born Englishmen" (Lowry 2014: 112–13).

If relations between the metropolitan powers and white settlers were often conflictual, we would expect, even more, to see this in the relation between the metropolitan rulers and the non-white, non-European, subjects that generally made up the majority of the overseas empires' populations. That certainly has been the presumption of much work on the subject populations of empires, especially that produced by the "postcolonial" school of historians and social scientists (Darwin 2013: 147–9). The frequently brutal form of the initial conquest, the ruthless suppression of all opposition and resistance, the denigration of the cultures of the indigenous peoples – this surely ensured that, whether or not overtly expressed, an attitude of hatred toward the imperial rulers was widespread among all classes of the native population. There would no doubt be some of Kipling's

Gunga Dins, who nobly lay down their lives for their white masters; but a far commoner attitude would be the insolence and seething resentment, punctuated by violence, portrayed by George Orwell in his *Burmese Days* (1934).

But, then, what are we to make of the repeated statements of many Indians that they too saw themselves as British, members of the same British Empire as the British at home and the other British communities scattered around the world? The Indian president of the Indian National Congress declared in 1912 that its object was "to create a nation whose citizens would be members of a world-wide empire. . . . Our great aim is to make the British Government the National Government of the British Indian people." The veteran Bengali nationalist Surendranath Banerjee protested against the view that the Congress sought outright independence, appealing rather to the sentiment that "we may all feel and realise, no matter whether we are Englishmen or Scotchmen or Irishmen or Indians, that we are Britishers, fellow citizens in a common empire" (in Darwin 2013: 163). No less a figure than Mohandas Gandhi, in urging Indians to fight for Britain in the First World War, proclaimed that "we are, above all, British citizens of the Great British Empire . . . our duty is clear: to do our best to support the British, to fight with our life and property" (in Kumar 2017: 359). Statements of this kind can be multiplied many times over, and they can be found not just in the Indian case but in those of several of Britain's African colonies. For instance, arguing the case for African representation, the Rhodesian African leader Esau Nemapare declared in 1945 that "we Africans have proved our loyalty to the Empire and the King by our own blood. The Empire is our house" (Lowry 2014: 143; see also Darwin 2013: 164).

In time, views of this kind became less common, both in the British and in the other European empires, as nationalists came to feel that the metropolitan governments were dragging their feet in allowing equal recognition to their non-European subjects. The Second World War speeded up this process. But we should not judge the relations between rulers and ruled in the overseas empires wholly from their end, from an outcome that was in no sense predetermined. Almost to the very end, it was unclear what form the settlement would take – whether independence was the only possibility or whether various forms of federation might be a preferable outcome. Native elites certainly wanted to share in power; whether that could be done within the framework of empire or only in an independent nation-state was a hotly debated issue.

We will consider this in more detail later. But, in general, we need to beware of dichotomous models of the relation between rulers and ruled in the empires – the view that opposition, latent or manifest, was the consistent and dominant thread of that relation. That model, it has widely been accepted, is false in regard to relations between classes within societies, and it is equally false in regard to relations between rulers and subjects in the empires. Collusion and complicity, or at the very least some form of working accommodation, were as common as resistance and rebellion.

That made for many complexities, even contradictions, in the kinds of identities that emerged among both the ruling and the subject peoples of the empire. The identities that emerged at the end of empire were in no sense pre-formed or pre-existing. They might even be said to have been made by empire. Empire permanently changed all the players. That is the subject of our next chapter.

4

Empires, Nations, and Nation-States

Nations, Nation-states, and Nationalism

Empires, as we have seen, have been with us for millennia; can we say the same about nations?

There is an immediate need to correct a common, though very understandable, confusion of two things: "nations" and "nation-states." This applies not just to everyday speech but to certain more or less official usages. Thus, we correctly speak of the United Nations – often abbreviated to UN – because that is how it has been designated since its foundation in 1945. But the United Nations is not an organization of nations, strictly speaking; it is an organization of nation-states (as was the preceding League of Nations). That is why relatively large groups such as the Scots (over 5 million), the Catalans (over 7 million), the Québécois (over 8 million), and the Kurds (15 million) are not members of the United Nations, even though they are almost universally recognized as nations; whereas tiny nation-states, such as San Marino (30,000), Monaco (35,000), and Liechtenstein (35,000), are full members of the UN. The former may be nations but they are not nation-states, though all have – at varying times – aspirations to be so. So, until and unless they become nation-states, they cannot be members of the UN. The latter have been recognized by the international community as sovereign and independent nation-states. So, despite their small size, they are entitled to membership, joining the other 193 nation-states that currently make up the United Nations.

We might think that, in the interests of accuracy, the UN might rename itself. But "United Nation-States" sounds bizarre, and "Union of Nation-States" has a sort of exclusionary ring to it, as of admission to an exclusive club. The founders of the UN were only acting in accordance with longstanding practice – especially in the English-speaking world – of conflating nations and nation-states. Perhaps – although this was never consciously spelled out – by calling itself United Nations it was holding out the hope that those groups that were currently nations might eventually form themselves into nation-states and so become members. There was, in other words, perhaps a generous and "democractic" motive behind the naming. But for those seeking precision in definitions and meanings, it has certainly not helped that one of the most important organizations in the world perpetuates the confusion between nations and nation-states.

Nations, or what are understood to be nations, are old; nation-states are new. They are the product of nationalism, a new ideology that developed in the nineteenth century, at first in Europe. It was nationalism that turned nations into nation-states, or at least formulated the doctrine that drove many nations to aspire to become nation-states, though relatively few actually achieved that goal. Taking language as the basis of nationhood, there are said to be something like 8,000 nations – actual or potential – in the world today; less than 200 of those have become nation-states, if we use membership of the United Nations as a measure of this (Gellner 2006: 43).

So what is the difference between nations and nation-states? Nations – the word derives ultimately from the Latin word *nascor*, to be born – are constituted by people who believe they share a common ancestry. Sometimes, they think they can name their ancestors, as with Romulus and Remus in the case of the Romans, though most people are conscious of the mythical nature of this belief. To this is added a sense of a common history, common customs, often a shared religion. Language is nearly always a key constituent of nationhood. Place often is, in the idea of a native homeland, but there are plenty of examples of nomadic or diasporic groups that consider themselves nations (Mongols and several groups of North American Indians, for example). Sometimes, usually deriving from their religion, nations have a belief in a special, divinely ordained, mission in the world, and may think of themselves as an "elect people." At various times, groups as diverse as Jews, French, English, and Americans have held such a view of themselves.[1]

Nations as thus defined have been in existence for hundreds, perhaps thousands, of years. They can be numbered in their thousands (Armstrong 1982). They are as old as empires and have accompanied them, either as part of or external to them. But what is crucially missing in this notion of nationhood is a specifically political dimension, some idea of a state. That is the principal difference – as the names imply – between nations and nation-states. There have been and still are many nations that are not states. Some wish to be, but by no means all. Many – perhaps most – nations are content with a reasonable degree of autonomy, allowing them the freedom to express their distinctive nationhood. This can take place within federations, as with the Swiss or Canadian Federation; it can even take place within empires, which are by definition multinational. This was true to a considerable extent of the Habsburg, Ottoman, and Russian empires.

What generally drives nations to seek independent status is when they feel that their aspiration to nationhood, or their ability to express themselves nationally, is thwarted by a superior power. Such is the case today, for instance, with Scots, Catalans, and Québécois, to name the best-known and most publicized examples. They may not achieve their goal; much depends on the political environment, the attitude of other states, and a host of other conjunctural factors. But what is important is the striving to achieve political independence. This is the new thing: the desire to become an independent nation-state. This is the fateful accomplishment of the new doctrine of nationalism. Nationalists feel that, without their own state, they are not a proper nation – one that they own and control. They fear that, without their own state, their national identity is at risk.

According to most accounts, nationalism arose in early nineteenth-century Europe, particularly during and as a result of the French Revolution.[2] Here was proclaimed the startlingly new doctrine that held, as Ernest Gellner put it, "that the political and national unit should be congruent" (Gellner 2006: 1). In other words, the principle should be "one nation, one state." Most importantly, while there might well be nations without states, all legitimate modern states must be based on the nation – ideally, just one nation. The state, in modern times, had to be the nation-state. National homogeneity was its principle, even if in practice that could rarely be achieved (though this didn't stop some from trying, often murderously through "ethnic cleansing").

Gellner – the most influential theorist of nationalism, along with Benedict Anderson – argued that such a principle was not just new, it conflicted radically with the principles and practices of the historic empires. Empires, like most premodern states, generally had rulers who were of different nationality from the majority of the people they ruled. States in Europe chose rulers from a handful of dynasties who were themselves often linked by intermarriage. Germany was one of the greatest exporters of ruling dynasties in the eighteenth and nineteenth centuries. Germans were to be found ruling the Habsburg Empire, the British Empire, Greece, Bulgaria, and Belgium; through intermarriage with Germans, the Russian Romanov dynasty was also mostly German. No-one thought there was anything strange about that. If anything, foreign rulers were preferred to native ones. They were less likely to interfere in local activities. They stood above the fray of sectional conflicts; they belonged to an international club of monarchs and mixed with each other at the favorite watering spots of Biarritz, Baden-Baden, Carlsbad, and Marienbad. They and their aristocracies had their own "high culture," usually cosmopolitan in character, and different from the various local cultures of most of their subjects. They kept the peace and administered justice; otherwise, the various "tribes" and "nations" – from their perspective, more or less the same thing – could get on with their own business (so long as they did not seriously threaten the power of their rulers).

It was this traditional order, Gellner argued, that was threatened by nationalism, which eventually overthrew it. For nationalists, "if the rulers of the political unit belong to a nation other than that of the majority of the ruled, this constitutes a quite outstandingly intolerable breach of political propriety" (Gellner 2006: 1). Frenchmen must be ruled by Frenchmen, Germans by Germans, Italians by Italians. This conviction swept through Europe during the nineteenth century, and, partly though European rule overseas, went on to conquer the non-European world. Its canonization, as the reigning political principle of the modern world – infinitely more powerful than Marxism or any other modern ideology – is by general agreement to be found in the principle of national self-determination proclaimed by President Woodrow Wilson in his "Fourteen Points" of 1918, intended to set the terms of the postwar world order.[3] It was under the banner of self-determination that the anti-colonial movement developed its critique and, in due course, its political energies in opposing empires (Manela 2009). For nationalists, there is no room and no justification for empire in the world.

Nation-States as Empires

Apart from opposing empire to nation, as sociological entities, Gellner controversially argued further that nationalism was a functional requirement of all modern industrial societies. Nationalism creates a common culture, a national culture, linking rulers and ruled as well as all classes in society. Industrial societies cannot function efficiently without this common culture. It enables individuals to be geographically and socially mobile. Such mobility is essential in the face of the ceaseless change – technical and occupational – that industrialization brings. The cultural divide that exists in empires, between the cultures of the elites and those of the many different groups they rule, is a fundamental obstacle to industrialization and modernization.

Empires, in other words, are out. They are incompatible with the requirements of modern society, and especially of a modern economy. They are an anachronism in the modern era. If they persist, they persist as archaic hangovers. In the twentieth century, one set of empires – the land empires of the Qing, the Ottomans, the Habsburgs, the Hohenzollerns, and the Romanovs – came to end just before and after the First World War. After the Second World War, it was the turn of the overseas empires, with the Dutch, the British, the French, the Belgian, and – somewhat later – the Portuguese empires all dissolving themselves. Even the Soviet Union – the new form of the Russian Empire – finally gave way, unable to keep up with the technical and social demands of a modern economy.

Gellner admitted that empires had clung on longer than one might have expected. But industrialization was uneven, as was the pace of development, allowing for a significant "time lag" between the original onset of industrialization in the early nineteenth century and the fall of empires in the twentieth century. Their fall was, however, inevitable. The foreseeable future was, he felt, still one in which nationalism and the nation-state would remain the central political elements of the modern world.[4]

Gellner's argument has been hugely influential.[5] In a very general sense, he is clearly right, in that the nation-state has become the norm of the contemporary world order. If empires still exist, they do so under other names, or deny their existence. Many people consider America – especially in its post-1945 role – as an empire. The Soviet Union was also widely described as an empire. Today, some people see China, with its "Belt and Road Initiative," reverting to its imperial past. All three countries vehemently reject the imperial label, as do other countries – e.g. India – also sometimes described as an empire. Empires are comprehensively discredited today. No-one wants to be an empire – or at least to admit to being one. If empires exist, they dare not speak the name.

But the ideological victory of nationalism can disguise many things happening beneath the name of "nation-state" – including the persistence of empire. We shall discuss this in our final chapter. But here we must note a number of things concerning the presumed move in recent times "from empire to nation or nation-state" – Gellner's argument, of course, but also a common formulation in much of the literature (e.g. Emerson 1962; Esherick et al. 2006). There are two presumptions here. One is structural: of the fundamental distinction between empires and nation-states, suggesting irreconcilable differences between them and the more or less inevitable hostility of one to the other, as harboring contrary interests (e.g. Spruyt 2001). The other is chronological: the assumption that there has been a more or less steady process of the replacement of empires by nation-states over the last century or so, the early twentieth century usually featuring as, if not the end, the beginning of the end (e.g. Maier 2007: 134, 154; Manela 2009: 11, 225). Both these presumptions are, if not wholly misleading, at least in need of severe qualification.[6]

First, are empires and nation-states so completely different, such inveterate foes?[7] Might they not have more in common than usually thought? We have already, in the previous chapter, had reason to consider the case of Britain, or the United Kingdom, as a kind of "mini-empire," an "inner empire" that then became the basis for the construction of an outer, overseas empire, the more familiar "British Empire." The English, having themselves been conquered by the Normans in 1066, merged with their conquerors and then, as Anglo-Normans, went on to conquer their near neighbors, the Welsh and the Irish. They almost conquered the Scots at the same time, and, though thwarted in this venture, they were able thoroughly to "anglicize" Scottish culture and institutions, making Scottish absorption in the more or less forced union of 1707 much easier. The "United Kingdom of Great Britain and Ireland," in other words, often thought of as a nation-state, has all the hallmarks of an "English Empire," an empire made by the English. Having done this, they brought their Celtic subjects – the Welsh, Scots, and Irish – into imperial partnership as they went on to create the vast overseas British Empire (Kumar 2003: 60–88).

Many other so-called nation-states have been formed by a similar process of "internal colonization." These include some of the oldest, best-known, and almost canonical examples of nation-states, such as France and Spain. "France" – the French nation – was created by the Capetian kings and their successors, expanding from their base in the Île-de-France and going on to conquer the neighboring principalities and kingdoms of Brittany, Burgundy, Flanders, Languedoc, Normandy, Gascony, Aquitaine, Provence, and several others. Such was the forcible making of "the hexagon," the French nation-state. As late as the French Revolution of 1789, France was still not a unified nation, divided as it was by strong regional languages and disparate traditions. It was not until the end of the nineteenth century that "peasants were turned into Frenchmen," in Eugen Weber's famous account, mainly through the agency of the schools and the army. As Weber says, "the famous hexagon can itself be seen as a colonial empire shaped over the centuries: a complex of territories conquered, annexed, and integrated in a political and administrative whole, many of them with strongly developed national or regional personalities, some of them with traditions that were specifically un- or even anti-French" (Weber 1976: 485).

Spain followed a similar course, of unification through conquest. Following the union of the kingdoms of Aragon and Castile in 1469, and the expulsion of the Moors in 1492, Spanish monarchs embarked on a mission to bring the adjacent Iberian territories into a unified state and to form a single Spanish nation. The incompleteness of this effort, and the clear evidence of the variegated nature of the "Spanish nation," can be seen in the repeated attempts by various parts – the Basques, the Catalans – to break away from Spain and form their own independent nation-states. The Spanish Civil War of the 1930s brought out many of the historic enmities, and Franco's draconian attempts to suppress them seem only to have driven them underground until a more auspicious opportunity arose to express once more their sense of difference and separateness. The sense of an "inner" Spanish Empire, which accompanied and in many ways launched the great overseas enterprises of the sixteenth century, creating the overseas empire, seems as clear here as in the English case.[8]

Two other, more recent, cases might be mentioned – again because they have come to be seen as representative examples of the creation of nation-states through nationalism. The unification of Italy (1860–70) and of Germany (1871) were long regarded as almost textbook-like illustrations of the triumph of nationalism in the nineteenth century. And yet more recent research has revealed them to be more like conquest states, akin to those of England/Britain and France. Italy was united from the top, and often against the popular will and the desires of other Italian states, by the Piedmontese monarchy under the direction of Camillo Cavour, who was no Italian nationalist (unlike Garibaldi and his Redshirts). Germany similarly, and more familiarly, was united by Prussian conquest of the other German states, many of whom were strongly opposed to joining a Germany under Prussian predominance. The later united German state of 1871 – which, after all, was called the "Second Reich," though often treated by historians as a nation-state – included not just these unwilling German members, but also non-German Alsatians, Danes, and millions of Poles.[9] The Prussian prime minister and new German chancellor, Otto von Bismarck, was deeply suspicious of German nationalism, and sought to undercut it by his exclusion of German-speaking Austria from the new Germany. For this old-style Prussian Junker, Germany was as much a dynastic state – the domain of the Hohenzollerns – as the Habsburg Empire. Hence the playing up of imperial symbols, and the frequent recall of the glories of the "Holy Roman Empire of the German People" (Berger 2004: 82–3).

One further example, from outside Europe, might illustrate well the overlap between nation – or nation-state – and empire. When the Chinese Empire collapsed in 1911, the republican state that replaced it was called a nation-state. It reflected the ideology of Chinese nationalism that – following Western models – had grown up in the late nineteenth century, basing itself on the idea of a predominant Han "race" (Dikötter 2015).[10] And yet both the Republic and the communist state that replaced it in 1949 held on to the same territories and groups of peoples as had the Qing Empire that fell in 1911 (just as the Soviet state that replaced the tsarist one in Russia in 1917 reconstituted the Russian Empire) (Esherick 2006: 229).[11]

China defines itself today as a "multinationality nation-state" (duo minzu guojia), with 56 recognized nationalities. The Han – the "majority nationality" – are said to constitute 92 percent of the population, with the remaining 55 "minority nationalities" making up the rest (Perdue 2007: 165). The awkward formulation, a "multinationality nation-state," reflects no more than the current disfavor into which the term "empire" has fallen today. No-one want to call themselves an empire, even if they are. Some of the "minority nationalities," like the Uighurs and the Tibetans, run into millions of people. Even the idea of a majority Han ethnicity is questioned by many scholars, as a construct invented by nineteenth-century theorists (Dikötter 2015: 61–78). Certainly, present-day China has as much the appearance of an empire as of a nation-state, as any Uighur or Tibetan will attest.

New nations as well as old display – if not the overlap – the close relation between empires and nation-states. This is true of many of the new nations of Africa and Asia, formed in the wake of decolonization in the twentieth century. These – Zimbabwe, Zambia, Malawi, Kenya, and most of the others, especially in Africa – are imperial creations, formed largely out of the geopolitical competition among European powers in the "scramble for Africa." They have almost no historical or ethnic basis, even though certain tribes predominate in many of them. In these cases, nations have been made by empires, from the outside; in the earlier European examples, nations have been made more by an inner process of "internal colonization." But in both cases, the old as well as the new, it is quite clear that the opposition between nation and empire will not hold up – at least in practice, whatever the theory or the principles might hold. Many nation-states are empires in miniature; they have been formed in the way that empires are usually formed, by the accretion of peoples and territories. Once formed, they can, of course, disavow their imperial origins. "Forgetfulness," as Ernest Renan said, "and I shall even say historical error, form an essential factor in the creation of a nation" (Renan [1882] 2001: 166). For nation-states, it is a necessity to present themselves as historic nations finding their "natural" completion in an independent state.

Empires as Nation-States

If nation-states have often been constructed as empires, and in their early years sometimes called themselves such (Kumar 2010: 124–5), might the reverse also be true? If nation-states can be seen as mini-empires, can empires be seen as (large) nation-states? Do nationalism and imperialism overlap?

Nation-states, as argued by Anthony Smith (1986), are generally constituted by core ethnies, dominant ethnic groups surrounded by other ethnic groups that act in a subordinate or subaltern capacity. Whether, for instance, we consider England itself or the British nation it created, it is clear that the English have been the dominant ethnie since at least the sixteenth century, with the Welsh, Scots, Irish, and later Jews, Indians, and Afro-Caribbeans, playing supporting roles. It is this ethnie that gives to the nation its "national character." It is that that supplies it with its ruling language, culture, and institutions (for other examples of dominant ethnies, see Kaufmann 2004).

Something similar can be said about empires, if not quite so unequivocally. In most empires, one can find a dominant people – the Romans, the Spanish, the English, the French, the Russians, etc. – who can be said to "name" the empire, who give it some of its principal characteristics.[12] They are the "state-bearing" peoples of the empire. They are its creators, and even if they are not dominant in terms of numbers – e.g. Germans in the Habsburg Empire – it is usually their language and culture that is the "high culture" of the empire, one that it is necessary to acquire if one wishes to make one's way in the empire (just as it is necessary to acquire the national culture in order to progress in the nation-state).

For the ruling or dominant peoples, it is not so much their nation as their empire that gives them a sense of themselves, just as in nation-states the nation identifies itself with the nation-state it creates. They are imperial peoples, not just national peoples. They take pride in their far-flung creations. But, just as nationalists often feel that there is something unique and special about their nation – that they may even have a providential mission or destiny in the world, as a "chosen people" (Smith 2003) – so too, even more, do the ruling peoples of the empire link themselves with a cause or a mission which they feel they have a duty to promote. We might call this "imperial" or "missionary" nationalism, always aware that to some extent that is a poetic description, and also that, since the ideology of nationalism did not emerge until the nineteenth century, there is something anachronistic in talking about imperial nationalism in empires that long predate that ideology (Kumar 2000: 30–5). Nevertheless, there do seem strong parallels between the ways nations and empires see their place and purpose in the world – including sometimes a sense of superiority.

For empires, the causes with which they identify themselves, and which gave an identity to the ruling people, have often been those of the great world religions. For the Indians of the Mauryan Empire, it was Buddhism; for the Chinese in their empire, it was Confucianism. The Arabs and the Ottomans made Islam their cause. The Romans first espoused the secular mission of civilizing – i.e. Romanizing – the world; later, though, they adopted Christianity and made its spread their mission. Western empires followed here, as in so many other respects, the Roman example, especially with respect to promoting Christianity. But the divisions within Christianity mean that different empires espoused different varieties. For the Habsburgs (Spanish and Austrian), the Portuguese, and the first French, North American, Empire, it was Catholicism; for the Byzantines and the Russians, it was Orthodoxy; for the Dutch and the British, it was Protestantism.

With the relative decline of religion in the nineteenth and twentieth centuries, the earlier Roman concern with civilizing returned. The French, in their second empire in Africa and Asia, explicitly named their mission as the *mission civilisatrice*; the British in theirs put the stress on the rule of law and parliamentarism. The rise of communism offered the secular cause in a new guise, one adopted by both the Russians and the Chinese in their resurrected empires.

The global, universalist, goals of these imperial missions might suggest a significant difference from nationalist ideologies, which tend to be more inward looking. But we must not forget that for early nationalists, such as Giuseppe Mazzini, nationalism did see itself in global terms. Nationalism for Mazzini was a first – though necessary

– step toward internationalism, a peaceful world of nation-states that respected each other's independence. The 1848 revolutions in Europe shattered many of those hopes, and later nineteenth-century nationalism increasingly took on a darker, more exclusivist, tone. Here what the nation increasingly celebrated was itself, its unique culture and character, not any wider or nobler purpose. National egotism became the order of the day, culminating in the murderous nationalism of the fascists and Nazis (Kumar 2012: 160–1).

But the parallel between imperial and national causes, and the peoples who promote the causes, is still suggestive. In both cases, we see the attempt to effect a fusion – a symbiosis almost – between a people and their political creation. Imperial nationalism plays down membership of a "mere" nation, with its tendency toward self-congratulation and self-importance; but it does so in order to insist on a higher form of nationalism – one that links the nation to a higher cause, one that goes beyond the nation.

There was indeed a moment, in the later nineteenth and early twentieth centuries, when imperialism and nationalism fused. But it was one that made imperialism the handmaid of the nation, rather than the other way round. This was the period in which, as the liberal writer J. A. Hobson saw it, nationalism threw off its liberal mantle and sought, on behalf of the nation, to crush other nations in the pursuit of world power. Like Mazzini, Hobson still looked to "genuine nationalism" as "the plain highway to internationalism." But he thought that in his own time it had debased into a form of imperialism, while imperialism itself – previously also internationalist, aiming at a world civilization – had been hijacked by nationalism, turning it into a hypertrophied or bloated nationalism (Hobson [1902] 1938: 11).[13]

In this view, both nationalism and imperialism have been diverted from their original, more generous, purposes. But it nevertheless indicates once more the many ways that empire and nation, imperialism and nationalism, can converge. If nation-states can be seen as empires, so too empires can be seen as no more than the nation-state writ large. The British Empire therefore – or "Greater Britain" as some termed it – is in this view no more than an extension of the English or British nation, an expression of British nationalism (e.g. Seeley [1883] 1971); the French Empire is no more than an expression of, and a compensation for, a wounded French nationalism in the wake of the crushing defeat at the hands of Prussia in 1871 (Schivelbusch 2004: 103–87). For many, this fatal conjunction of nationalism and imperialism was only confirmed by the fascist regimes of Italy, Germany, and Japan in the 1920s and 1930s, when nationalist regimes sought to enhance their power by imperialist land grabs (Arendt 1958: 123–302).

From Empire to Nation-State: A Natural Progression?

If nations can be seen as miniature empires, and empires as glorified nation-states, then that might throw into question the whole idea that the natural movement in modern times is "from empire to nation-state" – as we have seen, a very common assumption. In this view – as influentially propounded by Gellner and others – empires are archaic and premodern.[14] Their persistence can only be explained by a time-lag. They are hangovers from the past, destined to be replaced by the modern, up-to-date, nation-state.

But what if, with Frederick Cooper (2005: 153–203), we see empires and nation-states as "variable forms of the political imagination" in recent times – alternative possibilities, rather than an inevitable succession from one to the other?[15] What if one is not destined to be superseded by the other, but both remain possible ways of conceiving and organizing the world order? That, rather than some notion of a natural or inevitable succession, might help explain the otherwise puzzling fact of the long persistence of empires into modern times.[16]

Nationalism certainly challenged empires and the imperial principle in the nineteenth century. For smaller states and nations, or those which had historically been suppressed by more powerful neighbors – usually empires – striving for the nation-state seemed to be the best way to advance their cause and to protect or recover their freedom. Such was the case, for example, with Ireland, Norway, Poland, Italy, and the Slav peoples of the Habsburg Empire. Nationalism also appealed to some among the ruling peoples in the great empires, such as the "Little Englanders" in the British Empire, the Slavophiles in the Russian Empire, and Turks in the Ottoman Empire. In France, too, there was bitter struggle in the late nineteenth century between nationalists and imperialists. For these opponents of empire, empire was a wasteful and dangerous distraction, weakening the "soul" of the nation (Kumar 2010: 134–5).

But, at the same time, we have to note the resilience of empires against the nationalist threat, and their astonishingly long persistence into the modern era. The nineteenth century is often labeled the "era of nationalism," but we need to remember that formal empire lasted until well into the twentieth century, and that it is only with the end of the great overseas European empires in the 1950s and 1960s that the nation-state really came into its own: that is, over 180 years after the French Revolution had enunciated the principle of nationalism (Cooper 2005: 190; Osterhammel 2014: 405, 421–2). If, as Christopher Bayly says, the "period 1890–1940 was . . . the age of hyperactive nationalism" (Bayly 2004: 462), then we should remember that it was also and equally an age of vigorous imperialism.[17]

For who were the dominant players on the world stage in the nineteenth century? They were all empires: the British, the French, the Ottomans, the Russians, Austria-Hungary, China. Toward the end of the century, Germany, Japan, and the USA could be added to the tally of empires (American denials notwithstanding). The First World War was a war brought on by imperial conflicts and fought between empires (Burbank and Cooper 2010: 370). Many of the land empires collapsed at this time – the Qing, the Habsburg, the Ottoman, the Romanov, the Hohenzollern – but the overseas empires – especially the French and the British – emerged strengthened after the war, especially with the grant of several League of Nations "Mandates." In addition, the Russian Empire returned as the Soviet Union; Germany, after the interlude of the Weimar Republic, re-started with the Third Reich of the Nazis; the Italian fascists embarked on the construction of a new "Roman Empire"; and Japanese imperialism strengthened in the 1930s with the conquest of much of China. "The age of empires did not come to a close in 1919" (Osterhammel 2014: 466).

The Second World War was again mainly a war between empires: the "Allies" – Britain, America, the Soviet Union, France, China – and the "Axis Powers" – Germany, Italy, Japan. The war again resulted in a bonfire of empires – not just those of the defeated powers, but also those of the victors. This time it was the turn of the overseas empires. With startling speed, the Dutch, the British, the French, and the Belgians – Portugal took longer – wound up their empires (see, further, the next chapter). But the era of empires was by no means over. The USA and the USSR now emerged as the dominant imperial powers – again, denials on both sides notwithstanding. China revived under the communists, and recovered all the old territories of the Chinese Empire.

With the fall of the Soviet Empire in 1991, many commentators proclaimed "the end of empire" (along with "the end of history"). The Soviet Union, they said, was "the last empire." But others remarked that the fall of the Soviet Union left the field clear for the remaining superpower, the United States, to carry the imperial torch (Mann 2008: 37). Meanwhile, China's astonishing rise to economic power since the 1980s has encouraged her to wish to play a greater role on the world stage, to the extent that some see a new Chinese Empire emerging – while post-Soviet Russia too has seemed unwilling to act like a regular nation-state, but has shown distinct imperialist tendencies.

We shall look more closely at these recent developments in our last chapter. But for the moment what we must note is that the idea that there has been a worldwide progression from empires to nation-states wildly distorts the historical record. There has been no such clear movement. Empires have persisted alongside nation-states through-out the last two centuries, and undoubtedly have been the more powerful and influential actors. Far from being archaic or aberrant, they have virtually defined how the world has developed. Charles Maier (2002) has indeed argued that the stabilization of the world order, after the settlements of 1918, 1945, and 1989, turned criti-cally on imperial supervision and co-ordination, principally by the United States but also by the British and French empires, as well as the Soviet Union. The modern world, the world that was created after the eighteenth-century American and French Revolutions, has been as much a world of empires as of nation-states.

Empires and Nationalism

One can go further, and argue that it is not just that empires have co-existed with nation-states over the past two centuries, but that empires have actually nurtured nations and nationalism. Empires, in other words, are not necessarily only the antagonists of nations, as the received account has it. In many ways, empires have been the parents of nations.

This has occurred in two ways. The first has to do with the strategy of empires in playing off nations against each other, in order better to create stability and order within the empire. Nationalism is indeed a threat to empire, with its multinational or multicultural character. Its growth in the nineteenth century – whether among subject or ruling peoples – was regarded with alarm by all those charged with ruling the empires. Some, such as the Austrian statesman Clemens von Metternich, made opposition to nationalism, in the Habsburg Empire and beyond, the center-piece of policy. The 1848 revolutions throughout Europe indicated that simple opposition to nationalism, and attempts to suppress it, were likely to fail. Better to harness its force, and put it to use in strengthening the empire.

An indication of how that might be done was already given by the famous refusal in 1848 of the Czech nationalist, František Palacký, to join the German Frankfurt Assembly in its attempt to create an independent German nation-state. As a Czech, Palacký pointed out to Germans who took Czech support for granted, he had no wish to join the German nation. But, more to the point, he protested at the attempt to dismember the Austrian Habsburg Empire, which he regarded as the necessary safeguard of all small nations such as the Czechs against the designs of its powerful Slav neighbor to the East, the Russian Empire. In a famous statement, he declared that "if the Austrian state had not existed for ages, we would be obliged in the interests of Europe and even of mankind to endeavor to create it as fast as possible" (in Kumar 2017: 193).

Later Slav thinkers, such as Thomas Masaryk, were to add to this fear of Russia the designs of the newly powerful neighbor to the West, a united Germany, as an equal threat. From this way of thinking developed the powerful "Austro-Slav" movement among the Slav peoples of the Habsburg Empire. For them, empire was not the proverbial "prison house of nations" but – provided allowance was made for the development of their own ethnic cultures – a protective shell against the threats coming from both East and West (Kumar 2017: 193–5; see also Comisso 2006).

The Habsburg Empire's rulers took their cue from this approach. The nationalism of the ruling peoples – the Germans and the Hungarians – had to be put down, as likely to stir up the resentment of the other peoples in the empire. But a properly regulated Slav nationalism could be cultivated, as a balance to the nationalism of Germans and Hungarians, from whom the empire had the most to fear. Ideas of this sort were advanced from the very top, by such figures as the Crown Prince Rudolf, heir to the Habsburg throne; the Archduke John, brother to the emperor Francis I; and the Archduke Franz Ferdinand, who succeeded as the Habsburg heir on the suicide of his cousin Rudolf (Wheatcroft 1996: 165–7, 279–81; Judson 2016: 327–8). Such ideas were echoed, from a social-democratic position, by Austro-Marxists such as Karl Renner and Otto Bauer (Kumar 2017: 199–200). After the "Compromise" of 1867, giving rise to the Dual Empire of Austria–Hungary, they gave rise to hopeful proposals – never implemented – to add a formal "third leg" to the empire, making it "Austria–Hungary–Slavia."

The idea of balancing nationalisms against each other proved particularly effective in the case of Austrian Galicia. Here, Poles were the wealthiest and most powerful group, dominating their Ruthenian (Ukrainian) co-residents. The Poles here, as elsewhere in the region, were intensely nationalistic. In 1846, they rose against their Austrian rulers. The rebellion was put down ruthlessly, but, following it, the Austrian government saw fit to promote Ukrainian nationalism, as a counter to that of the Poles. Many Ukrainians date the rise of Ukrainian nationalism from this time. The Galician city of Lemberg (later Ukrainian Lviv) became the heartland of Ukrainian nationalism – and remains so today.

The Russian Empire appears to have taken a leaf from their Habsburg neighbor's book. It too had its Polish problem, on an even bigger scale. The Poles had risen in rebellion in 1830, and again, more threateningly, in 1863. The Russian response was not just repression, but the stimulation of alternative nationalisms where the Polish presence was strong. Thus, in Lithuania, as a means of offsetting Polish influence, the Lithuanian language and Lithuanian culture were encouraged. Even their Catholicism was tolerated, despite its being also the religion of the Poles. Hence, once more, a new nationalism, Lithuanian nationalism, was brought into being by the active intervention of an empire (Weeks 2001). Dangerous as the strategy was, it proved successful here, as in a number of other cases; and, as we shall see later, it was not nationalism that brought down the Russian Empire (nor, indeed, any other).

Following the well-tried imperial recipe of "divide and rule," other empires have also employed the strategy of stimulating one nationalism to offset another. The British were almost too successful in fomenting Muslim nationalism to counter the growing force of Hindu-majority Indian nationalism in their empire. Jinnah and the other Muslim leaders, right up to the Second World War, had no intention or desire to create a separate Muslim state out of the British Raj. But they certainly responded to British encouragement to develop their own cultural identity and to make demands for at least designated Muslim provinces within an independent India. In the upshot, and speeded up by developments in the Second World War, the outcome was indeed a separate, almost wholly Muslim state, Pakistan, created out of the bloody conflicts of the "Partition" of 1948 (Brendon 2007: 396–420; Clarke 2008: 425–53, 493–6).

The Second World War also gave the Japanese Empire an opportunity to exploit the forces of nationalism against their enemies – the British, the French, the Dutch, and the Americans (Burbank and Cooper 2010: 404–11; Kennedy 2016: 32–3). The Japanese did not create Indonesian, Burmese, or Malayan nationalism. But, under the banner of "Asia for the Asians" and the "Greater East Asia Co-Prosperity Sphere," they used their kinship with other Asian nations to promote themselves as the liberators of these nations from Western colonial rule. Their incorporation of French Indochina as a Japanese protectorate, their crushing victories over the British in Hong Kong, Singapore, Malaya, and Burma, and over the Americans in the Philippines, provided them with the opportunity to back nationalist leaders such as Achmed Sukarno of Indonesia, Aung San of Burma, and even some of India's nationalist leaders, such as Subhas Chandra Bose (Ho Chi Minh of Vietnam was less persuaded, in the light of Japanese support of the Vichy regime in Indochina, but he too took advantage of Japan's removal of French power). The sight of an Asian power defeating the erstwhile impregnable West was bound to be invigorating to Asian nationalists of all kinds. Japan was defeated, of course; but the nationalism that it had promoted and strengthened in the end proved formidable (Albertini 1969: 29–31). In their weakened circumstances after the Second World War, most of the European empires found that they had neither the strength nor the will to resist nationalist demands.

There is yet another way in which empire and nation stood not as antagonists, but as partners. John Darwin has argued that "empire created distinctive kinds of ethnicities, not just by promoting a 'tame' indigenity, but by subsuming local sources of meaning in a new supra-local identity." He calls these new identities "imperial ethnicities": "the assertion or acceptance of an ethnic identity that promised (or seemed to) a privileged access to the resources and opportunities that an empire could afford" (2013: 150, 165). His view is that older native identities often lacked the resources – material and ideological – to construct the kind of nationhood that was required for the modern nation-state. Native elites in the overseas empires willingly collaborated with their European imperial rulers in governing the empire; as Gallagher and Robinson (1953) showed some time ago, such collaboration was essential in the running of the far-flung and diverse empires. Darwin argues that such collaboration had an educative effect on native elites, leading them to adopt much of the language and the techniques of European nationalism. This did not necessarily mean rejecting older identities – it mostly meant fusing them with the new ideas and new possibilities. Out of this interaction came new national identities and such modern movements as Indian, Indonesian, and Vietnamese nationalism.[18]

We might, finally, note that one of the most spectacular examples of "imperial ethnicity" took place in the Soviet Union – the "Soviet Empire." Here, once more, the effect was the result of collaboration between Soviet and local elites. Bolshevik leaders such as Lenin, and especially Stalin, accepted that many of the native peoples of the

Soviet Union had not yet achieved the level of "civilization" necessary to make them full functioning Soviet Socialist Republics (the prelude to the higher product of the single socialist "Soviet People" of the future). Stalin, as Commissar for the Nationalities, and later as Soviet leader, embarked on an extensive program of *korenizatsiia*, or "indigenization." The aim was to stimulate local cultures and, through an ambitious program of education, to bring the native peoples up to the level of modern nations. A number of groups were selected as "titular nationalities" – Ukrainians, Belorussians, Georgians, Armenians, Azerbaijanis, Uzbeks, Kazakhs, and several others – and their language and culture were officially promoted, through national festivals, "folk" museums, broadcasting, and political and educational institutions. In several cases, there were no existing written languages or any of the usual emblems of nationhood, and so they had to be, and were, invented by Soviet scholars and bureaucrats. The result was the "upgrading," and in some cases the actual invention, of nations where – especially in the Central Asian republics – none had existed before (Kumar 2017: 291–300).

Local elites were the main beneficiaries of this policy of indigenization. They staffed the local Soviet institutions and had extensive control of their republics. For much of the history of the Soviet Union, they were content to act in these roles. But the seeds of nationalism had been planted by the Soviet state. When, in the 1980s and 1990s, the Soviet Union unraveled, the local elites were ready to step forward as national spokesmen. They exchanged their sober Soviet suits for more colorful ethnic garb. But Belorussian, Uzbek, Kazakh, Turkmen, and a good number of other nationalisms had been born within, and at the instigation of, the Soviet state. So, too, to a good extent, was Russian nationalism – this time because Russians, supposedly the dominant ethnic group, felt they had been the victims of the Soviet state, ignored when all the other nationalities had been cultivated. Either way, the Soviet Union can be held to have nurtured the national groups that took over as its successors – though, again, it was not nationalism that brought down the Soviet Union, any more than it did any of the other modern empires.

"We live," as John Darwin says, "in a world largely made by empires and among ethnic identities as often forged in collaboration with those empires as rallied against them" (2013: 168). It is an understanding frequently lost or distorted in the common habit of pitting nation against empire. Empires make nations, as much as they are, on occasion, opposed by them.

Empire Against Nation-State: Divergent Principles

It has been important to show the similarities and overlaps between empires and nation-states because of the persisting tendency to see them as rivals, sworn enemies. Perhaps the strongest underlying feeling, not always made explicit, is that empires are old-fashioned, archaic, part of humanity's past but not of its present or future. Empires and modernity, it is thought, make awkward bed-fellows. There is no room for empires in the modern world. "This is," declares Michael Mann (2008: 41, 43), "no longer the age of empires but of nationalism and the nation-state. . . . Empires are no longer normal."

The preceding account should dispel such an illusion. Empires have been as much a part of modern times as nation-states – arguably, more so. Not only have nations often been made by empires, they have been overseen by them for much of their history. In the twentieth century, empires were the dominant players almost as much as they were in the nineteenth century, supervising, through their directing roles in such organizations as the League of Nations and the United Nations, the emergence and fortunes of nation-states (Mazower 2009a). Nation-states have for much of the time lived in the shadow of empire. Only since the 1960s, perhaps, has it been possible to say that we live in world of nation-states – and, as we have seen, even that statement needs severe qualification.

We might go further. Nation-states might seem the norm of the present time. But to many observers, a world of competing nation-states is a recipe for continuing conflict, one that, in the nuclear age, threatens not just the peace but the very existence of humanity. In the wake of the collapse of the "last empire," the Soviet Union, Charles Maier remarked that "I do believe that we relied on something very like an empire in the postwar period, that it provided an undergirding of peace and prosperity, and that we shall need some equivalent territorial ordering to emerge successfully in the era that has followed 1989" (Maier 2002: 62).

We shall consider some of those prospects and possibilities in our final chapter. But here we might simply note that nation-states are a late and recent development, and that, compared with empires, the period of their dominance has been remarkably short so far. Their future remains uncertain. Over a century ago, the great theorist of the nation, Ernest Renan, observed that nationalism is "the law of the age in which we live." But, he continued, "nations are not something eternal. They have had their beginnings; they shall have their end" (Renan [1882] 2001: 175). For some, that end – at least insofar as it applies to a world made up of a multiplicity of nation-states – cannot come too soon, for humanity's sake. Even Ernest Gellner, as we have noted, despite his stress on the functional necessity of the nation-state in modern society, came to yearn for something different, returning in his last years to something like the Habsburg Empire – the region of his upbringing – as a model for a future world order (Kumar 2015).

At any rate, we need, in the end, to stress the differences between empires and nation-states, despite their many resemblances. As principles of political organization, they point in very different directions. The principle of the nation-state is one nation, one state. Its drive is toward uniformity and homogeneity. There should be one national people and one national culture. Every people has its own unique and singular culture. "No nation," as Benedict Anderson says, "imagines itself coterminous with mankind" (2006: 7). If there is diversity, it is at the international level. The world is a world of nation-states, each cultivating its own culture. There is a recognition of difference and particularity, but only between nations, not within them.

Empires go the other way in almost every respect. As we have noted a number of times, empires are universalist, unitary, and multiethnic or multinational. They aim at the spread of a particular civilizational idea in the world, of which they see themselves to be the unique carriers. In principle, there can be only one empire in the world, and one imperial mission. Their aim, unlike nation-states, is indeed to be "coterminous with mankind." They are also irreducibly plural. Unlike nation-states, this plurality is internal, not external. Empires rule over many lands and peoples. The task of managing such diversity is one of their principal challenges. As soon as empires feel the need to "nationalize" themselves, to become something like large nations, as happened with several empires in the late nineteenth century, they have signed their own death warrant.

The most dangerous nationalism, from the point of view of the health and persistence of empire, is that of the ruling people itself. Nationalisms from below it can usually cope with. But that of its own *ethnie*, of the people who oversee the empire (though generally with much cooptation of other groups), threatens its very principle of existence. It has to be above the fray, to allow for the diversity that characterizes it. The ruling people certainly aim to guide the empire in a certain direction, toward the greater and greater realization of the imperial mission. A certain degree of assimilation, especially among local elites, is necessary for the orderly running of the empire. But for the ruling people to stress the culture and superiority of their own nation, to make it the goal of the empire to promote that, risks stirring up resentments among the other national groups in the empire. When, in the late nineteenth century, Turks in the Ottoman Empire, and Russians in the Russian Empire, began to agitate on behalf of Turkish and Russian nationalism, they threatened the viability of the whole imperial enterprise. The empire's rulers and advisers sought, as far as they were able, to head off this dangerous development. To a remarkable degree they were successful, until they were drawn into the maelstrom of the First World War.

J. A. Hobson, writing at the time of the Boer War, and alarmed at the increasing fusion of nationalism and imperialism, made it clear at the outset of his great work, *Imperialism*, that such a development was a perversion of both principles. He was particularly keen to emphasize this point in relation to empire – for, despite the use made of his work by anti-imperialists such as Lenin, he was fundamentally pro-empire, and thought the British Empire had an important role to play in the future.

What was particularly important about empire, according to Hobson, and what had been its essential principle in the past, was its universalism and its unitary nature. It was this that was undermined by its collusion with a power-hungry and competitive nationalism. This had produced the novel phenomenon of a world of competitive empires.

The notion of a number of competing empires is essentially modern. The root idea of empire in the ancient and medieval world was that of a federation of states, under a hegemony, covering in general terms the entire known recognized world, such as was held by Rome under the so-called *pax Romana*. When Roman citizens, with full civic rights, were found all over the explored world, in Africa and Asia, as well as in Gaul and Britain, Imperialism contained a genuine element of internationalism. With the fall of Rome this conception of a single empire wielding political authority over the civilized world did not disappear. On the contrary, it survived all the fluctuations of the Holy Roman Empire. Even after the definite split between the Eastern and Western sections had taken place at the close of the fourth century, the theory of a single state, divided for administrative purposes, survived. Beneath every cleavage or antagonism, and notwithstanding the severance of many independent kingdoms and provinces, this ideal unity of the empire lived. It formed the conscious avowed ideal of Charlemagne . . . Rudolf of Habsburg not merely revived the idea, but laboured to realize it through Central Europe, while his descendant Charles V gave a very real meaning to the term by gathering under the unity of his imperial rule the territories of Austria, Germany, Spain, the Netherlands, Sicily and Naples. In later ages this dream of a European Empire animated the policy of Peter the Great, Catherine, and Napoleon. (Hobson [1902] 1938: 8–9)

The whole discussion in this book so far should indicate the fundamental accuracy of this masterly sketch of the imperial idea, at least in the West. It is confirmed by more recent studies of the idea (e.g. Folz 1969; Muldoon 1999; Münkler 2007). Hobson saw the persistence of the idea into the nineteenth century, sustained by the "humane cosmopolitanism" of the Enlightenment and the French Revolution. Even nationalism did not, in its early guise, threaten this ideal, since its ultimate goal was an orderly world society of independent nation-states. But its degeneration into an aggressive and competitive form, and imperialism's adoption of a nationalistic outlook, together worked to undermine the universalist dimension of empire.

Hobson saw little hope or possibility of reviving the universal empire. But, faced with the murderous nationalism of the 1930s, in the third edition of his *Imperialism* (1938) he expressed his belief that "any reasonable security for good order and civilization in the world implies the growing application of the federation [i.e., imperial] principle in international politics." He strongly championed the idea, which had attracted Seeley and others in the late nineteenth century, of turning the British Empire into an "Imperial Federation," "a voluntary federation of free British states, working peacefully for common safety and prosperity," which "might indeed form a step towards a wider federation of civilized States in the future" (Hobson [1902] 1938: 332).

Hobson was, of course, not alone in looking beyond the nation-state as the organizing principle of the modern world. The League of Nations was already an effort, if not to de-throne the nation-state, at least to subject its operations to some sort of regulation and oversight. The weakness and eventual failure of the League led to fresh efforts, after the Second World War, with the United Nations, this time given more teeth and more effective central control in the form of the Security Council. There are other supranational organizations too, most importantly the European Union – which some have compared, approvingly, to an empire (e.g. Münkler 2007: 167).

We shall later want to consider these parallels and analogies, and the question of how far empire – in some guise – remains a possibility. First, however, we need to consider how these far-flung and long-lasting entities met their end, at least formally. What brings about the end of empires? How has it come to be that, for many people, empires are now history, not a relevant part of our current condition? How did we come to say farewell to empire?

5
Decline and Fall

A Rhetorical Device?

It has been customary, since the earliest times, for empires to bemoan their fate. Their educated classes nearly all expect the empire, sooner or later, to decline and fall. Charles Maier writes of "the melancholy of empire, the intimations of mortality that tinge all its triumphs" (Maier 2007: 286; see also Ferguson 2010). Virgil may have written that the gods had given Rome "empire without end," in both time and space. But Roman emperors such as Marcus Aurelius were acutely aware of the problems facing Rome, and feared for its future. Roman writers such as Tacitus excoriated the empire and praised the "barbarians" who wished for its overthrow. Christian thinkers of the fourth and fifth centuries looked forward to the end of Rome as the sign of the anticipated Second Coming of Christ and his millennial rule.

At the other end of Eurasia, Chinese literati at regular intervals expressed their fears for the future of their ancient empire. Every significant dynastic change, as from the Song to the Yuan, or the Ming to the Qing, was accompanied by lengthy analyses of the trials and tribulations of empire, and the likelihood that this time there would be no recovery, that China would succumb to the "barbarians" (as indeed they did in these cases, though the empire recovered under the new rulers). In the nineteenth century, as the Qing came up against the power of Western nations, there was now a new perceived threat from barbarians, this time ones armed with formidable military power. Urgent reforms of the empire were required if it were to survive – but statesmen and scholars alike felt little hope that this would be achieved. Over 2,000 years of empire would soon come to an end, as the defeats by Europeans in the Opium Wars, and the great rebellions of the time – such as the White Lotus and Taiping – were already portending. "In late 1860," it was thought, "the Great Qing empire was near extinction" (Rowe 2012: 201).

Similar gloomy prognostications can readily be found in the modern Western empires as well. Luis de Camões's great sixteenth-century epic, *The Lusíads* (1572), while it celebrated the historic Portuguese voyages of Vasco da Gama and others, at the same time, as its modern editor notes, it sounded "a note of elegy," emitting "the odour of an empire in decline." Arriving in Lisbon after many years away in the East, Camões finds Portugal "given over / To avarice and philistinism / Heartlessness and degrading pessimism." It has "lost that pride, that zest for life" that formerly animated it and made its great achievements possible (Camões [1572] 1997: x, 226). Portugal's empire seems a thing of the past. Indeed, shortly after *The Lusíads* was published, Portugal suffered the catastrophic defeat of Alcácer-Kebir in Morocco (1578), with the death of King Sebastião and the loss of over 20,000 men, followed two years later by Portugal's absorption by Spain. Camões, it seemed, had been very prescient.

Seventeenth-century Spain, too, was full of writers and artists pronouncing doom on Spain's great empire (Elliott 1989: part IV). Spanish thinkers accepted the classical idea that all states went through a cycle, which made a phase of decline inevitable. As early as 1600, a prominent commentator, González de Cellorigo, observed "how our Spain is subject to the process of decline, to which all other republics are prone" (in Elliott 1989: 219). Spain, it was felt by many, was now in its stage of decline, as shown by rampant inflation, the loss of Portugal in 1640, and the revolt of the Catalans. And, as with Portugal, there was an epic, *Don Quixote* (1605–15), on hand to express the mood of disillusion and disorientation, the sense of a Spain – as with the bemused knight – "having lost its bearings in a changing world" (Elliott 1989: 265).

For the Islamic world, the great statesman and scholar Ibn Khaldun (1332–1406) had already formulated a law of decline, as hardy nomads – Arabs, Mongols, Ottomans – took over sedentary empires and were in their turn corrupted by the riches and comforts of urban life. Decline and demise of empires were as inevitable as the decay and death of human bodies (Shawcross 2016). In the seventeenth century, in the wake of the great triumphs of Suleyman the Magnificent in the previous century, Ottoman thinkers too began to worry about the future of the empire, and to discern the signs of decadence and decline all around them (Lewis 1962). The burden of complaint was, as so often, the decline or neglect of traditional practices and institutions – in this case, the abandonment of use of *kanun* or customary law, and an overreliance on the strict religious rule of the *sharia*; the decline of the *devshirme*, the levy of Christian youth that had produced some of the best of the sultan's ministers; the rejection of the *timar* system of land tenure which had provided the basis for the sturdy cavalry, the *sipahi*, the force behind some of the Ottomans' greatest victories (Kumar 2017: 116–17). By contrast, the elegiasts looked back to the golden age of Suleyman and, more generally, the period of the "first ten good sultans." The path since then had been downwards; the end would be soon.

Russians, too, at this time were contemplating a dismal future, and sounding the apocalyptic note (Hosking 2012: 131–74). With the death of Fedor I in 1598, the Riurikovich dynasty that had ruled Russia since its inception came to an end. The rule of his successor, Boris Godunov, ended in violence and chaos, to be followed by the well-known "time of troubles" (1604–13). The election in 1613 of Mikhail Romanov as the new tsar was subsequently seen as a turning point – but virtually no one at the time saw it as such. The "time of troubles" could be said to have extended to the end of the seventeenth century, with violence and uncertainty as its hallmark. In 1610, the Poles invaded and occupied Moscow, and the Swedes took Novgorod. Russia appeared to be on the point of dismemberment by its most powerful enemies. A succession of pretenders aimed at the throne, leading to almost continuous civil war. The Cossack Stepan Razin led one of the greatest peasant rebellions in Russian history, lasting more than four years and drawing in people from all parts of the empire. The "Great Schism" between the Reformers and the Old Believers convulsed the Orthodox Church. It was not surprising that the great Russian composer Modest Mussorgksy, in his two powerful operas *Boris Godunov* (1872) and the unfinished *Khovanshchina*, should use this period to illustrate Russia's seemingly irresolvable difficulties in achieving peace and harmony.

The seventeenth century generally has been seen as a "time of troubles" for societies all over Eurasia. "Declinism" has to be seen in this context. Historians have written of "the general crisis of the seventeenth century," a time of economic hardship, religious wars, and endemic rebellion and revolution. From the English Civil War, the *fronde* in France, the Thirty Years' War in Germany, revolts – Dutch, Catalan – throughout the Spanish Empire, over to the other side of Eurasia with the bloody conflicts attending the end of the Ming dynasty and the rise of the Qing, it has seemed impossible to think of this time as other than apocalyptic – as, indeed, it seemed to many participants at the time. Much has been attributed to the great climatic shift associated with the "Little Ice Age" of the seventeenth century (Brook 2013; Parker 2013; Goldstone [1991] 2016).

But the gloom and doom of the seventeenth century was followed by the sunny uplands of the eighteenth-century Enlightenment in Europe. The European empires – including the Ottoman – recovered (if they had ever declined) and continued for more than another two centuries, while at the same time conquering ever more of the world. In that time, the British and the French constructed the two largest empires in world history. In China, the Qing dynasty doubled the extent of the territory of the Chinese Empire and brought about one of the most prosperous periods in Chinese history (Rowe 2012: 1–2). If all this was "decline," every state should suffer it.

It is obvious, in fact, that "decline" is a rhetorical trope in the history of empires. It is a poetic mode that is readily available to intellectuals and statesmen when the going gets rough, on a par with the oft-repeated and equally rhetorical cry of despair, "*o tempora! o mores!*" ("oh, the times! oh, the customs!"). One can usually trace its antecedents in a tradition of "declinist" literature in the society in question – as, for instance, during the period of the "Warring States" in early Chinese history, or, for European societies, the laments of late Latin authors as the problems mounted in the later Roman Empire (arguably Christianity, with its early stress on the "end of time" and the dissolution of worldly society, was one such powerful source of "declinism" for these societies).[1]

There are many functions of this declinist literature, a principal one being to sound the alarm and call for reform (or return). What we cannot do is to take it at its face value. The prediction of the imminent end of empire is not generally based on a realistic assessment of its chances of survival but more on a moralistic sense of outrage or, often, simply on the sense that one's own group or class is losing out in the struggle for power. The Roman senatorial class regarded with horror the rise of non-Romans and non-Italians in the imperial bureaucracy and army, and their literary spokesmen duly proclaimed the imminent end of the empire.

In seeking to understand how and why empires decline and fall, therefore, we would be well advised to look beyond contemporary expressions of alarm. We need to examine the actual political and social forces, usually in the context of the international system, that undermined the empire and brought about its demise. Wars and revolutions are part of that story, as is the rise of nationalism and other modern ideologies such as socialism. Natural causes can play their part too, as is suggested for the fall of the Ming dynasty in China with its succession of devastatingly bad harvests and other weather-related disasters (Brook 2013: 238–61).

The range of empires is huge, and the causes and manner of their fall equally complex and varied. For the West, with the dominance of classical studies for so long, the "fall of Rome" has received an almost inordinate amount of treatment. The canonical work here is Edward Gibbon's *History of the Decline and Fall of the Roman Empire* (1776–88) – written at the height of the European Enlightenment, when, sustained by the Industrial Revolution, Europe was just about to take off into self-sustaining economic and technological growth and conquer the world. Gibbon may have been issuing some kind of warning to Europe, with Rome as the parallel. But his *History* – despite later misconceptions – is not really about the fall of Rome at all, or at least not the Rome that most people have in mind. For, as Gibbon shows, if Rome fell in the fifth century, it fell only in the West; it continued for another thousand years as the Byzantine Empire, which always saw itself as the continuation of the Roman Empire. The "fall" that Gibbon chronicles, for the greater part of his work, is not so much that of the western Roman Empire as that of its eastern part, the Byzantine Empire that fell to the Ottoman Turks in 1453 (and the famous "triumph of barbarism and religion" that he sees as the principal cause may refer therefore not, as is usually thought, to the German tribes and Christianity, but to the Arabs, Turks, and Islam).

Gibbon was very confident about the causes of the decline of the Roman Empire in the West. It was "the natural and inevitable effect of immoderate greatness. Prosperity ripened the principle of decay; the causes of destruction multiplied with the extent of conquest; and as soon as time or accident had removed the artificial supports, the stupendous fabric yielded to the pressure of its own weight." Indeed, for Gibbon, "the story of its ruin is simple and obvious; and instead of inquiring why the Roman Empire was destroyed, we should rather be surprised that it had subsisted so long" (Gibbon ([1776–88] 1995, II: 509). This "simple" account of Rome's downfall has been echoed by numerous commentators since, and made the basis of several general theories of "the rise and fall of great powers," to employ the Gibbonesque title of Paul Kennedy's well-known book. For Kennedy, as for Gibbon, states and empires fall through "imperial overreach," a striving for conquest and expansion that goes beyond the material base that was responsible for the initial rise (Kennedy 1989: xxiv–xxvii, 566–76, 693–8).

Gibbon's work was enormously influential in nineteenth-century

Europe. It was the source of many of the melancholy reflections on the possible decline of the British and other European empires, with Rome as the inevitable comparison (Kumar 2017: 340–7). We need, to some extent, to distance ourselves from that overwhelming presence. Rome is but one example of a general phenomenon that has received extensive treatment from historians and sociologists.[2] It is impossible to ignore Rome, given its enormous importance in the "tradition of empire" in the West – the sense that each empire was merely re-capitulating the Roman experience. Its "decline and fall" will always repay inquiry.[3] But, if we are casting our net on a global scale, clearly there is something limiting in confining our attention to what can be learned from that one example, however brilliantly and influentially studied.

There seems, finally, despite the conventional wisdom, nothing inevitable about the fall of empires.[4] Or, perhaps, one might better say, if their fall is inevitable, no one has come up with any general theory as to why that might be so. Cyclical theories, on the analogy of the natural processes of the seasons or the individual life-cycle, were once popular, but have long been out of fashion. Ideas such as "over-reach" are suggestive but too vague to be of much use, and in any case do not fit all the examples, including some of the most important ones.[5] All states, like all humans, ultimately fail. Empires are no exception to that general rule. But neither is their fall something deserving special treatment. They are subject to the same contingencies, and the same general processes, as all states. Each empire has its own history. But there are times when whole clusters of empires are subject to the same forces. Here we might be able to discern some general features.

China and the End of Empire

In a short treatment of the kind attempted in this book, we can deal with only a handful of cases of the fall of empires. For their obvious relevance to our own times, the fall of the European empires in the twentieth century has a special claim on our attention. That is especially true of the end of the overseas empires after 1945 – the process known as "decolonization," on which there is now a voluminous literature. The impact of that is still being felt the world over.

But a brief treatment, first, of the end of the Chinese Empire, the most venerable of the empires and the longest-lasting, seems in order. With the fall of the Qing dynasty in 1911, 2,000 years of Chinese imperial history came to an end. That was not necessarily the end of the Chinese as an imperial people; as we shall see later, the Chinese after an interregnum of some 30 years re-constituted their empire under a new name, the "People's Republic of China." But, in both a formal and symbolic sense, something definitely ended in 1911.

It suited the interests of both republicans and communists – the successors to the empire – to present the Qing Empire as stagnant and in long-term decline. As such, it was common to call it "feudal." The "May 4 Movement" that started in 1919, with its Westernizing and modernizing turn, energetically promoted such a view. Western opinion, for its part, readily accepted this assessment. In such a view, the 1911 revolution was not only inevitable but long overdue.

This view has been decisively refuted by recent research.[6] There were, it has been shown, vigorous attempts at reform, first in the "Hundred Days Reforms" of 1898, and later, more successfully, in the "New Policies" (*xinzheng*) of 1901–10. Learning from the Japanese example, the Qing government proposed, and implemented, new representative institutions at the local and provincial levels. In 1910, it also laid out a scheme for a National Assembly (to be convened in 1917); in the meantime, it established a Provisional National Assembly and arranged for representatives to be selected by the local and provincial assemblies. Responding to pressure from the numerous constitutionalist societies that sprang up after 1905, the court also announced its intention of promulgating a constitution – again, on the Japanese model of a constitutional monarchy – in 1917.

To stimulate commerce and promote industrialization, the government sought to establish and co-ordinate chambers of commerce in the provinces and major cities. By 1909, there were about 180 of these, actively engaged in promoting economic activity, often in partnership with foreign companies. The chambers were also important in giving businessmen a voice, and creating a sense of solidarity among them, just as the provincial assemblies strengthened and solidified the local gentry groups who dominated them.

There were radical reforms also in the central administration and in education. The venerable and quaintly titled "Six Boards" were replaced by cabinet ministries on the Japanese and Western model. In 1905, the Qing court abolished the longstanding examination system for selecting officials. In its place, it established schools with Western curricula; their number grew from about 4,000 in 1904 to 52,000 by 1909. More than 4 million students passed through these new schools: "Almost overnight, the modern school diploma replaced the examination degree as the most basic credential for entering government service and achieving social status" (Rowe 2012: 260; see also Zhao 2006: 16–18).

Important changes also took place in the army, instituted by the Commission on Military Reorganization set up in 1903. The old banner forces and the Green Standard Army were abolished and in their place – under the direction of Yuan Shikai – appeared the westernized Beiyang Army, which became the best-organized and most efficient fighting force in China in the early decades of the twentieth century. New military academies were established, often with Japanese instructors, and "New Armies," officered by graduates of the new academies, were set up in the provinces. For the first time, perhaps, military service began to acquire prestige among the educated elite.

What is important to note is that the forces that eventually overthrew the Qing Empire were themselves direct creations of that empire, the product especially of the reforms that began in earnest in 1901. It was customary at one time to attribute the success of the revolution of 1911 to Sun Yat-Sen and his "Revolutionary Alliance." But Sun was out of China – mostly in Japan, Hawai'i, and the United States – for most of the first decade of the twentieth century, and was actually in Denver, Colorado, when the revolution broke out (Schiffrin 1971). Like Lenin and the Bolsheviks, Sun and his followers inherited the revolution but they did not make it (nor, in the end, did they control it for very long).[7]

The driving force of the revolution was not the radical students and the professional revolutionaries, who had mostly faded by 1908, but the "reformist elites" that were the products of the "New Policies" of the early 1900s: the gentry in the provincial assemblies, the business elites in the new chambers of commerce, the military officers that emerged from the new academies. Of course, these developments were not entirely new; they built on social and economic changes that had been taking place in the empire for a generation or more. But the New Policies, initiated as they were from the top, gave an added stimulus and encouragement to the groups that had been benefitting most from the changes. They became impatient with the delays and resistance that were the inevitable accompaniments of such radical policies. The empire, they felt, no longer served its purpose; some sort of constitutional republic would be the best vehicle to implement the necessary changes.

In 1911, they took the opportunity of an army mutiny, together with some localized disturbances caused in the main by floods and bad harvests, to accomplish a more or less bloodless revolution that ended the empire (Esherick 2006: 233–4; Rowe 2012: 280–3; Spence

2013: 249–54). Sun Yat-Sen, recently returned from the United States, and a nationally – and internationally – recognized symbol, was invited by a representative group of provincial elites, convened by Yuan Shikai, commander of the Beiyang Army, to become the provisional president of the new Republic of China, inaugurated on January 1, 1912. Actual power remained very much with Yuan Shikai and his army, as Sun himself acknowledged in a message to Yuan expressing the hope that he would soon succeed Sun as president. The Qing court, to whom Sun was anathema, in announcing the abdication of the 7-year-old Emperor Puyi, "the last emperor," on February 12, 1912, in fact made it a condition that Yuan Shikai should take over the presidency from Sun, as he quickly did – with Sun's consent – on March 10, 1912. It was clear, too, that the international powers – Britain especially – would accept no one but Yuan as the president of the new Republic (Schiffrin 1971: 467–73; Young 1971: 434–5; Spence 2013: 254).

It would be wrong, despite the persuasiveness of this generally revisionist account, to ignore the blows that the empire had suffered in its later years. There was the great wound of the massive and long-lasting Taiping Rebellion (1850–64), in which the rebels occupied great swathes of the central areas of the country, and in which it is estimated as many as 20 million Chinese may have died. In the midst of this occurred the "Second Opium War" (1857–8), following which in 1860 the British and French forces took Beijing and burned to the ground the Yuan Ming Yuan – the exquisite Summer Palace built by the Qianlong emperor in the eighteenth century. By the Treaty of Tianjin (1858), extraordinarily strict and punitive terms were imposed on the Chinese, including a huge indemnity and the opening of several more treaty ports (thus adding to the humiliation already heaped upon them in the "First Opium War," 1839–42). Foreigners – mainly British – also controlled the lucrative Imperial Maritime Customs.

Other foreign powers took the opportunity to prey on China. The Sino-French War of 1884–5 led to the French annexation of Vietnam, long regarded as a tributary state of the Chinese Empire. Far worse was to follow. In the Sino-Japanese War of 1895, Taiwan was lost to the Japanese, Korea became an informal (and, from 1910, formal) colony of Japan, and the Japanese established a strong presence in Manchuria. Manchuria – the Qings' homeland – was also the main site of the Russo-Japanese War of 1904–5, which ended with the Russians and Japanese effectively dividing Manchuria between them. The British at the same time, fearful of Russian designs on India, sought to occupy Tibet, dispatching the Younghusband expedition to Lhasa in 1903–4. Germany, not to be outdone, in 1897 seized the bay of Jiaozhou on the southern shore of the Shandong peninsula and secured a 99-year lease on it; German colonists then built up the model city of Qingdao on the adjacent territory (where they founded the Tsingtao Brewery!) (Conrad 2012: 58–62; Rowe 2012: 235).

Everywhere, China appeared to be under siege from foreign powers. The widespread anti-foreign sentiment that developed led to the disastrous "Boxer Uprising" of 1900, ill-advisedly backed by the court under the direction of the Dowager Empress Cixi. The rising was bloodily put down by a multinational "Allied Expeditionary Force," with Japan supplying the largest contingent of over 8,000 men. Crushing reparations and even more concessions to the foreign powers followed in the "Boxer Protocol" (1901): "Following the Boxer Protocol, the national sovereignty of the Great Qing empire was a myth that almost no one any longer believed" (Rowe 2012: 246).

It was not, despite frequent assertions to the contrary, nationalism that brought down the Chinese Empire in 1911, any more than it was the activities of professional revolutionaries such as Sun Yat-Sen. "Chinese nationalism" is, in fact, a very strange thing, almost as strange as "English nationalism."[8] There was certainly a strong current of anti-Manchuism that developed in the late nineteenth and early twentieth centuries, and a corresponding championing of Han ethnicity and the assertion that only the Han were "true" Chinese (Perdue 2007: 144–7, 158–64).[9] But this seems to have been the result mainly of the sense that China's Manchu rulers had become unfit to rule. The blame for the apparently endless series of humiliations suffered at the hands of foreign powers was laid at the door of the Qing dynasty. It was easy then to vilify the Qing by labeling them "foreigners," akin to the foreigners who were preying on China. The queue, the pig-tail imposed on all male subjects by the Manchus, became the hated symbol of "alien" Manchu rule (as best shown in the stories by the popular writer Lu Xun).

Once the Qing had been deposed – through the adroit maneuverings of the provincial elites, acting with the New Army units, and with minimal resistance from the court – calmer and more realistic views prevailed. The view that the revolution had been for the creation of "China proper" (*Benbu Zhongguo*), that is, for Han China, gave way to the recognition that China had over the centuries – and especially under the Qing – become what the influential scholar Kang Youwei called "Greater China" (*Da Zhongguo*). "China" included not just Han, but also Manchus, Mongols, Muslim groups (such as the Uighurs of Xinjiang), and Tibetans. China was in effect a multinational state, and the Chinese were composed of many ethnic groups, not just the Han majority. Kang's views won out over those of the arch Han nationalist Zhang Binglin – who had signaled his anti-Manchuism by publicly cutting off his queue – and his fiery follower Zou Rong (Perdue 2007: 159–64).

Individuals and groups as opposed to each other as Sun Yat-Sen and the revolutionaries, on the one hand, and the Qing court on the other, both issued strong statements in support of such a view. Sun, formerly a passionate critic of the Manchu dynasty and advocate of Han China, by the time he became (provisional) president of the new Republic had had a change of heart and accepted that China was "Greater China." In his inaugural address as president on New Year's Day, 1912, he proclaimed that "the people are the foundation of the state. Unifying the Han territories, Manchuria, Mongolia, the Muslim lands, and Tibet means uniting the Han, Manchu, Mongol, Hui [Muslim] and Tibetan ethnicities (*zu*) as one people (*yiren*). This is called the unity of the nation (*minzu*)" (in Esherick 2006: 245; see also Perdue 2007: 145).

The idea that China constituted "the five races as one family" was emphatically restated by the Qing court, echoing a similar pronouncement of the multiethnic character of China by the Qianlong emperor in 1755. In their abdication edict of February 12, 1912, they declared: "We welcome the establishment of a great Chinese republic that integrates all of the territories where dwell the five ethnic groups, that is, Manchus, Han, Mongols, Muslims, and Tibetans" (in Zhao 2006: 16). Gang Zhao has persuasively argued that such a view represented the triumph of Qing imperial ideology over Han nationalism, as initially expressed by Sun and his followers: "Thanks to the rise and spread of 'greater Chinese nationalism', the official Qing view of China as a multiethnic entity has persisted into the twentieth and twenty-first centuries, contributing directly to the construction of the modern Chinese national identity" (Zhao 2006: 23). Certainly, the Chinese communists, as their actions in Tibet and Xinjiang have repeatedly proved, show no inclination to deviate from this longstanding view of who the Chinese are and what China is. The unity of China, an overriding goal that goes back to the earliest years of the empire, means the inclusion of all its historic territories – "China proper," as well all the acquisitions beyond that make up "Greater China" (hence, no renouncing of the claim to Taiwan, for instance).

War, or the threat of foreign intervention, were major causes of the fall of the Qing Empire. The fear of being "carved up like a melon" – a frequently recurring phrase in the critical commentary of the time – was the dominant concern in reformist circles in the early twentieth-century China (Schiffrin 1971: 443). The loss to France in the Sino-French War, the repeated incursions of other Western powers, the swingeing punishment imposed by the occupying powers in putting down the Boxer Rebellion: all these severely weakened the Qing government and undermined its legitimacy in the eyes of large sections of the population. If the dynasty could not protect its own people, what was the justification for its continuance? Clearly, these disasters signaled that it had lost the "Mandate of Heaven."

Especially wounding – indeed, traumatic – was defeat in the Sino-Japanese War of 1895.[10] It not only "showed the world for the first time how astonishingly weak the Great Qing Empire . . . really was"; to the Qing's own subjects, "for whom defeat at the hands of the Japanese had been inconceivable," loss in the war "to such a puny and previously despised neighbor demonstrated to many the absolute necessity of Japanese-style Westernization" (Rowe 2012: 230). The "constitutional movement," demanding something like the Japanese Constitution of 1889, followed hard on the heels of defeat in the war, leading eventually to the end of empire in 1911. But it was significant how much, even in 1911, all eyes – those of Sun especially – were on the foreign powers. Their neutrality and non-interference were crucial. When they showed their acquiescence in the establishment of the Republic, all actors could celebrate the triumph of the revolution. It was also telling that Sun should meekly yield the presidency to Yuan Shikai because that is what the powers, especially the British, insisted.

The Fall of the European Land Empires

We have seen that nationalism was only one – and, in many ways, a minor one – of the causes of the fall of the Chinese Empire. Defeat in a succession of wars, and the threats of more, were far more important in weakening the Qing and depriving them of legitimacy than was the growth of Chinese nationalism (much as that was the product of these defeats). Was the case different in the fall of the great European land empires – the Habsburg, the Ottoman, the Romanov, the Hohenzollern – that fell in 1918 or soon after? Was nationalism the force that brought down these empires?

Certainly, that was the claim, for obvious reasons, of the national politicians who took power in the nation-states that succeeded the empires. It suited them to regard the empires as the "prison-house of nations," and to celebrate popular nationalism as the great "democratic" force that overthrew the autocratic and dynastic empires. Even the Bolsheviks, whose communism made them regard nationalism as a "bourgeois" and potentially counter-revolutionary force, felt the need to pay their respects to the principle of nationality, and, as we have seen, in the policy of *korenizatsiia* – "indigenization" – embarked on an ambitious and far-ranging policy of awakening and strengthening the nationalities in the new Soviet Union. For many commentators, that proved their undoing in the later years of the Soviet Union.

The verdict of those nationalists has been echoed by a host of scholars considering the fall of these empires. It has become almost axiomatic to see nationalism as the main dissolving force, the principle whose fundamental incompatibility with empire ensured that, once nationalism had established a popular base, it became the main threat to empire and finally its executioner.[11] In a highly sophisticated and partly quantitative analysis, two recent scholars have tried to show that nationalism was the main cause of the collapse not just of the land empires in 1918, but also of the overseas empires after 1945 (Hiers and Wimmer 2013).

It was not, in fact, in any of the cases of the Ottoman, Habsburg, and Romanov empires, nationalism that brought them down. Nationalism – both of the subject peoples and of the ruling peoples themselves – did become a challenge to imperial rule, and rulers struggled to contain and control it. But in no case was it strong enough by itself to destroy the empire. In most cases, whether in the Balkans, or Central or Eastern Europe, nationalist movements in the nineteenth century remained an affair of elites, often arising in diasporic communities outside the empires. They held little appeal to the mass of the people, who were more likely to look to the traditional rulers – the Ottoman sultan, the Habsburg emperor, the Russian tsar – for the alleviation of their problems than to the nationalists.[12] Moreover, until the First World War, most nationalists sought not outright independence for their nations, but autonomy within the empire. For many of the nationalities, such as the Slavs in the Habsburg Empire, or the Ukrainians and the Baltic nations in the tsarist empire, there was more to fear from the designs of other states than from their host empire. Timely concessions were made to nationalist sentiment in all the empires in the later nineteenth and early twentieth centuries. Empires had every reason to hope that they could weather the nationalist storm.[13]

What made that impossible, for some at least, was war – in this case, the cataclysm of the First World War, a war between empires. The victors in the war – the British and French, especially – were able to emerge with their empires intact, and even strengthened. Nationalism had arisen in those empires as much as in the land empires. But the British and the French showed that such nationalism could be contained, and even re-directed to the defense of empire when it came under threat from its enemies. Troops from all the British and French colonies fought loyally for their empires throughout the First World War, earning the gratitude and respect of their rulers, and at least some concessions after the war.

The same was true initially for the land empires. Troops from all the nationalities fought for the Habsburg, Ottoman, and Romanov empires in the First World War. But as the war went on, and defeat loomed, the nationalities jumped ship. Unable, and in most cases unwilling, to demand national independence previously, the conditions of war gave them both the opportunity and the motive for seeking independence. Their only hope for the future seemed to lie in being independent nation-states. The impending collapse of the empires made them change direction. Now they competed among themselves to be the leaders of the new nations that appeared to be the only outcome of the bonfire of empires resulting from the war (Roshwald 2001).

In this, they found strong support among the victorious powers, notably the United States and its president, Woodrow Wilson. Wilson had in the early years of the war been against the break-up of the empires. He saw them as a force for stability in the region. As the war went on, and the defeat of the land empires appeared inevitable, Wilson too changed direction and came out in favor of national independence (Roshwald 2001: 159–60). The new thinking was expressed in the famous "Fourteen Points" of 1918 and the principle of "self-determination" (discussed in the previous chapter). War had weakened the empires to the point where the nationalists saw both the need and the opportunity to assert themselves. But it is possible that, without Wilson's powerful support, backed in a more self-interested way by the British and the French, the new nations might not have emerged so easily from the wreckage of empire (as can be seen from the Russian case, where the limits of Western power allowed the Soviets to re-establish the Russian Empire in a new guise).

War and the international context: both of these were indispensable in the break-up of the land empires in 1918 (Kennedy 2016: 16). This provides probably the clearest case for the importance of these factors in the fall of empires. But we can see this in the overseas empires as well, both in later cases and in earlier ones too. The Spanish and the Portuguese empires provide good examples from an earlier time. In the early nineteenth century, Spain and Portugal both lost a good part of their Latin American empires. Once more, the success of the independence movements has often been attributed to "creole nationalists," such as Simón Bolívar, José de San Martín, Agustín de Iturbide, and Miguel Hidalgo (Anderson 2006: 47–65). Their statues, as the heroic founders of the new nations of Mexico, Venezuela, Bolivia, Peru, Brazil, Argentina, and a score of others, are to be found all over Latin America.

It takes little away from the struggles of the creole, "European," elites – though often in isolation from the parallel struggles of the non-creole Indians – to argue that these by themselves would never have been enough to defeat the metropolitan powers of Spain and Portugal (Van Young 2006). There had been many risings in the past – such as the great Peruvian revolt in 1780–3 of Túpac Amaru – and all had been suppressed. What now made the difference was the crushing of the metropolitan powers by the new French Empire of Napoleon: "The factor that triggered the collapse of the Spanish and Portuguese empires was without any question Napoleon's military occupation of the Iberian Peninsula" (Uribe-Uran 2006: 83; see also Kennedy 2016: 10–11). The Spanish king, Ferdinand VII, was dethroned, and Spanish liberals went on to issue the ultra-liberal Cadiz Constitution of 1812 that further encouraged the revolutionaries in the overseas empire (Fradera 2018: 65–9). The Portuguese king, Dom João VI, decamped to Brazil to set up a court in exile, but this lasted little more than a few years before, in 1822, under his son Pedro I, Brazil declared itself independent.

In 1826, the British foreign secretary, George Canning, defending British support for the former Spanish and Portuguese colonies, famously boasted that "I called the New World into existence to redress the balance of the Old." Latin American commemorations of independence regularly celebrate Canning and the British for their aid and support. There is some justice in this. British support for the independent Latin American republics was important in sustaining them after independence, and in preventing the return of the colonial powers. British support and, in a somewhat different context, that of the Americans, with the "Monroe Doctrine" of 1823 warning off Europeans from interfering in the affairs of the American continent, illustrate well the significance of the international context in bringing about the end of empires.

But Latin Americans might with more justice celebrate not so much – or not only – Canning and the British, but also Napoleon and the French. It was the French who, by eliminating the power of the metropolitan centers of the empires in the Iberian peninsula, created the space and the opportunity for the colonial subjects of Spain and

Portugal to make their bid for independence. French colonial subjects, by contrast, did not get such an opportunity, which makes even
more remarkable the eventual success, against all the odds, of the
Haitian struggle for independence.[14]

Spain did not lose the whole of its empire in 1810–21. It was left
with Cuba – "the jewel in the crown of the empire" – Puerto Rico,
and the Philippines, the first proving particularly lucrative for most
of the nineteenth century (Balfour 2004: 153). But another war, with
another Western power, put paid to that. Following Spain's defeat in
the Spanish–American War of 1898, Spain lost its last major colonies
(for the Spanish this was widely glossed as a "catastrophe," and Spain
entered on an agonized period of postcolonial self-interrogation).[15]
Again, before that war, no nationalist movement in those colonies
had been able to throw off Spanish rule, despite several attempts.
Most notable was that of the Cubans in 1895–8, bloodily suppressed
by Spain and the main spur to the Spanish–American War (Blackburn
2005: 74).

This also explains why Portugal, despite the loss of Brazil, was able
to hold on for so much longer to its remaining colonies, especially
in Africa. Portugal did not engage in any major wars after the early
nineteenth century. Although, despite being initially neutral, it joined
the Allies in the First World War, it remained neutral in the Second
World War. Bitter struggles in Angola, Mozambique, and Guinea-
Bissau availed nothing until the Portuguese military overthrew the
Portuguese dictatorship in 1974 and rapidly made its peace with the
independence movements in its African colonies. Once more, the key
to colonial independence was defeat at the center, the removal of
metropolitan power and control.

One further example, from the earlier history of the Ottoman
Empire, can show the importance of war and the international
context in determining the fate of empires. The Ottoman Empire did
not collapse until 1918; but, earlier, it had suffered a severe trunca-
tion that undoubtedly weakened it. The cause once more was war:
the Russo-Turkish War of 1877–8, which was a disaster for the
Ottomans. At the Berlin Congress of 1878, the British, French, and
Germans prevented the Russians from acquiring all the gains that they
had forced upon the Ottomans in the earlier Treaty of San Stefano
(1878).[16] But, under international pressure, the Ottomans nevertheless had to accept the loss of many of their Balkan possessions, Serbia,
Montenegro, Romania, and Bulgaria, while the Habsburgs gained the
right to occupy and administer Bosnia-Herzogovina (finally annexed
by them in 1908). Following earlier patterns, to be repeated in the
First and Second World Wars, nations that had struggled without

success to achieve independence did so by courtesy of the inter-national community and the defeat of the imperial powers in war.[17]

Decolonization and the End of the Overseas Empires

After the dissolution of the land empires following the First World War came the turn of the European overseas empires after the Second World War. In what appeared at the time unceremonious haste, the European powers divested themselves of their empires mostly between 1945 and the 1960s (Portugal held on to its African empire until 1974, and to what was left of its Asian empire – Macao – until 1999; Britain, too, did not hand over its colony Hong Kong to China until 1997). With the fall of the "Soviet Empire" in 1991, and America's unwillingness to call itself an empire, it appeared as if the era of empires was indeed over. Japan still has an emperor, but the "Empire of Japan" was officially declared dead in 1947, and the emperor is currently a ceremonial figurehead with even less power than the British monarch.

No more than in the case of the land empires was the fall of the overseas empires inevitable or inscribed in the laws of history. In fact, many of the overseas empires emerged from the First World War expanded and strengthened. What had brought about the destruction of the land empires was their defeat in war. The victors – the British, the French, the Italians – picked up the pieces and simply added them to their territories (Louis 1998: 94–5; Abernethy 2000: 105–16; Pedersen 2015: 17–44). From the wreckage of the Ottoman Empire, the British salvaged Iraq, Jordan, and Palestine, which it held as League of Nations Mandates, but over which it had in practice almost complete power. The French did similarly with Syria and Lebanon. The German overseas empire was dismantled and the components – German South-West Africa, German East Africa, Cameroon, Togo, and German possessions in China and the Pacific – were distributed among the victorious powers. Britain and France once again got the lion's share, but the United States and Japan also shared in the spoils. While these countries increased their territories, the Belgians, Dutch, and Portuguese had at least the satisfaction of having their empires confirmed, despite Allied concern about the character of their rule.

There had been nationalist movements in all of the overseas empires before and during the war, just as there had been in the land empires. Many commentators have seen in these the seeds of the imminent decline and fall of these empires. This is a clear case of being wise after the event. Because the overseas empires fell after 1945, it has seemed obvious that they must have been "falling" – in a state of stasis or suspended animation – since 1918 or earlier (see, e.g., Abernethy 2000: 117–26; Manela 2009: 11; Jansen and Osterhammel 2016: 38–42).[18]

There is little evidence of this. Most nationalist movements, such as those in India or Algeria, sought autonomy or a greater degree of participation for the native population, not independence. Wilson's call for national self-determination applied mostly to Europe; in Asia or Africa, it seemed to matter less to him and the Western Allies, as the Chinese, Egyptians, Indians, and Koreans found to their cost (Manela 2009: 177–225). The League of Nations appeared more a vehicle for the preservation of empire – "empire by other means" – than for ending – or even, to any appreciable extent, regulating – it (Mazower 2009a: 29–103). It can even be argued that, in the interwar period, the European overseas empires reached their apogee. Never before had there been greater support for empire among the metropolitan population; never before had the metropolitan governments come to feel so strongly that their security and their economic prosperity depended on their possession of empire. Great efforts were made to bring the administration of the empires into greater order, and to develop colonial economies more efficiently.[19] Giving up empire was the last thing on people's minds.

That, nevertheless, was what happened after 1945, and with astonishing speed, as European empires, one after the other, "decolonized."[20] Once more, war was the great solvent of empires (Albertini 1969; Kennedy 2016: 25–34). This time it was the victors as much as the defeated who found it impossible to hold on to their empires. The empires of the Axis Powers – Germany, Japan, and Italy – ended with their defeat in war. Their conquered territories were returned to the empires of the victors, the British, the French, the Dutch, the Americans. In Central and Eastern Europe, the pre-war nation-states were resurrected, but in many cases with severely altered boundaries – Poland was the great example – and, for most of them, consigned to informal rule by the Soviet Union as part of the "Soviet bloc." The end of the empires of the Axis Powers also involved a massive disentangling of populations, as millions of Germans, Japanese, and Italians were forcibly "repatriated" to their homelands – even if, as with most of the Germans, they had left them hundreds of years ago.

The return of lost territories to the victorious Allies did not in the end mean the long-term survival of their empires. Not that their resolve had flagged. None of them wished to give up their empires (Ward 2016: 247–8). There was even a renewed effort, in the immediate postwar period, to continue the pre-war policies of "rationalizing" the administration of their empires, which included making major concessions to nationalist demands. In all the overseas empires, citizenship was now held out as a real possibility for all the subjects of the empire, non-European as well as the already franchised Europeans. There were ambitious and elaborate schemes of economic development in the colonies, again picking up on pre-war policies. The colonies were to be made more productive, partly for the sake of their own populations but also to help the metropolitan powers in their postwar recovery efforts. The aim, as Tony Smith has said, was not to decolonize but to "reform in order to preserve" (in Ward 2016: 248; see also Shipway 2008: 114–38; Kennedy 2016: 37–8).[21] All the European imperial powers would have agreed with the sentiment famously expressed by the British prime minister Winston Churchill in 1942, when he said that he had "not become the King's First Minister in order to preside over the liquidation of the British Empire."[22]

What made that resolve ultimately inadequate was the decisive effect of the world war. France was occupied, as was much of the rest of Western Europe, and Britain subjected to massive bombing, then engaged in a long-drawn-out struggle on all fronts across the world. For all the European powers, the war was financially, militarily, and psychologically exhausting. The Allies might emerge victors, and the Europeans determined to hang on to their empires, but their ability to do so was severely compromised by the damage that the war had inflicted on them in all aspects of their societies. The urgent task after the war became the reconstruction of those societies. The colonies were meant to play a part in this; but if the cost, in terms of managing and policing them, became too great, then they would have to be sacrificed in the greater interest of the home country.

It did not help that the strongest power to emerge from the war, the United States, was – so long as Franklin Delano Roosevelt was president – passionately opposed to the European empires and determined to wind them up as soon as possible. The so-called Atlantic Charter, issued in 1941 as a joint statement by Roosevelt and Churchill of Allied war aims, explicitly declared – in terms precisely taken up by the United Nations later – that "all people have the right to self-determination." For Churchill, the principle applied only to the states under German occupation; for Roosevelt, it had universal applicability, and he made it clear that it applied especially to the colonies under European rule (Mazower 2013: 250).

Under Roosevelt's successor, Harry Truman, that attitude was moderated somewhat, and the Americans pursued a policy of shoring up the European empires as part of the strategy of "containment" of the communist threat represented by the Soviet Union and its Third World allies. But France and Britain's reckless adventure over the Suez Canal in 1956 – their "last hurrah" – ended this exercise in the "imperialism of decolonization" (Louis and Robinson 1994). America lost patience with its European allies. From that time on, it felt it better to conduct its foreign policy directly, as an imperial power in its own right, rather than through the agency of the European empires.

The effects of the Second World War, combined with the withdrawal of American support and growing nationalist movements in the colonies, brought about what appeared in retrospect a linked chain of devastating colonial losses. The European overseas empires tumbled one by one, starting in Asia and the Middle East – where the impact of the war was most intensely felt – and then continuing in Africa and elsewhere. In Asia, it was Japan that did the greatest damage to the European empires. The Dutch were expelled from Indonesia; the British from Hong Kong, Singapore, Malaya, Burma, and Borneo. The Japanese first controlled the Vichy regime in French Indochina, then displaced it. The myth of European superiority was permanently shattered – not just in those countries where the Japanese ruled directly, but all over Asia. Nationalists throughout the region felt emboldened to take up the struggle for independence – in many cases, with Japanese support. The wholly unexpected collapse of European power in the region "awakened millennial expectations which were immediately identified with the expulsion of foreigners . . . Ties of loyalty were broken, the passive endurance of an established system of rule rejected, whilst on the other hand mass forces were released which lent an undreamed-of impetus to the emancipation movement" (Albertini 1969: 28–9).

The empires might return after Japan's defeat, but in their weakened state they were unable to contain the forces stirred up by the war. First to go were India and Pakistan in 1947, followed speedily by Ceylon (Sri Lanka) and Burma in 1948. In just two years, the great British Raj had disintegrated. In 1949, following a bitter war, the Dutch were forced to give Indonesia its independence.

In the Middle East, Syria and Lebanon gained their independence from France. Britain conceded independence to Jordan in 1946, and in 1948 all-out conflicts between Jews and Arabs prompted the British to surrender the Palestine Mandate, leading to the creation of Israel and a rump Palestinian state. Egyptian independence was confirmed after the Suez debacle of 1956. Iraq, nominally independent of the British since 1932, achieved effective independence with the overthrow of the Hashemite monarchy in 1958. Thus were the French and British empires in the Middle East wound up.

Suez seems to have been a turning point, at least as far as the British were concerned. The "winds of change" blew strongest in sub-Saharan Africa, with gathering speed in the later 1950s and 1960s. Practically all the British colonies in Africa had gone by 1965, though the white settlers in Southern Rhodesia fought a grim delaying action, until forced to concede independence in 1979. The British Caribbean colonies also, with a few exceptions, became independent states in the 1960s.

The British were wont to congratulate themselves on the relative peacefulness with which they gave up their empire, compared with the violence and bloodshed which they saw as attending the break-up of the other European empires. A characteristic view was that of the eminent British scholar Noel Annan: "The peaceful divestment of the Empire was the most successful political achievement of my generation. Unlike France who fought bloody battles in Indo-China and Algeria, which divided the French nation and shook the army's allegiance, Britain withdrew from her dependencies in good order and left little resentment behind" (Annan 1991: 483). This compla-cent view has more recently been questioned by those who point to the violent anti-colonial struggles in Malaya and Cyprus, and to the harsh actions of the British authorities in repressing the nationalist movement in Kenya. But a fair judgment seems to be that of Elizabeth Buettner: "Britain had no single decolonization episode that came even remotely close to French Algerian proportions, and staged its succession of colonial exits without becoming tainted by violent after-maths comparable to those afflicting the Belgian Congo" (Buettner 2016: 59; see also Darwin 1988: 328; Spruyt 2005: 117–44).[23]

Of all the European powers, France was certainly the one that fought most determinedly to retain its empire. Hundreds of thousands of French, Algerians, and Vietnamese died in the colonial wars that raged in Indochina and Algeria between 1945 and 1960. Eventually the French withdrew, defeated by Vietnamese forces under Ho Chi Minh in 1954, and by the calculation of Charles de Gaulle – brought in to "save" Algeria for the nation – that the struggle in Algeria was endangering the French republic and that Algeria had to be given up. With the loss of Algeria, it seemed only logical to give up the other French possessions in Africa, which one after the other became inde-pendent between 1956 and 1962.

The Dutch, too, fought desperately to hold on to their colonies, chief of which was Indonesia (Buettner 2016: 78–105). There was no talk about giving up the Dutch East Indies, which for generations had been regarded as indispensable to the Dutch economy. Indonesian nationalism, which had been growing since the 1930s, was not taken seriously. A bitter colonial war ensued after 1945 when Indonesian nationalists, led by Sukarno and encouraged by Japanese defeat of the Dutch in the Second World War, declared Indonesia an independent republic. By 1947, 170,000 men were committed to the defense of Dutch rule in Indonesia – "the greatest war ever fought by the Dutch army" (Wesseling 1980: 125). Despite the brutal tactics – similar to those of the French – employed by the Dutch army, and under pressure from the Americans who were re-assured by the anti-communist stance of the nationalists, the Dutch were forced to concede independence to Indonesia in 1949 – though not without a short-lived attempt to retain Dutch influence through a federated "Republic of the United States of Indonesia" linked to the Netherlands (Wesseling 1980: 135–6; Buettner 2016: 95–6).

The speed of post-1945 decolonization has astonished everyone, at the time and since. Empires that had been in existence for 200 or 300 years lost most of their colonies within a space of 20 years, from 1945 to 1965. Writing just after the dizzying changes, Rupert Emerson observed:

> Here was a system of world-wide dimensions which only a few years earlier still had a look of solidity and permanence to it and which had ordered – or disrupted – the affairs of very large segments of mankind for centuries in some instances, for decades in many others. Is there any other occasion on which so global and commanding a scheme of things was swept away in so brief a time? (Emerson 1969: 3)[24]

The formal climax of this movement might be said to be the UN General Assembly's 1960 "Declaration on the Granting of Independence to Colonial Countries and People," in which it was solemnly affirmed that "all peoples have the right to self-determination," and which proclaimed "the necessity of bringing to a speedy and unconditional end colonialism in all its forms and manifestations" (in Emerson 1969: 5).

Some have sought the sources of this striking phenomenon in a longer historical arc, arguing that "decolonization" had started as long ago as 1776, when the North American colonies threw off British rule. Decolonization, fed by the ideas emanating from the American and French revolutions, had continued by fits and starts ever since, in "waves" that included the early-nineteenth-century decolonization of parts of the Spanish and Portuguese empires, the late-nineteenth-century decolonization of parts of the Ottoman Empire and the rest of the Spanish Empire, and the post-1918 decolonization of the great European land empires. The post-1945 decolonization of Asia and Africa was in this perspective simply the latest wave of this longstanding anti-colonial movement that found its inspiration in those very Western societies whose rule it sought to throw off (Strang 1991; Kennedy 2016: 8–24).[25] One could even say that it was the West delivering on its promise to free the colonies after a due period of "education" in governance.

There is some force in this kind of analysis. But it operates at a level of generality that mostly leaves unanswered the question of why particular spurts of decolonization occurred at the moments that they did. It is particularly weak on the latest, incredibly rapid, round of decolonization, which certainly needs explaining in its own terms. Above all, it ignores the fact that the rulers of the European empires were for the most part, and for most of the time, supremely self-confident about their right and their ability to manage their empires. They did not see themselves as engaged in some kind of defensive, "holding," operation, shoring up their empires against an irresistible and rising tide of decolonization. On the contrary, almost right to the end, they engaged in various strategies to secure and strengthen their hold on empire. Its rapid loss was as surprising to them as it was, in most cases, to the anti-colonial forces that sought to bring down the empires. That was one reason why the postcolonial settlements in so many cases were rushed and improvised, containing the seeds of innumerable future conflicts.

It is clear in any case that the post-1945 wave of decolonization, rapid and remarkable as it was, was not the end of the story of empire. The European empires may have gone, at least formally. But not only did that not mean that they did not continue to exercise a formidable degree of informal influence and control over their erstwhile colonies – in many cases, with the willing consent of at least the elites of the newly independent states. There was also the continued existence of the American and Soviet empires, much as they disowned the name of empire. They dominated the international scene after 1945, as global powers that acted frequently as the European empires of old. The Europeans, for their part, came together in a "European Union" that was a kind of substitute for their lost empires, and which in the eyes of some actually had the characteristics of some of the older forms of empire.

Empire had, and has, an after-life that continues to affect both the metropolitan societies and the territories over which they formerly ruled. It is to that continuing story of empire that we must now, in conclusion, turn.

6
Empire after Empire

Imperial Legacies

The "end of empire "was not the end of empire. It is difficult to see how it could have been, or been thought to be so. Empires have dominated the world for millennia, though generally in particular regions of the world. In their latest form, the European empires of land and sea, they extended their sway over the whole world, transforming the societies – both those of the metropolis and of the colony – that they incorporated. In many cases they lasted for centuries. It would be strange to think that, once the Europeans gave up formal rule of their empires, the impact and influence of empire would not continue to resonate through the societies that had experienced these centuries of imperial rule. "The empires of our time were short-lived," wrote the novelist V. S. Naipaul, "but they have altered the world forever; their passing away is their least significant feature" ([1967] 1985: 32). "Short-lived," perhaps, in comparison with some of the empires of the ancient world – but transformative, undoubtedly.

To speak of "legacies of empire" has become conventional, but also controversial. The controversies are often of a methodological kind: how does one demonstrate clearly that such-and-such a practice is an imperial hangover rather than a new creation, suited to the new circumstances, or a persistence or resuscitation of a pre-imperial pattern? Some Asian thinkers, for instance, repudiate the idea that it was European rule that taught them how to be a nation; they had their own indigenous traditions that they were able to put to use

– in a new form – in constructing their nations after independence (Chatterjee 1993).

The use of "legacies" can also often be a lazy gesture. Legacies are assumed rather than shown. One talks vaguely of "legacies" in, say, accounting for the frequent occurrence of authoritarian populism in the societies of Eastern Europe. This is traced back to their experience as subject nations in the Habsburg, Russian, or Soviet empires (or sometimes the Nazi Empire). Such experience is undoubtedly relevant, as we shall see. But one needs to demonstrate the persisting political and sociological forces that give rise to such movements, not simply put them down to some sort of unchanging legacy, an apparently permanent memory-imprint in the culture.

The inheritance of empires can undergo modifications, often profound ones. In societies which were the heirs to old civilizations, as well as often to ancient established states, as in much of Asia, the experience of empire was bound to be different from that of societies lacking such a background. Indians, Sri Lankans, Burmese, Vietnamese, and other Indochinese, had preserved memories and practices deriving from times – often distant ones – when they had their own state, usually one based on one of the historic "world religions," Hindu, Muslim, Buddhist, Confucian (or sometimes a combination of these, to which might be added varieties of Christianity). The European empires – principally, in these cases, British and French – affected these in myriad profound ways. There was never any real going back to the past, however much nationalist leaders – themselves, for the most part, creations of Western education and experience – might claim to be doing so. But there could be a genuine recovery of ideas, attitudes, and practices drawing upon these resources from the past.

These could give a distinctive character to the new state. Hinduism in India, Islam in Pakistan, Buddhism in Sri Lanka, Myanmar, and many of the south-east Asian states, which could also call upon Confucian traditions, achieved a far greater prominence in the new states than was ever possible when they lived under European rule. The influence of old traditions could go well beyond religion. Mohandas Gandhi – trained as an English barrister – called upon his fellow Indians to renounce practically all Western ways and return to the beliefs and practices of traditional Indian civilization. Other nationalist leaders in India, such as Jawaharlal Nehru, disagreed, and, with Gandhi's assassination in 1948, India took a different, more modern, path. But Gandhian ideas have had a profound influence on India since independence, even featuring in the ideology of the ruling ultra-Hindu nationalist party, the Bharatiya Janata Party.[1]

Things were different in those states that were in effect created *de novo*, where there were no longstanding state traditions to draw upon. This was particularly the case in Africa and the Middle East. There, the leaders had to draw up blueprints for the new states that were heavily dependent on relatively recent imperial experience. In Africa, this was because there was no serviceable state tradition to draw upon; in the Middle East, it was because the ancient civilizations of Mesopotamia and Egypt had long been absorbed in long-lasting empires – Macedonian, Roman, Byzantine, Ottoman, British, and French. As the latest and most "modern" imperial rulers, it was the British and French who most directly contributed to state-formation in the Middle East after independence, though Otttoman traditions played a considerable part as well.

Imperial legacies are naturally to be found in the metropolitan societies of the European rulers as well. Here, too, the argument is complicated by contradictory tendencies. Empire, once it was gone, could come to appear shameful – something to forget, if not to apologize for. There was a chorus of denials and attempts to rewrite history. Empire had not been planned; it happened by accident; it had been thrust upon Europeans as a burdensome necessity. Europeans – unlike others – were "reluctant imperialists." The loss of empire had had no perceptible effect on metropolitan society (see, e.g., Porter 2004b).

On the other hand, with time, there began a perceptible re-appraisal of the empire story. Empire had not been all bad. It had brought incalculable improvements in the lives of its subjects. The "civilizing mission" was not just hypocrisy and a cover-up for exploitation. Societies that had lived under arbitrary and oppressive rule had been brought under the rule of law. Education had been established at all levels. A vital infrastructure of roads, railways, and shipping had been laid. The beneficence of empire was clearly shown by the chaos and disorder that broke out in so many of the independent states after the imperial rulers had departed. A nostalgic glow began to settle over the memory of empire, as shown in many films, TV series, and works of popular literature.

We will need to examine all sides of this complex inheritance of attitudes and memories, and the way they may have affected behavior, in both the formerly subject societies and those of their European rulers. For reasons to do with their global reach and significance, it is the after-life of the European overseas empires that has attracted most attention. But first we should look at the land empires. Many of them disappeared in the early twentieth century, including the one long-lasting non-Western empire, the Chinese Empire. But they left behind a host of issues and questions that continued to affect their constituent parts for long afterwards, right up to the present.

Imperial legacies are real. The difficulties of establishing them, the dangers of reading too much into them, should not stop us from attempting to trace their lineaments and trying to assess their effects on post-imperial societies. Empires have been among the longest-lasting phenomena in world history. The idea that their influence would abruptly stop when they were formally dissolved strains credulity. Human societies do not work like that. They are accretions of past and present. The past of empire is part of the present of societies that once lived empire.

Legacies of Land Empires

In the years following the end of the First World War, nearly all the Eurasian land empires collapsed. Before the war, in 1911, the Chinese Empire had already given way to the Chinese Republic. Its fate was followed after 1918 by the Habsburg, Romanov, Hohenzollern, and Ottoman empires. The fall-out from all these empires was considerable, and complex.

The Habsburgs had ruled much of east-central and south-eastern Europe. Their empire was often thought of as ramshackle and archaic, though it also generated much affection, and was rightly admired for its astonishing cultural vitality (what would European music be without Vienna?). No one was very surprised when it fell, though many felt a sense of foreboding as to what might follow.

This sense of foreboding, and expressions of regret for the passing of the Habsburgs, grew almost into a literary industry in the inter-war period (Kozuchowski 2013). Acclaimed works such as Robert Musil's *The Man without Qualities* (1930–2) and Joseph Roth's *The Radetzky March* (1932) were by no means uncritical of the empire. But, at the same time, they found many qualities to admire, and, as the political débris of the 1930s piled up, were in no doubt about what had been lost. Particularly revered was the figure of the long-ruling and (almost) last Habsburg emperor, Franz Joseph, as emblematic of the tolerance, fairness, and sense of duty that characterized the Habsburg Empire at its best.

Nostalgia for the lost empire could only grow as its central elements, Austria and Hungary, were drawn into the 1930s maelstrom. Austria, the rump state formed in 1918, could only see a future for itself in a "Greater Germany," and duly allowed itself to be swallowed up by the Nazi state in the *Anschluss* of 1938. Its reward was to share in that state's dramatic downfall, followed by years of occupation by the Allied powers. Not till 1955 did the troops leave (Beller 2011: 231–60).

Hungary, the other main prop of the Austro-Hungarian Empire, fared perhaps even worse. A brutal communist republic under Béla Kun was quickly overturned by Admiral Miklós Horthy, who inaugurated a 20-year reign of authoritarian personal rule in which fascist elements increasingly came to the fore. Horthy was unable to prevent the Allied-imposed Treaty of Trianon (1920), by which Hungary lost 71 percent of its territory, 58 percent of its population, and 32 percent of its ethnic Hungarians. But he vowed to reverse it, reviving dreams of "Greater Hungary" and seeking to restore Hungary's historic role in the region (Macartney [1937] 1965). Since Hitler encouraged such ambitions, Hungary readily sided with the Axis Powers in the Second World War and, like Austria, shared in their fate. But, while Austria ultimately emerged a neutral state from the ashes of 1945, Hungary, physically devastated and economically exhausted, ended up a satellite state of the Soviet Union. Only in 1989 did it recover its independence.

The two metropolitan powers, Austria and Hungary, might be said to have suffered the normal consequences of loss of empire: a search for a new role, while at the same time brooding over the loss of their once great status and power. The results were not pre-ordained, but there were strong pressures to take measures that, in the short to medium term at least, might spell disaster. Austria was able, after a nightmare period, to find a snug place for itself as a small, neutral, Central European country, whose beautiful countryside, plentiful mountains, and graceful cities made it an attractive tourist destination and so contributed greatly to Austria's postwar prosperity. There have been occasional bursts of Habsburg nostalgia, and no lack of pride in Austria's great past. The centenary of Franz Joseph's death, in 2016, stimulated many historical exhibitions and works celebrating his reign. But there have been no attempts to restore Austria's imperial past, except in carnival floats and night-club satire.

Darker ghosts haunt Hungary, and the existence of the 3 million ethnic Hungarians in the "near abroad," mostly in Romania, Slovakia, and Serbia, continue to stimulate movements of Hungarian nationalism and revanchism. One consequence has been a revival of the authoritarian populism reminiscent of the interwar period. Unlike Austria, Hungary seems unwilling to settle for a backseat on the European scene. Although a late-comer, it aspires to represent the Central European presence in the European Union, and even to suggest that it stands for the real "Europe" in a way that other members no longer do.

For the subject – as opposed to the metropolitan – peoples of the Habsburg Empire, the effects of empire are more directly observable. The empire in many cases shaped them both physically and psychologically. The boundaries of most of the successor states to the Habsburg Empire were outlined in the federal scheme for the re-organization of the Austro-Hungarian Monarchy proposed by the Emperor Charles in 1917, itself an echo of many such plans drawn up by Austro-Slavists and Austro-Marxists in the late nineteenth and early twentieth centuries (Judson 2016: 420–33). The empire had named, if not conceived, its heirs. It had also left them with many perplexities.

Austrian Galicia is a good example. A province of the Habsburg Empire since the eighteenth century, it contained Poles, Ukrainians (Ruthenians), and Jews. The Habsburgs practiced a largely successful act of accommodation between the different groups. After 1918, most of Galicia ended up in an independent Poland, to the chagrin of the Ukrainians. After 1945, it was divided more or less equally between Poland and Ukraine.

Both Poland and Ukraine continue to show the clear marks of empire – not just the Habsburg Empire, within which Galicia was contained, but also the Russian tsarist and Soviet empires which provided the other elements of the two states (Kumar forthcoming a). Thus, Ukraine has a clear dividing line, culturally and politically, between western Ukraine, centered on the old Galician city of Lviv, and eastern Ukraine, centered on the Donetsk region and the Crimea. Western Ukraine was part of the Habsburg Empire, eastern Ukraine part of the Russian and later Soviet Empire. Since the fall of communism, the fault lines have shown themselves dramatically, with western Ukraine steadily supporting liberal, pro-European Union leaders such as Leonid Kravchuk, and eastern Ukraine looking eastward and supporting pro-Russian leaders such as Leonid Kuchma. This has resulted tragically in a long-running civil war with thousands dead and the annexation of the Crimea by Russia.

Poland, too, has its two halves, reflecting the dual imperial legacy. They are often referred to as "Poland A" and "Poland B," with the Vistula as the line of demarcation. Poland A is more prosperous, more urbanized, closer in character to the societies of Western Europe. Poland B is less developed, more rural, more conservative and nationalist. The sources of these contrasting attitudes are equally clear. Poland A was for most of the time part of the Habsburg (Galicia), and also the Hohenzollern, empires (Silesia and Pomerania). It had a "western" imperial experience – more liberal and economically progressive. Poland B was part of the Russian Empire, and had a typically "eastern" experience – more repressive and backward economically. The communist experience did not erode these differences, which have continued to show like dye marks the contrasting experiences of empire.

With the Ottoman Empire, we can also distinguish between the post-imperial experience of the metropolitan power and that of its subject peoples. Reduced, after a bruising civil and international war between 1918 and 1923, to the rump state of the Republic of Turkey, the old Ottoman core has struggled to find an identity. Under Turkey's founder, Mustafa Kemal "Atatürk," a draconian attempt was made to erase all traces of the Ottoman past. Mosques were closed, the caliphate abolished, and Islam lost its privileged status. Atatürk strove to create a modern secular republic on the Western model.

Certainly, a good deal of that was accomplished, as is very clear in the large Turkish cities of Ankara, Izmir, and Istanbul. But equally clear is the incomplete nature of that effort, and the return or revival of many beliefs and practices of the Ottoman past. Particularly marked is the return of Islam, under the long-running rule of President Recep Tayyip Erdogan and his Justice and Development Party. There are also signs that Turkey is not finished with empire – that, as its relations to the West come under increasing strain, it aspires once more to an imperial presence in the region (Onar 2015). In 2013, the former foreign minister Ahmet Davutoglu declared that "Turks will once again tie Sarajevo to Damascus, Benghazi to Erzurum to Batumi. This is the core of our power. These may look different countries to you, but Yemen and Skopje were part of the same country a hundred and ten years ago, as were Erzurum and Benghazi" (Adil 2019: 12). Turkey is increasingly turning its back on Europe, with declining support for membership of the European Union, and seeks instead to restore itself – as in the Ottoman period – as the defining power in the Middle East and Central Asia. "Ottomania" is a discernible feature of both popular and high culture in contemporary Turkey.

As with the Habsburg Empire, the Ottoman Empire's erstwhile subject nations have struggled to come to terms with their long experience of empire (Brown 1996). For over four centuries, the Arab peoples lived under Ottoman rule. Though aware of their differences from the Ottoman Turks – "as was their custom or habit" was their stock way of acknowledging these differences – Arabs shared with their imperial rulers the common faith of Islam that was the ruling culture of the empire. The Ottomans even designated the Syrian capital Damascus as the fourth holiest city of Islam, after Mecca, Medina, and Jerusalem. Under Sultan Abdulhamid II (1876–1909), as part of his pan-Islamic strategy with the loss of most of the Ottomans' Christian provinces, Arabs were increasingly appointed to high office (Barbir 1996: 104-6).

Arab nationalism was a late development, coming only in the early twentieth century after the Young Turks renounced an imperial vision for the Ottomans and sought, especially under Atatürk, to construct a purely Turkish national state. Even during the First World War, few Arabs supported the "Arab revolt" orchestrated by Sharif Husayn and the British. The replacement of Ottoman imperialism by British and French imperialism after the First World War was a cruel disappointment to most Arabs. It caused many to look back with some nostalgia to that period when they were constituent parts of the Ottoman Empire. Particular interest attached to the mid-nineteenth-century Young Ottoman model of a federated empire of peoples and religious communities within an overarching Islamic-Ottoman framework (Barbir 1996: 108). For it was British and French rule that brought about their most immediate concerns – most notably the creation of the state of Israel in their midst. But with the creeping Islamicization of Turkey, there is some indication that the Arab nations will once more seek to form a common front against the perceived enemy and its Western backers. Islam is a powerfully revived force. The Ottoman Empire was once the seat of the caliphate, keeper of the Holy Places of Mecca and Medina, leader of the Islamic *umma*, the world community of Muslims. There are today other claimants of the caliphate in the Middle East – but none can speak with such longstanding authority as the Ottomans.

Ottoman legacies are equally, and more directly, to be found in the Balkans, whose peoples were shared between Ottoman and Habsburg rule (Rusinow 1996; Todorova 1996). One clear fault line is that to be found between the Catholic nations of Slovenia and Croatia, on the one hand, and Serbia, Bulgaria, and the other Orthodox nations, on the other. The former were part of the Habsburg Empire, the latter of the Ottoman. Despite many shared features of culture, including in some cases that of language, the different imperial experiences have thrown up a host of differences that ultimately proved fatal to the attempt to unify them all in the joint state of Yugoslavia. A brutal and bloody civil war in the 1990s finally put paid to that experiment.

What also was revealed in that civil war were not simply profound differences between the Christian nations, but also the question of the Muslim populations in many of the Balkan states. Ottoman rule had led to conversions and large settlements of Muslims in

Bosnia-Herzegovina, Bulgaria, Albania, and Serbia (Todorova 1996: 62–5). In July 1995, members of the breakaway Bosnian Serb "Republic of Srpska" massacred over 8,000 Bosniaks – Bosnian Muslims – in the eastern Bosnian town of Srebrenica. In addition, they drove more than 20,000 civilians from the region. This horrific episode, more than anything else in the civil war, brought home to the outside world the living presence of Ottoman rule in the Balkans. They were further reminded of it by the civil war in Serbia itself, which resulted in the creation of the independent state of Kosovo, made up largely of Albanian Muslims. Not so very long after Muslims, who had lived for over 600 years in Spain, had been expelled from Europe, they returned and have continued to be an active presence in the European borderlands of the south. Through the Ottoman as much as the earlier Arab empires, they make the point that Islam is a part of Europe, not some foreign and alien presence that has to be expunged.

In one further country, Ottoman rule shows its long reach. The Ottomans ruled Hungary for over 150 years, from the early sixteenth to the early eighteenth centuries. When the Protestant Reformation occurred, the Habsburgs took the lead in the Catholic Counter-Reformation in Europe. But they were unable to prosecute it in Hungary, most of which was under their other antagonist, the Ottomans. The Ottomans, in fact, gave support to the Hungarian Protestants. Many of these were Calvinists, which accounts for the persistence of Calvinism in southern and eastern Hungary today. The eastern city of Debrecen is still today called "the Calvinist Rome," and Protestantism is the most popular religion in that region of Hungary (Pálffy 2001: 120). The Ottoman legacy in Hungary is not just Turkish baths and Turkish cuisine.

What of the Russian Empire, the other great land empire that fell in 1917? What has been its legacy in the vast region of Eurasia that it covered? That legacy has been complicated by the fact that what succeeded the tsarist empire was another Russian Empire, the Soviet Empire known as the Soviet Union. The Soviets systematically rebuilt the Russian Empire to almost its original size. After the Second World War, they even extended its influence by creating an "informal empire" in Eastern Europe, the group of countries – including Poland, Hungary, Czechoslovakia – that came to be called the "Soviet bloc," and that for over 40 years were more or less directed by Moscow.

The Soviet Empire was, however, not just another Russian Empire. Russian nationalism was discouraged – except briefly during the "Great Fatherland War" of 1941–5 – and Russians, in fact, came to feel that, though clearly the predominant force within the Soviet Union, they had also been its sacrificial victims (Kumar 2017: 300–8).

As we have seen, other nationalities, under the policy of "indigeni-zation" (*korenizatsii*a), were encouraged to develop their national cultures; the Russians, as is typical with ruling peoples, were asked to play theirs down, as likely to cause resentment among the subject peoples.

With the fall of the Soviet Union in 1991, the Russians – like other imperial peoples – have suffered the natural consequences of this inhibition of their own national identity. An imperial people for centuries, they have never developed a strong tradition of thinking of themselves as simply a nation – in pursuit, therefore, of a nation-state. Within days of proclaiming that the Soviet Union no longer existed, the Russian government of Boris Yeltsin adopted the double-headed eagle, the old symbol of the tsarist empire, as the state emblem of the new Russian Federation. The preamble to the new Constitution, intro-duced in 1993, declared, "We, the multinational people of the Russian Federation . . ." Although ethnic Russians make up 82 percent of the Russian Federation, some 25 million ethnic Russians live outside it in the "near abroad," in the Baltic states and Central Asia.

Russia is not alone in this, of course; most so-called nation-states are multiethnic or multinational, and many have large diasporas living outside the eponymous nation-state. But formerly imperial states develop habits of mind and behavior that make it peculiarly dif-ficult for them to settle down as nation-states – as just one state among others. Certainly, present-day Russia, under President Vladimir Putin, seems strongly inclined to flex imperial muscles. In 2008, Russia established a protectorate over the former Soviet territories of Abkhazia and South Ossetia, detaching them from an independent Georgia. It also continues to prop up the "Pridnestrovian Moldavian Republic" (Transnistria), refusing to accept it as part of an independ-ent Moldova. In 2014, Russia annexed the Crimea, declaring it a Russian territory that had unfortunately been transferred to Ukraine in the 1950s by the Ukrainian-leaning President Nikita Khrushchev (reputedly after a night of drinking with his Ukrainian friends). It was as Russian, they claimed, as the region of east Ukraine that the Russians supported, with arms and men, in its struggle with the Westward-leaning Ukrainian government. President Putin is on record as having declared that the break-up of the Soviet Union was "the greatest geopolitical catastrophe of the [twentieth] century" and a "genuine tragedy" for the Russian people. There will be no new "Russian Empire," by name at least – but Russia will probably remain incapable of distinguishing between its interest as a nation, strictly speaking, and the re-building of empire as the natural theater of its national life.

So much for the legacy of empire in the metropolitan core of the Russian and Soviet empires.[2] What of the "peripheries," the peoples and territories that since the sixteenth century were incorporated in the successive Russian empires? For the Asiatic part of the Russian/ Soviet Empire, we might say that one clear legacy is the very existence of the peoples and territories there as separate nation-states today (Morrison 2015: 164–6). Before their conquest by Russia, the Uzbeks, Kazakhs, Kyrgyz, Tajiks, and Turkomen roamed Central Asia as nomadic tribes, mostly of Turkic origin. The Russians reorganized and territorialized them in the nineteenth century. Later, in the 1920s and 1930s, the Soviet Union made of them full-fledged "Soviet Socialist Republics" – the "Uzbek Soviet Socialist Republic," the "Kazakh Soviet Socialist Republic," etc. With its Stalinist policies of "indigenization," it also equipped them with "national" languages and promoted their "national" cultures. In both cases, neither had existed before in any discernible way.

Central Asians did not, unlike some other parts of the Soviet Union, press for independence. But, when the opportunity presented itself – and when, in truth, they had not much choice in the matter as the Soviet Union imploded – the leaders – mostly former Communist Party *apparatchiks* – of the Central Asian peoples found themselves in possession of ready-made national states. They quickly repositioned themselves as nationalists, in most cases emphasizing the Islamic character of their nation. The old Soviet Socialist Republics reappeared, their boundaries mostly unchanged, as the five "Stans" – Kazakhstan, Uzbekistan, Kyrgyzstan, Tajikistan, Turkmenistan. They inherited the Soviet development of their not inconsiderable resources of oil and gas. Mostly multiethnic – Kazakhstan recognizes 131 ethnicities – they adopted the language of the "titular" nationality – Uzbek, Tajik, etc. – as the national language, but also kept Russian as a second official language and the one that most were adept in. Many ethnic Russians remained in the region, playing an important role in its development. The legacy of Russian rule in Central Asia is as profound as it is unmistakable. There is almost no clearer case of empires as builders of nations – the very nations that succeed them.

In the western, European, borderlands of the Russian and Soviet empires, the peoples in the empire had in some cases prior experience as nations, and even states. That was particularly true of the Poles and Lithuanians, who had formed the core of the great Polish–Lithuanian Commonwealth before its dismemberment at the hands of the Austrians, Prussians, and Russians in the eighteenth-century partitions of Poland. But the influence of the Russian/Soviet Empire is as evident in the region as the impact of the Habsburg and Hohenzollern empires previously considered. Ukraine – "Little Russia" to the Russians – had a shadowy existence before its incorporation in the Russian Empire in the seventeenth century. Its national consciousness owed not a little to Russian attempts to stimulate it as a counter to the more dangerous threat of Polish nationalism. In the late Soviet period, it emerged as the most ardently nationalist republic, and was the first to declare its independence from the Soviet Union. But its radically divided character today clearly indicates the continuing power of the Russian presence in its character and culture.

Contemporary Poland, too, owes it very shape to the Soviet Union. Resurrected after the First World War as an independent state, in the Second World War it lost its western part to Germany and its eastern part to the Soviet Union (before being wholly conquered by Germany). After Germany's defeat, Poland was bodily shifted westward, more than recovering the German sections, but at the cost of permanently losing its eastern section to the Soviet Socialist republics of Ukraine and Belarus. Those sections then became part of the independent states of Ukraine and Belarus. Poland, as we have seen, still carries traces of its Russian past. But its largely Western character – its loss of historic elements of its past, such as the old cities of Lviv/Lwov and Vilnius/Wilno – is the result of the tectonic shifts brought about by the operations of empires on its territories. Contemporary Poland is an imperial creation almost as much as contemporary Ukraine, Belarus ("White Russia," also a Russian/Soviet invention), and the Baltic states of Lithuania, Latvia, and Estonia (where large numbers of Russians remain to remind the inhabitants of their past as imperial subjects).[3]

We can also finally note, in this consideration of the imperial legacies of the land empires, the case of the Chinese Empire. Following its dissolution in 1911, China embarked on a period of more or less intermittent civil war that lasted until 1949. The republic that succeeded the empire maintained the boundaries of the empire but was constantly under threat from within by feuding "warlords." Eventually, the Nationalist Kuomintang, under Chiang Kai-Shek (Jiang Jieshi), took control, but confronted a stubborn opponent in the Chinese communists organized by Mao Zedong. Even more dangerous was the threat from outside. Japan invaded and conquered Manchuria in 1931, setting up the puppet state of Manchukuo and controlling most of the rest of China. Mao led the communist forces in resisting both Japan and the Kuomintang, eventually prevailing to establish the communist People's Republic of China in 1949.

Under Mao, the communists repudiated the whole Chinese past, denouncing it comprehensively as "feudal." The Chinese were taught to despise all the old beliefs and customs, from Confucianism to foot-binding. For a while, during the "Cultural Revolution" (1966–76), they were even urged to reject their scholars and intellectuals, as reminiscent of the old scholar-gentry.

Since Mao's death, and the "liberalization" of the Chinese economy and society that began with Deng Xiaoping's reforms of the early 1980s, a new attitude has begun to develop toward the Chinese past. Confucianism has found a place as a bulwark to communism, instilling respect for authority. There is pride in China's place for so many centuries – before the "century of humiliation" imposed by the West in the nineteenth century – at the center of the world economy. Chinese museums now celebrate the great voyages of Admiral Zheng He in the early Ming period, and Chinese scholars speculate on what might have been, had China continued those voyages and perhaps embarked on colonization.

Most far-reaching of all is the "Belt and Road Initiative" (BRI), launched with much fanfare by President Xi Jinping in 2013.[4] The aim is to spread China's influence throughout the world through an ambitious and elaborate program of investment and construction on all continents, though Africa, the Middle East, South America, and parts of Asia loom particularly large in Chinese thinking. BRI involves large infrastructure projects such as roads, railways, bridges, and ports. Sometimes whole cities are constructed. The aim is to replicate – by the same peaceful means, but now on a world scale – the great trading routes known as the "Silk Roads" in centuries past, of which China was the hub.

China denies any "imperial" intention in all this ("a bid to enhance regional connectivity and embrace a brighter future" is its colorless description of its purpose). It declares that it wishes to use its increasing wealth and power to produce a better, more equal, and more harmonious world. But others have seen in BRI echoes of empire, China re-asserting itself as the "Middle Kingdom" – the kingdom at the center of the earth.[5] The difference is that, while the earlier Chinese Empire tended to remain restricted and regional, the new Chinese Empire has global aspirations. China is soon set to take over from the United States as the world's largest economy.[6] Its people now travel all over the world; its students are to be found in the schools and universities of all the major Western countries. It has founded Confucius Institutes on many foreign university campuses, to promote the Chinese language, culture, and civilization. Its spectacularly successful hosting of the Summer Olympic Games in Beijing in 2008 announced its "coming out" to the world.

No more than any other state will the Chinese construct a new formal empire – though in many ways it already has one. The Chinese communist state inherited the old republican boundaries, which in turn took these over more or less unchanged from the empire. There is an extraordinary continuity here from at least Qing times, with China ruling over the vast non-Han territories of Tibet, Xinjiang, and Mongolia, just as did the Qings. The official 57 ethnicities in the People's Republic of China testify to its multiethnic and multinational character. China does not call itself an empire, any more than does the United States. But, in the eyes of many, the one is as much so as the other.

The new thing is China's reaching out to the world, something it has resisted for much of its history. This can be interpreted – and has been – as an attempt to create an "informal empire," just as the British created one alongside their formal empire in the nineteenth century. Time alone will tell if that is the case, and whether in fact they will succeed (there have already been numerous hiccups). But there are certainly enough indications already to suggest that, whatever it is called, the results of BRI could well be a new kind of global empire – "an empire with Chinese characteristics," just as what is practiced at home is called "socialism with Chinese characteristics."

The Overseas Empires: The Postcolonial Condition

The European overseas empires covered the world. Their ending is within the memory of many people still alive. That very recentness makes it difficult to assess their long-term legacies. That applies to both the subject nations and to their metropolitan rulers. In the immediate aftermath of "decolonization," there were responses and re-adjustments that made sense in the heat of the moment. The metropolitan societies seemed to want to put their empires behind them. The subject societies wished to show that the break was complete. They were now in control of their own destiny; they were making new societies. They dramatized it with changes of names – of the country, the city, the streets. Statues of the old European rulers were toppled; in their place were the heroes of the independence movements.

Some of those changes were bound to be superficial and ephemeral. The centuries of imperial rule could not simply be shrugged off, either by the subjects or by their rulers. Now, 50 or so years on, we are still not in a position to assess the real, long-term, consequences of the experience of empire. But we can at least make a start.

Much of the thinking about the effects of empire has gone under the label of "postcoloniality." This refers to a body of writing that has tried to lay out a systematic way of studying the persisting influence of empire in the thought and behavior of postcolonial societies. It is somewhat unfortunate that much of it is concerned only with the impact of empire on the subject, mostly non-Western, societies of the "Third World," or what is now commonly referred to as the "global South." It is tied, that is, mainly to anti-colonial thought and movements, and to trying to show how empire continues to shape much of the life of the postcolonial societies that were once part of the European empires. So Julian Go says that "postcolonial thought is primarily an anti-imperial discourse that critiques empire and its persistent legacies" (Go 2016: 1). Others stress the activist impulse behind postcolonial thought – the fact that it is meant not just to point to persistencies, but also to stimulate action to throw them off, to get rid of the imperial incubus. Postcolonial critique, says Robert Young, is "a form of activist writing that looks back to the political commitment of the anti-colonial liberation movements and draws its inspiration from them" (2001: 10). It is "quite simply, what Walter Benjamin called 'the tradition of the oppressed'" (Young 2015: 149). Not surprisingly, its key documents contain ringing titles such as Frantz Fanon's *Black Skin, White Masks* (1952) and *The Wretched of the Earth* (1961).[7]

Belatedly – mainly because, in the metropolitan societies, empire was neglected for so long after its passing – scholars have begun to apply postcolonial perspectives to the ruling societies. Empire is a persisting fact in European societies too.[8] That should have been obvious, but there were good reasons to ignore it. When the master has finished his meal, the servants squabble over the scraps. The master moves on to other concerns, largely oblivious of the effects of the meal on his thought and behavior. But master as well as servant have partaken of the same meal, and its effects can be seen in both.

The legacy of the overseas empire is most obvious in the non-Western societies that were subject to European rule. That is why postcolonial studies have focused mostly on them. The effects are so patent and palpable. Peoples were bodily moved; borders were fixed; economic, cultural, and political institutions were put in place. All these bore the stamp of Europe. Indigenous traditions might modify them, or persist alongside European practices, but the societies that emerged after empire carried the unmistakable imprint of the Europeans that had ruled them.

The empires, in many cases, made nations where they had not existed before. It gave them a national identity, often a national language where none of the indigenous ones could command the assent of all the constituent parts of the new nation. Languages in most of the African colonies were local, regional, tribal. To impose any of them would be to impose the rule of particular tribes, an unacceptable solution in most cases. Better, to still divisions, to accept at least for the time being the language of the erstwhile European ruler. Hence, many of France's West and Central African colonies continued to use French after independence, forming a wide-ranging francophone community that included metropolitan France along with many of its former colonies. So, too, the British "Commonwealth of Nations" included many African and Asian nations who continued to use English as the official language long after independence. Even where there were historic languages reflecting longstanding high cultures, as in India, the absence of a unifying language after independence led to the de facto adoption of the European ruler's language – in this case, English – as the common national language, one that all were prepared to share.

Even where the new nations self-consciously adopted new names – Zimbabwe for Southern Rhodesia, Burkino Faso for Upper Volta, Myanmar for Burma – it was obvious that the actual state forms derived directly from imperial rule. Africa showed this most clearly. Before the coming of the European empires, there were various tribal groupings and federations, but it was the Europeans who put them into the political forms that gave shape to the newly independent nation-states. Once established, these state forms showed remarkable tenacity. It has frequently been remarked that, despite the many civil conflicts that have wracked Africa since the departure of the Europeans, the state borders established by the empires have remained largely intact (C. Young 2001: 172).[9]

This has not surprisingly given rise to endless conflicts, mostly of an ethnic kind. The Europeans made colonial states that suited their convenience, and according to the distribution of power in Europe. Lines were drawn on the map of Africa that often bore no relation to past history or ethnic composition. Nigeria, Africa's largest and most populous state, can stand as a good example. Nigeria was named and created by the British, finding its existing boundaries in 1914. It was formed out of three regions very different in character and composition. It contains over 250 ethnic groups, the largest of which are the Hausa ("Northerners"), Igbo ("Easterners"), and Yoruba ("Westerners"). These ethnic groups map onto the main religious divide, with the northern Hausa and Fulani being mainly Muslim, and the eastern Igbo, Christian – the Yoruba being almost half and half. Political parties divided after independence in 1960 mainly along ethnic lines, and have remained so. The official language is

"Nigerian English," an attempt at a common bond amidst the diversity (Kwarteng 2012: 273–303).

Ethnic diversity does not necessarily lead to conflict. But where, as in Nigeria, traditional enmities and divisions have been papered over in a state created by outsiders, it is highly likely to occur. Nigeria's political instability, born mainly of religious and ethnic conflict, has been endemic. For three years, between 1967 and 1970, a bitter civil war raged between the Igbos, who declared the Eastern Region the independent state of Biafra, and the other ethnic groups. It is estimated that between 1 and 3 million people died during that war. Its end solved little. From 1966 to 1999, Nigeria was ruled by a series of military strongmen basing themselves on particular ethnic groups. Since that time, a precarious democracy has prevailed, but ethnicity remains the basis of political power.[10]

A legacy of ethnic conflict, often fueled by rival interests among outside powers, is one of the clear results of the kind of political formations left by the European rulers in their former colonies (Fearon and Laitin 2003: 88). "Nation-states" they may be, but national homogeneity is even more lacking in their case than it is in those many other nation-states that are also marked by ethnic diversity. Equally clear is the degree of economic dependency that has followed the end of empire. For many commentators, what followed European rule was not real independence for the new nations, but a kind of indirect rule in which the powerful states and large private corporations of the former imperial rulers continued to exercise real power over the fortunes of the supposedly new sovereign states. Employing a term that was to have wide currency, the Ghanaian leader Kwame Nkrumah in 1965 called this condition – with an echo of Lenin – "neo-colonialism: the last stage of imperialism" (in Gildea 2019: 98). Echoing this, Frantz Fanon, one of the best-known of the anti-colonial writers, declared that "colonialism and imperialism have not paid their score when they withdraw their flags and their police forces from our territories" (Fanon [1961] 1967: 79–80).

Here was a species of "informal empire" very similar to the kind that was practiced especially well – according to Gallagher and Robinson (1953) – by the British during the era of free trade in the nineteenth century. Formal empire could be dispensed with when informal means served the same purpose, more cheaply and more efficiently. The new states might bid their former masters goodbye, in elaborate ceremonies involving the lowering of the old imperial flag and the raising of the flag of the proud new nation. But the cruel reality was continuing dependence on the old rulers – for aid, for investment, for expertise, often even for basic security. The global institutions of the new world order instituted after 1945 – the United Nations, the International Monetary Fund, the World Bank, the World Trade Organization – might seem to give parity to all nations, old and new. But in their operations they were clearly managed by, and in the interests of, the major Western powers.[11]

In the event, the degree of dependence has varied considerably. Some former colonies – formal and informal – such as India and Brazil have established a real degree of independence and become major players in the world economy. China, semi-colonized for over a century, has gone even further, and in an extraordinary and unprecedented burst of development has come to challenge even the most powerful economy in the world, that of the United States. Most of the African states, on the other hand, have remained heavily dependent on outside powers – China now, as much as America or Europe. There is, it is clear, no one "Third World" of postcolonial societies, but many worlds of development. European states will continue to try to maintain a "special relationship" with their former colonies – the French with the French-speaking countries of *francophonie*, the British with the Anglophone countries of the Commonwealth – but their ability to dictate policy will depend now on many circumstances that they cannot control.[12]

If economic and political dependence has been one feature of the postcolonial condition, for many an even more significant legacy has been the state of psychological and cultural dependency. The "empire of the mind" has, in their view, been even more tenacious than that of the economy or polity.[13] Colonialism, they argue, did not just shackle the body; it ensnared the mind, delivering up the colonial subjects as re-engineered creatures with a deep-seated colonial cast of mind. Colonialism had entered the soul of the subject peoples. Such an inheritance was infinitely more difficult to throw off than economic or political dependence.

Many of the themes elaborated in this vein were stated in the terse poetic prose of Aimé Césaire's pioneering *Discourse on Colonialism* ([1950] 2000): a "declaration of war" against Europe and on behalf of the Third World, it has been called. Césaire, from French Martinique, set the tone by declaring that the colonizers were as much infected by colonialism as the colonized. "Colonization works to decivilize the colonizer, to brutalize him in the true sense of the word" (2000: 35). That is what Césaire calls "the boomerang effect": the colonizer, in treating the colonized man as an animal, "tends objectively to transform himself into an animal" (2000: 41).

But his urgent concern was with the plight of the colonized, not that of the colonizers. Colonial subjects had become infected with the poison of colonialism. They had come to accept the superiority of the white man, and to see themselves as inferior beings, dependent on white leadership. Throwing off European political rule was never going to be sufficient by itself. The more important task was "decolonising the mind" – to use the title of the 1981 book by the Kenyan novelist Ngugi wa Thiong'o. It was to free the colonial subject of the mental dependence that had accompanied political dependence. Colonization has meant "thingification" – the turning of the colonized into mere "instruments of production" for the colonizers, a mental brutalization that has been the other side of physical brutalization: "I am talking about millions of men in whom fear has been cunningly instilled, who have been taught to have an inferiority complex, to tremble, kneel, despair, and behave like flunkeys" (Césaire 2000: 42–3).

It was another Martinican, Frantz Fanon, who, in his book *The Wretched of the Earth* ([1961] 1967) spelled out the message in the form that gave it the greatest impact. Fanon, a trained psychiatrist who committed himself to the anti-colonial struggle in Algeria, was indebted to Césaire, but laid out their common ideas in a more programmatic way. Psychological and mental dependency was, indeed, the problem. But the solution, Fanon controversially proposed, was not simply critical self-reflection but a purging act of violence, violence as "a cleansing force": "The colonized man finds his freedom in and through violence." It is only through the act of violence – "to work means to work for the death of the [white] settler" – that the colonized will be able to throw off the incubus of colonial attitudes ([1961] 1967: 67–8).[14]

It helped in spreading Fanon's message that the original French edition included an extended preface by the famous French philosopher Jean-Paul Sartre. In Fanon, declared Sartre, "the Third World finds itself and speaks to itself through his voice." Endorsing Fanon's call for violence, Sartre wrote:

The native cures himself of colonial neurosis by thrusting out the settler through force of arms. When his rage boils over, he rediscovers his lost innocence and he comes to know himself in that he himself creates his self. Far removed from his war, we consider it as a triumph of barbarism; but of its own volition it achieves, slowly but surely, the emancipation of the rebel, for bit by bit it destroys in him and around him the colonial gloom. . . . The rebel's weapon is the proof of his humanity. For in the first days of the revolt you must kill: to shoot down a European is to kill two birds with one stone, to destroy an oppressor and the man he oppresses at the same time: there remains a dead man, and a free man; the survivor, for the first time, feels a national soil under his feet. (in Fanon [1961] 1967: 18–19)

Sartre's endorsement of Fanon's message – seen as a kind of "revolutionary messianism" by critics – helped to ensure that it would be heard around the world, among American blacks in the United States as much as among revolutionaries in Latin America and South-East Asia. All saw in Fanon's diagnosis of the colonial condition a reflection of their own predicament. The analysis was given further publicity, this time at the level of academic discourse, by the distinguished Palestinian-American literary scholar, Edward Said. In his widely read *Culture and Imperialism*, he declared that Fanon, "more dramatically and decisively than anyone ... expresses the immense cultural shift from the terrain of nationalist independence to the theoretical domain of liberation" (1994: 323–4). What Fanon showed was that national independence for colonial subjects was never enough, that it might even be a trap, for "orthodox nationalism followed along the same track hewn out by imperialism" (Said 1994: 330).

The Afterlife of Empire in the Metropolitan Societies

In his earlier, equally influential book *Orientalism* (1979), Said had examined the impact of empire on the metropolitan peoples, the peoples who ruled the empires. There, he was largely concerned with the way the experience of empire had formed for the colonizers a particular image of the Orient – Said used mainly the example of Middle Eastern cultures – in which it was counterposed to the Occident as degenerate and inferior, a region of weakness, effeminacy, and dependency: "Orientalism, which is the system of European or Western knowledge about the Orient, [is] synonymous with European domination of the Orient" (Said 1979: 197). The consequences of this way of thought could be seen in contemporary attitudes and policies, especially in regard to peoples in the Arab world. Said wrote before the terrorist attacks of September 11, 2001, on the World Trade Center in New York and the Pentagon in Washington DC – the events that unleashed the American "war on terror" in Iraq, Afghanistan, and elsewhere. But he had anticipated the virulent Islamophobia that seized much of the Western world in the wake of those events.

The Islamic world had had much reason to be aware of the European empires. By the time of the First World War, Britain ruled – in India, Africa, and elsewhere – over half the world's Muslims. This number increased with the establishment of the postwar League of Nations British Mandates in Iraq, Jordan, and Palestine, making Britain "the greatest Muhammedan power in the world" at the time (Aydin 2017: 83). Many Muslims were also to be found in the French Empire in North Africa, and the Dutch Empire in Indonesia. It was this experience of the European empires, with the accompanying European disparagement of Muslim civilization as uncreative and backward, that was responsible for the renaissance of Muslim thought at the end of the nineteenth century, and the elaboration – for the first time ever, according to Cemil Aydin (2017: 65–98) – of the idea of a common Muslim civilization that had at one time led the world in scientific development and enlightened thought. Set against that background, the recent reassertion of Muslim pride, and the search for a new caliphate – vacant since the end of the Ottoman Empire – make sense, even if their expression can take violent and even terrorist forms.[15]

Muslims were also a significant part of the phenomenon that for many people represents the most obvious and visible legacy of empire in the metropolitan societies: what has been called "colonization in reverse," the immigration of millions of people from the former European empires to the imperial heartlands in Europe. For France, this has meant mainly Muslims and others from North Africa and sub-Saharan Africa; for the Dutch, immigrants from Indonesia and the Caribbean; for the British, immigrants from the subcontinent of India, Pakistan, and Bangladesh, as well as from Africa and the West Indies. Together, these now make up substantial minorities in many of the major cities of Britain, France, and the Netherlands. Belgium and Portugal, too, are now home to significant numbers of immigrants from their former empires.

Not all the immigrants are black or brown. There are also the white "returnees" and repatriates who lived as farmers, traders, teachers, administrators, and soldiers in the former empires. "Returnees" and "repatriates" are, however, misleading terms. Many of these people of European descent – *criollos* they would have been called in Latin America – had been born outside Europe and had not even ever visited their "home" countries. For them, the encounter with their "home" societies has often been disorienting and disturbing. Many British repatriates, for instance, found their home societies so uncongenial that they rapidly moved on to one of the white societies of the "Britannic world" – Australia, New Zealand, South Africa (Buettner 2016: 226–7).

Of the between 5.4 and 6.8 million people from the former colonies who arrived in Western Europe in the 40-year period after the Second World War, between 3.3 and 4 million were Europeans or Eurasians – that is, more than a half of the total. Portugal alone took in 1.5

million *retornados*, increasing Portugal's population of 9 million by over 5 percent – the largest decolonization migration of any European society. France, too, between early 1950s and the mid-1960s took in 1.5 million repatriates, who came to form over 3 percent of the 44 million French citizens of the "hexagon" – metropolitan France. A million of these were the *colons* or *pieds-noirs* from French Algeria. For Britain, the 1991 census recorded that more than 560,000 whites had been born in former British colonies, in addition to some 25,000 Eurasians, mostly Anglo-Indians. In the Netherlands, there were 300,000 Europeans and Eurasians from former Dutch colonies, mostly from Indonesia; they included some 180,000 "Indisch Dutch," of mixed-race origin. In the case of Belgium, the violence and chaos that followed the precipitate withdrawal from the Congo in 1960 led to the mass emigration to Belgium of nearly all the 89,000 Europeans formerly resident there (Buettner 2016: 213–50).

Few scholars – Elizabeth Buettner is an exception – have explored the experience of these white returnees. They were thought either to have been easily absorbed by their "home" countries, or to have been too few in number to bother about. More often, they were figures of fun, seen as living out colonial fantasies in Cheltenham or Bath (or Marseilles). In any case, their problems paled by comparison with those of the several millions of black and brown immigrants, or descendants of immigrants, from the former colonies. In Britain, in 2017, about 5 million – some 7 percent of the population – were either first- or second-generation Asian, West Indian, or African immigrants from the former British Empire, mostly from India, Pakistan, and the Caribbean. A comparable number in France – about 7.8 percent of the total population – also hailed from the former French Empire, mostly North Africa and sub-Saharan Africa. The Netherlands, Portugal, and Belgium, too, have received significant numbers of non-Western immigrants from their former colonies, in Indonesia, Africa, and the West Indies.

The experience of these "colored" immigrants has been chequered, to put it mildly.[16] Some societies, such as the Dutch and the British, hoped to create "multicultural" societies, allowing each group its own traditions and ways. Integration, not assimilation, was the watchword. Much of this came unstuck, especially in the wake of "9/11," as Muslims in the European cities experienced increasing suspicion and hostility on the part of the white population. The response, not surprisingly, was a radicalization of the Muslim communities, especially among the young, some of whom opted to join extremist Muslim organizations such as Al-Qaeda and ISIS. Much of the radicalization took place at home, in the prisons, mosques, and *banlieues* – virtual Muslim ghettoes in French cities – of the home communities.

In London, on July 7, 2005 – "7/7" – three young British Muslims killed 56 people in a bombing of London buses and underground trains. On March 22, 2017, a converted mixed-race Islamist killed 5 pedestrians and knifed a policeman on London's Westminster Bridge; two months later, on May 26, 2017, a British Muslim suicide bomber killed 22 people and injured 59 at a pop concert in Manchester. On June 23, 2017, a Pakistan-born British Muslim mowed down pedestrians on London Bridge, killing 7 and injuring 48. All these attacks were seen as revenge against the British for supporting US-led raids in Iraq, Syria, and Libya.

France, which rejected "Anglo-Saxon" policies of multiculturalism, and declared for time-honored practices of assimilation, fared even worse. Particularly shocking was the killing by French Muslims of 12 journalists of the satirical magazine *Charlie Hebdo* in Paris on January 7, 2015. A few months later, on November 13, 2015, French Muslims killed 130 people at the Bataclan concert hall in Paris. On July 14, 2016, a Tunisian-born Muslim drove his truck into a crowd in Nice, killing 86 people and injuring 458. Since the attacks were ostensibly a response to French interventions against ISIS in Syria and Iraq, some commentators found in them echoes of empire, of the long French presence in the Middle East. "It is now clear," wrote the veteran French sociologist Edgar Morin, "that the Middle East is now present in the heart of France." But some of the perpetrators were also of Algerian origin, and when the Paris police invaded the *banlieue* of Saint-Denis where the Bataclan attackers were holed up, many commented that "it was as if the Battle of Algiers, fought to clear the kasbah of FLN terrorists in 1957, was now being fought in the *banlieues* of Paris" (Gildea 2019: 228; see also 200–2, 223–31, 240–1). This was the empire striking back, with a vengeance.

Multiculturalism, it is clear, is dead, at least in the form in which it has been practiced hitherto (Kumar 2008).[17] Its result has been communities cut off from each other and unaware of what takes place in each. "Integration," legal and civic, may have been an honorable goal, but perhaps an impossible one if groups live in mutually uncomprehending communities. Assimilation, French-style, also seems to require a different approach. French views of *laïcité* and secular republicanism have come to look too rigid, too unable to accept the degree of cultural diversity that is inherent in all post-imperial societies. Nevertheless, to many commentators, some version of assimilation seems increasingly to be the necessary response to the fragmentation and compartmentalization that currently threatens many European societies (see, e.g., Brubaker 2015: 119–54).

"Colonization in reverse" is merely one – though clearly the most visible and, in some ways, the most significant – aspect of the afterlife of empires in the metropolitan societies. Traces of empire have also been found in many other spheres – architecture, popular culture, cinema and TV, sport, fashion, the monarchy, foreign policy.[18] Nostalgia is one feature of this, but by no means the predominant one. What is more important is the changing shape of the international environment, and the sense that empire may have something to teach us about how we come to terms with it.

Has Empire a Future?

A British public opinion poll in July 2014 found that 59 percent of respondents thought the British Empire "something to be proud of"; only 19 percent thought it a source of shame (Gildea 2019: 235–6). This follows a trend going back several years. Empire, after having suffered a period of amnesia and indifference, has experienced a renewal of interest and attention. Why might that be so?

The nation-state was long thought to be the natural successor to empire. In the twentieth century, as symbolized by the League of Nations and the United Nations, it became the standard form of the modern state, the only one accepted as legitimate. Increasingly, though, it seems to be the source of our problems, not the solution to them. Nation-states have unleashed violence on an unparalleled scale in recent decades, such as in the Yugoslav wars of the 1990s, the Rwandan genocide of 1994, and the murderous wars – such as the Iran–Iraq war of the 1980s – in the Middle East of the late twentieth and early twenty-first centuries. Earlier in the twentieth century, the nation-states of Germany and Italy – both newly united in 1870 – were the agents of some of the most barbaric acts in human history. Today, nationalist passions continue to fuel conflicts all over the world. They are on the rise even in those societies that were thought to have gone beyond them, in the United Kingdom, France, Germany, Italy. In Spain, they have revived historic enmities between the regions. In the United States, "America first" has become the rallying-cry of a populist nationalism that has bitterly divided the country.

Empires had their quotient of violence, but they acted as much to restrain as to cause it. For them, nationalist rivalries were a threat to their stability, and to the very principle of supra- or multi-nationality by which they ordered themselves. By contrast, the Wilsonian principle of self-determination, liberal in essence as it was, has been a recipe for endless conflicts and wars, many of them civil. Civil war has, in fact, taken over from international war as the typical conflict of our times (Fearon and Laitin 2003: 75; Armitage 2017: 1–8). David Armitage has noted the paradox that "the closer the world comes to the cosmopolitan ideal of universal humanity, the more intimate have international and even global wars become" (Armitage 2017: 198).

Much of that "intimacy" relates to ethnicity and nationhood. Any group that can make a reasonable claim on the world community that it is a nation feels legitimated in its struggle for national independence and statehood. Group after group – from Québécois, Catalans, and Scots to the peoples of East Timor, Kosovo, South Ossetia, "Transnistria," and the "Republica Srpska" of Bosnia – have declared themselves a separate nation with the right to form their own nation-state, by force if necessary. Thousands have died in the ensuing conflicts. Never mind if the resulting nation-state is too small or too weak to be viable by itself, and needs the protection of powerful patrons – Russia in the case of South Ossetia and Transnistria, the United Nations in the case of Kosovo, Serbia in the case of the Republica Srpska. If the Scots and Catalonians secede from their respective composite states, they too will need the European Union to secure their survival.

Whatever the legitimacy and validity of the claims, the principle of nationalism promises – or threatens – a future of unremitting and unending conflict. This, perhaps, is sufficient to explain the search for political arrangements that go beyond the nation-state, or are an alternative to it. The League of Nations and the United Nations were attempts to restrain or to supervise the operations of the nation-state, in the wake of what were thought to be its catastrophic consequences in two world wars. Neither proved very successful – the League of Nations because of its structural weakness, the United Nations because the great powers effectively controlled it through the Security Council, leaving the General Assembly as little more than a talking shop. In the 1990s, NATO forces bombarded a sovereign state, Serbia, without a UN mandate; and in 2003, the United States and its allies invaded Iraq, again without UN sanction – a war that the UN Secretary-General Kofi Annan declared "from a [UN] Charter point of view . . . illegal" (BBC News, September 16, 2004).

It is not, perhaps, surprising that, in this search for non-national principles of political organization, the history and structure of empires have been scrutinized as offering possible models. Empires were, after all, almost by definition, supranational and multinational.

Might they have something to teach us? In an early statement of such a view, the veteran American statesman and historian George Kennan observed in 1979 that "the Austro-Hungarian Empire still looks better as a solution to the tangled problems of that part of the world than anything that has succeeded it" (in Kozuchowski 2013: 168). The Austro-Hungarian Empire – the Habsburg Empire – has remained a favorite with many commentators (see, e.g., Miller-Melamed and Moreton 2019). The Ottoman Empire, with its *millet* system of self-governing communities and general tolerance of different religions and cultures, has also found favor, in the light especially of the current Turkish government's Islamicizing propensities (Onar 2015: 151–2). The historian Niall Ferguson saw the British Empire as an early instance of globalization – "Anglobalization" – and suggested it as a model for current attempts to grapple with the phenomenon (Ferguson 2004: xx–xxviii). The harsh treatment by China's communist leadership of the Muslim Uighurs in the Chinese province of Xinjiang has been critically compared to the much more intelligent and successful policies that prevailed in the old Chinese Empire (Millward 2019).

Writing in 1917, on the eve of the fall of the Habsburg Empire, the great Austrian poet and dramatist Hugo von Hofmannsthal wrote that "this Europe that wants to shape itself anew needs an Austria." Hofmannsthal, an ardent believer in "the Austrian idea," saw the Habsburg Empire as possessing that "structure of genuine elasticity" that allowed it to be a bridge between Eastern and Western Europe. Its "fluid boundary" allowed for the cross-movement of peoples and cultures – Germans, Latins, and Slavs (in Le Rider 1994: 122). Years later, in the 1990s, another great Central European intellectual, Ernest Gellner, somewhat revised his earlier view of the necessity of nationalism and now, in the face of what he saw as the regrettable fall of the multinational Soviet Union and the multiethnic Yugoslavia, called for a re-organization of the world on something like the Habsburg model: "a global Habsburg Empire." Inspired by the enthusiasm of the anthropologist Bronisław Malinowski, born in Habsburg Galicia, for the Habsburg Empire, which Gellner characterized as "the League of Nations with teeth," Gellner provocatively proposed that the solution to the irreducibly multiethnic and multinational condition of the world was to "colonise simply everybody – i.e. deprive their political units of sovereignty – while allowing them absolute cultural freedom of expression, thereby incidentally depriving boundaries of some of their importance and symbolic potency" (in Kumar 2015: 80).[19]

A "Europe without borders" has always been one of the declared aims of the European Union (EU). Hence, it is not surprising that comparisons between past empires and the European Union have become increasingly common – uncomfortable as that might be for some of its members. In fact, it can be persuasively argued that, for many of the European states that formed it, the European Union was indeed a substitute for the empires that they lost in the 1940s and 1950s. "The empire is dead, long live the EU," was the sarcastic comment of the Portuguese dissident Antonio de Figueiredo, in exile from Salazar's Portuguese Empire, which clung on until the 1970s. When Portugal finally gave up its empire, it was quick to seize on the EU as an alternative source of largesse and as providing a new identity (Buettner 2016: 208–10). More ambitiously, the French saw the EU not just as a way of containing their old enemy, Germany, but also of giving France a leading role in what General de Gaulle and others saw as a revived Napoleonic Empire, stretching from the Low Countries to Central Europe. For them, as for other former imperial powers, "colonies were lost, but a new future in Europe beckoned" (Gildea 2019: 260, see also 145; Wesseling 1980: 131–2).[20]

As a multinational or supranational organization – despite its travails, one of the most successful to date – the European Union has frequently invited comparison with the Habsburg Empire. The EU, with its eastward expansion, now embraces practically all of the old Habsburg lands, and the "federalization of Europe" has seemed to many strikingly close to the many schemes to federalize the Habsburg Empire in its later years (Kozuchowski 2013: 19). Even more popular has been the analogy with the institution that the Habsburgs domi-nated for centuries, the Holy Roman Empire. It was, therefore, fitting that it was the Habsburg heir, Otto von Habsburg, a member of the European Parliament, who in 1989 announced that "Europe is living largely by the heritage of the Holy Roman Empire."

James Leigh, who quotes this, indeed sees the EU as "a continental-sized revival of the Holy Empire" (Leigh 2005: 3, 17). Leigh is troubled by this, as a reincarnation of a 2,000-year tradition of the "European Empire" that began with Rome and that, drawing on its Christian inheritance, sought to impose itself on the world. But for Jan Zielonka, the Holy Roman Empire is an admirable example of what he calls "the neo-medieval empire," the model which he wishes to promote for thinking about the EU. The EU should not, he argues, be seen as a superstate, a "neo-Westphalian state" which incorporates the principle of absolute state sovereignty established at the 1648 Treaty of Westphalia. Rather, it should follow the pattern of the medieval European empire, which was "a patchwork of various quasi-sovereignties and overlapping hierarchies whose powers were defined in complicated contracts and oaths" (Zielonka 2007: 145).[21]

The "American Empire," America as Empire?

If "Europe" – that is, the European Union – can be thought of as a new empire, and if China and Russia are showing imperial inclination, are there are other instances of empire today? Of course, none of them is likely to call itself an empire; empire is, indeed, a dirty word today. But one can perhaps be an empire without necessarily calling oneself such. One can behave as an empire, even think of oneself in such terms as recall empires. The concept of "informal empire" is based on this very perception; and, though we have chosen not to pursue that very tricky path, in at least one case it seems worthwhile to consider the argument. This is because of the global and historical importance of a country that, for some, irresistibly summons up the image of empire. That country is America – the United States of America, to be precise.

In the wake of the events of "9/11," and especially following the American invasion of Afghanistan in 2001 and Iraq in 2003, there was much talk of an "American Empire."[22] In vain did official spokesmen deny the label. "We're not an imperial power," declared President George W. Bush. His Secretary of Defense, Donald Rumsfeld, emphatically agreed: "We're not a colonial power. We've never been a colonial power" (in Ferguson 2005: ix, 1). But for many, as for the British historian Niall Ferguson, "the United States today is an empire." Indeed, given its overwhelming economic and military power, "there has never been an empire mightier than the United States today" (Ferguson 2005: 286, 289). But it is "a peculiar kind of empire," "an empire that dare not speak its name," "an empire in denial" (Ferguson 2004: 381). Frequently quoted were the dreamy musings of a senior adviser to President George W. Bush: "We're an empire now, and when we act, we create our own reality. And while you're studying that reality . . . we'll act again, creating other new realities . . . We're history's actors . . . and you, all of you, will be left to just study what we do" (in Suskind 2004: 51). It was a remark highly reminiscent of similar bombastic ravings by the senior Party official O'Brien in George Orwell's *Nineteen Eighty-Four* ("we make the laws of nature," "we control life at all levels," etc.). Particularly during the years of the younger Bush's presidency (2001–8), America seemed to have reverted powerfully to a recurrent aspiration to reshape the world in its own image – a task seemingly made easier now that the main rival, the Soviet Union, had collapsed in 1991, leaving America the "lonely superpower." World empire – in fact, if not in name – beckoned (Bacevich 2002; Vivek 2004: 435–6).

The assertion that America is an empire, or should be treated as such, goes against a longstanding tradition of thought that argues that America could not and cannot be an empire, because that would deny its own foundation in an eighteenth-century anti-colonial revolt against its colonial ruler, Great Britain. Created against empire, how could it be, or aspire to be, an empire? Such arguments have been heard repeatedly since that time, most notably at the time of the Spanish–American War of 1898, when America possessed both the opportunity and the power to establish an overseas empire. In a poem of 1899, when America was contemplating the future of the recently captured Philippines, the British poet Rudyard Kipling called upon Americans to take up "the white man's burden," to take over the imperial role from an exhausted Europe and continue the task of spreading civilization in the world. The fact that America chose not to seize that opportunity has been taken as eloquent testimony to its anti-imperial character. There is frequent reference to the strong anti-imperial statements by presidents Woodrow Wilson and Franklin D. Roosevelt, both of whom were genuinely opposed to the European empires and sought to wind them up.[23]

It is, indeed, important that, when faced with the choice in 1898, America chose not to make the Spanish colonies of the Philippines and Cuba American colonies (though not without decades of occupation in the former case, and a good deal of informal control in the latter). Also important is that the Spanish colony of Puerto Rico, though annexed, was not made into an American colony, but incorporated in the American state (though with the rather anomalous status of "commonwealth" rather than as a full constituent state). Apart from a few relatively small "territories" (significantly not called "colonies") – Guam, American Samoa, the US Virgin Islands, Northern Marianas, and some other Pacific possessions – America does not and has not possessed an overseas empire, unlike its main European rivals.[24] That, for some, is conclusive (e.g. King 2006).

But having overseas colonies is not, of course, the only way of being an empire. Might not America be thought of as a land empire, having extensive parallels particularly with the vast Russian land empire constructed by the tsars, and continued by the Soviets? Or, as was a common view among early commentators, might not America be the new Rome, with the same imperial destiny and civilizing mission (Ferguson 2005: 33–5)? That has been the conviction of those who have discerned a consistently imperial impulse in American history – but directed more at its near neighbors than at distant overseas territories. From its very beginning, even before it threw off British rule, America looked both westward, beyond the

Appalachian mountains, and southward, toward the Caribbean and Latin America. Emancipation from Britain in 1783 – among the causes of which was precisely this desire to burst the geographical bounds established by the imperial ruler, not to mention the threat to the institution of slavery posed by the powerful abolitionist movement in Britain – freed Americans to pursue this dream (Taylor 2016). It also presented America with another tempting target, this time to the north. Why not complete the sweep of British North America by taking its last stronghold, Canada?

Some of the territorial expansion of the new United States was achieved through purchase – of Louisiana from the French in 1803, Florida from Spain in 1819, and Alaska from Russia in 1867. But all of these purchases were embedded in wider designs, to the west, south, and north-west. With the acquisition of the vast territory of Louisiana – which doubled the size of the young republic – linked to the transcontinental Lewis and Clark expedition sponsored by President Thomas Jefferson, Americans began their rapid drive to the Pacific. The filling in of the continent was achieved to a good extent by means that had much in common with the creation of the European empires: removal – sometimes near-extermination – of indigenous peoples, and war with neighbors. Just as Britain had built up its overseas American empire by restricting or removing the Indians, and by defeating the French, so Americans in their turn developed their land empire by similar means.

By a series of treaties, regularly broken, and some bloody Indian wars, white Americans steadily drove the Indians out of their ancestral lands and corraled them in reservations, often in the least hospitable regions of the continent. In the process, the number of Indians shrank to virtually negligible proportions; the remnants lived diminished and demoralized lives, a prey to disease and alcoholism. Confidently seeing this as the fulfillment of America's imperial mission, a frontier newspaper declared: "The same inscrutable Arbiter that decreed the downfall of Rome, has pronounced the doom of extinction upon the red men of America" (Kiernan [1978] 2005: 103–4, and, generally, 29–41, 79–104; see also Mann 2005: 83–98; Weitz 2019: 83–121).

The same fate might seem to have been marked out for America's southern neighbor Mexico, newly emancipated from Spain. First came the annexation of Texas – independent from Mexico since 1836 – in 1845: "the fulfillment," as John O'Sullivan portrayed it in the *Democratic Review* in 1845, "of our manifest destiny to overspread the continent" (Ferguson 2005: 38; McPherson 2013: 32). "Manifest Destiny" was a more aggressive version of the "Monroe Doctrine" of 1823 that had warned Europeans to keep out of the

Americas. America was solely for Americans. But many have seen that as a covert claim by the US to hegemony in the continent, with a right to intervention whenever it saw the need. It should, they say, "more properly have been termed the Monroe Manifesto of Empire" (McCoy and Scarano 2009: 65; see also Ferguson 2005: 42, 52–3).

Such an impulse was felt in 1846–8, when the United States provoked a war with Mexico which ended with Mexico forced to cede New Mexico and California: a move that doubled the size of the US and stripped Mexico of a third of its territory.[25] There were impassioned demands that the US should not stop at this but go on to take the whole of Mexico. That was resisted, but there were similar calls for the US to press its claims to the north, to British Canadian territory in the Pacific North-West. "Fifty-four forty or fight!" had been the slogan of President James Polk during his campaign, thus reviving the cry for the annexation of Canada that surfaced at regular intervals during the nineteenth century (first in the 1812 war with Britain). In the end, America purchased Oregon from Britain and confirmed the 49th parallel as the border with Canada; but evidence that the dream remained appeared when the call to invade Canada was heard yet again during the war fever that accompanied the Spanish–American War of 1898.

Destiny was to the fore again in that war. "Duty," said President McKinley, justifying the Spanish–American War, "determines destiny" (Hofstadter 1965: 177). America, it was proclaimed, by its God-given "errand in the wilderness," its Anglo-Saxon inheritance, its manifest success in the world, was marked out with a sacred duty to spread its civilization in the world. "We Americans," Herman Melville wrote in his novel *White Jacket* (1850), "are the peculiar, chosen people – the Israel of our time; we bear the ark of the liberties of the world." That was Duty. Destiny meant that America had the will and the means to succeed, as its past history already showed. It meant that "expansion was a national and 'racial' inheritance, a deep and irresistible inner necessity" (Hofstadter 1965: 177). Such a view also justified the annexation of Hawai'i in 1898 – already more or less colonized by American settlers, but now an important complement to America's growing presence in the Pacific (Ferguson 2005: 46–7).

But Hawai'i eventually – in 1949, along with Alaska – became a state of the Union, not an American colony. And, as we have seen, Cuba, though occupied, was not kept, and the Philippines too – whose people were passionately championed by no less a person than Mark Twain, among other anti-imperial dignitaries – were let go after a generation of sometimes bitter conflict. Puerto Rico was indeed kept, but as a "commonwealth," not a colony. The anti-imperialists in the end won out in 1898, though feelings in favor of empire ran high (Hofstadter 1965; Ferguson 2005: 45–60). America did not become an overseas empire on the model of Britain or France, the leading imperial powers of the time.

But Hawai'i is good evidence that, if America did not become an overseas empire, it has good cause to be considered a land empire. Despite being thousands of miles away in the Pacific, Hawai'i was incorporated into the American federal state in the way all mainland territories were incorporated, as a full constituent state after a period of "trial" as a territory. In this sense, Hawai'i was no different from Kansas or Montana. America's westward drive is the true imperial instinct in America. It did not necessarily stop at the Pacific, as even Frederic Winslow Turner, formulator of the famous "frontier thesis," admitted. The frontier, said Turner, had imbued American life with an "expansive character . . . Movement has been its dominant fact, and . . . the American energy will continually demand a wider field for its exercise" (Turner [1920] 1962: 37). When, in the twentieth century, Americans dreamed of colonizing the moon, it was this long-standing expansive spirit that they appealed to.

In the twentieth century, as America grew to be the dominant world power, there were many other ways in which outsiders in particular discerned an imperial strand to its character. There were the frequent open armed interventions in Latin America, and later in the Middle East and Asia, resulting usually in regime change. There was the covert armed support for allies, as in the overthrow of Prime Minister Mohammed Mossedeq of Iran in 1953 and the deposition of Salvador Allende of Chile in 1973. There were the hundreds of military bases, on all continents, with which America encircled the globe. There was the economic power of America's great multinational corporations, imposing stringent terms of price and labor conditions on a multitude of nations. There was American "soft power" across the world, the enormous popularity and influence of the products of America's mass entertainment industries, from Hollywood studios to the Disney Corporation. All these were forms of what Gallagher and Robinson (1953) had influentially called "informal empire," in their account of nineteenth-century British power in the world that went beyond the formal British Empire. Even if commentators were unwilling to agree that America had, or was, an empire in the formal sense, many conceded that America had all the signs of informal empire – "empire by other means."

"The United States have been the cradle of modern Anti-Imperialism, and at the same time the founding of a mighty Empire." That was the paradox noted by the German economist Moritz Julius

Bonn in 1947 – one echoed by many observers (Ferguson 2005: 62). More recently, David Armitage (2018) has spoken of America as "the anti-imperial empire." In the end, it does not really matter whether or not we agree that America can be called an empire. The plain fact is that it has acted imperially for much of its history. It has expanded, on the North American continent, in ways that bear close similarities with the expansion of other land empires, such as those of tsarist Russia and Qing China. While not acquiring a significant number of overseas territories, it has been active in promoting its power and influence across the world – by informal means and "soft power" so far as that was possible; by more active armed intervention when that was deemed necessary. In other words, empire in fact, if not in name. There is no indication, in the conditions of the early twenty-first century, that it has ceased to think and act in these terms.

It is indeed hard to imagine that the era of empires is over. The "triumph of the nation-state," in any case, appears very short-lived in retrospect – if, indeed, the independent, sovereign, nation-state was ever more than an aspiration, rather than a reality. The nation-state certainly acquired legitimacy in the nineteenth and twentieth centuries. But for practically the whole of that period, nation-states were accompanied, and indeed overseen, by empires – right up to the 1960s and beyond. When the European empires dissolved, their role was taken over by the American and Soviet empires. When the Soviet Empire in its turn went in 1991, the Americans were for a while "the lonely super-power." But other contenders have since risen – the Chinese above all, with possibly the European Union and a revived caliphate, led by Iran or Saudi Arabia, as other rivals. All in all, it is difficult to deny the truth of Niall Ferguson's conclusion to his book on the British Empire: that "like it or not, and deny it who will, empire is as much a reality today as it was throughout the three hundred years when Britain ruled, and made, the modern world" (Ferguson 2004: 381).

We began this book by noting, with John Darwin, that empire has been the "default mode" of political organization for most of human history. We should surely not therefore be surprised to find that it continues to find favor today. This is undoubtedly to the dismay of many. But some will also see that, in some form, it may well be of the kind that we need to find order in an increasingly disorderly world. The nation-state is not and cannot be the terminus of world history. Its victory, if ever fully achieved, spells international anarchy and continual violence within and between states. Everyone is searching for the post-national state. Empires, in one variety or another, have long supplied a model – one that pre-dates the rise of the nation-state but that has proved its staying power well beyond that. This would not be the first time that the future of modern societies might lie in some retrieval from their past.

Notes

1 Empires in Time and Space

1 The newer term "colonialism" expressed a different analysis, and a different attitude, from the older "colonization," used to describe the practice of ancient Greeks and Romans – as well as early-modern Europeans – of "planting" settlements of their own citizens overseas. For attempts to distinguish colonialism analytically from imperialism, see Finley (1976) and Osterhammel (2005: 21–2; but cf. 2014: 430–4). Most people prefer to use the two terms as synonyms, or at least as closely related (e.g. Robinson 1986; Cooper 2005: 26–30; Burbank and Cooper 2010: 325–9). On the "Third World" origins and deployment of "colonialism," see Fieldhouse (1981: 6–7), who sees colonialism as a specifically historical phase of imperialism, lasting from *c*.1870 to *c*.1945, and relating mainly to European rule over non-European peoples in Asia, Africa, and the Pacific. This seems a sensible use, if one wishes to distinguish imperialism and colonialism. See, further on this, Kumar (forthcoming b).

2 Putting empires in a wider context, that of worldwide *colonization* as a process that began with civilization itself and continued with the colonial empires, Herbert Lüthy has said that "the history of colonization is the history of humanity itself" (1961: 485).

3 The best way to get a sense of the overall historical and geographical reach of empires is through historical atlases of empires, with their maps and illustrations. Two good ones, covering the whole world, are Farrington (2002) and Davidson (2011).

4 For critical discussions of Jasper's Axial Age concept, see the essays in Eisenstadt (1986), Arnason et al. (2004), and Bellah and Joas (2012). Some scholars, anxious to include Christianity and Islam, have – somewhat cavalierly – extended Jasper's designated period of 800–200 BCE to make it last until 600–700 CE (see, e. g., Mann 1986: 301,

341; Goldstone and Haldon 2010: 3). They do not seem to grasp that, quite correctly, Jaspers regarded Christianity and Islam as offshoots of Judaism, and that therefore they are embraced by his inclusion of the Jewish prophets.

5 It seems to have been Naram-Suen (*c*.2190–*c*.2154 BCE), grandson of Sargon of Akkad, who had the first recorded title of a ruler who was both divine and "The Mighty, king of the four corners of the world" (Mann 1986: 135; Davidson 2011: 16). Such designations – "King of Kings," rulers of the whole known world – became common throughout the region of the early Near Eastern empires, suggesting much copying from illustrious predecessors. These titles were to stretch for thousands of years more, both in the region and beyond, illustrating one of the grand continuities of the imperial tradition in world history.

6 Good accounts of these "classical" empires, again with excellent maps and illustrations, can be found in Larsen (1979), Alcock et al. (2001), Harrison (2009), Morris and Scheidel (2010), Davidson (2011: 36–81), and Benjamin (2018). See also Garnsey and Whittaker (1978), Burbank and Cooper (2010: 23–70), and, for Greeks and Persians, Morkot (1996).

7 The extent to which the Persian Empire systematically promoted Zoroastrianism is much debated, but the current consensus seems to be that they were restrained in their efforts by pragmatic considerations – nor do they seem to have had a sense of "mission" comparable to later empires (see, e.g., Llewellyn-Jones 2009: 120; Wiesehöfer 2010: 88). But see, for a stronger statement of the importance of Zoroastrianism to the empire, Mann (1986: 241–2).

8 "The Assyrian Empire was bringing into earthly political reality the order that obtained in the heavenly realm where the gods of all the peoples and polities of western Asia acknowledged Ashur as their lord" (Bedford 2010: 48). "The imperialistic expansion of the [Assyrian] central kingdom is ... the prevailing of cosmos over the surrounding chaos, it is an enterprise that brings order and civilization" (Liverani 1979: 307). See also, on Assyria and Babylon, Mieroop (2009: 94); and, on Egypt, Kemp (1978: 8).

9 The idea of a world-changing "break" around 1500, a historical watershed, can also be found in the work of Immanuel Wallerstein and other "world-system" theorists, as well as more generally in the work of several other world historians. Jerry Bentley, for instance, speaks of the "modern age, extending from 1500 to the present," "a period during which all the world's regions and peoples ultimately became engaged in sustained encounter with each other, thus a period that inaugurated a genuinely global epoch of world history" (Bentley 1996: 768–9). William Green similarly says that, "prior to 1492, history at its grandest level could only be hemispheric. A completely integrated world history is only possible after the hemispheres were in permanent contact ... To me, 1492 is a commanding moment of global transition" (Green 1995: 101,

111; see also Green 1992: 46, 50). See also Herbert Lüthy (1961: 485–6, 494), who says that the overseas European empires "created the world in which we live . . . Europe's colonization of the world . . . was the painful birth of the modern world itself." For a dissenting view, regarding 1800 rather than 1500 as the real turning point, see Frank (1998, esp. 12–34, 258–320). Kenneth Pomeranz (2000) also puts "the great divergence" between China and the West as starting around 1800, not earlier.

10 See Blanshard (2009: 128) and Morris (2010: 128–34). For the assertion that there was an Athenian Empire, though largely of an informal kind, see Finley (1978) and Doyle (1986: 54–8).

11 For the European encounter with the lands and peoples of the New World, variously conceived, see – all published to mark the 500th anniversary of Columbus's first voyage to America in 1492 – Elliott (1992), Greenblatt (1992), Todorov (1992), and Pagden (1993). For Michel de Montaigne's searing condemnation of the European conquests, see his essay "On Vehicles," and, for the superiority of the New World "barbarians" over the Europeans of his own time, his "Of Cannibals," both in Montaigne ([1580] 1958: 105–19, 264–85).

12 For the Portuguese Empire, see Boxer (1977), Newitt (2005), Dias (2007), Disney (2009, II), Crowley (2015), and Elliott (2016).

13 John Elliott considers that this view is held mainly by English-speaking historians and commentators, and that they ignore the vast amount of work on the Portuguese Empire done by Portuguese and even English scholars (Elliott 2016: 76). That might be so – but it is still the case that, in most general treatments of empire, the Portuguese experience is seen mainly as a prelude to the better-known Spanish achievement in the New World: see, e.g., Hart (2008: 50–60). The Portuguese Empire has remained the Cinderella among the European overseas empires.

14 For the Spanish Empire of the Habsburgs, see Elliott (1970; 2007); Kamen (2003); Fradera (2007); Kumar (2017: 147–66, and the further references there).

2 Traditions of Empire, East and West

1 "The coalescence of the idea of the Germanic kingdom with the concept of the everlasting Empire is the most conspicuous fact in the history of the term *imperium* during the period which we call the Middle Ages" (Koebner 1961: 33). Rome was the *imperium*; Germany the *regnum*.

2 The element of disrupture, and discontinuity, was that, unlike Charlemagne, Napoleon took the crown from the hand of the pope, Pius VII, and crowned himself, thus declaring that his empire also began a new era, a break with the past. Napoleon called himself "Emperor of the French," not of France; he claimed to embody the popular element of the French Revolution (Koebner 1961: 281). For Charlemagne's coronation as Holy Roman Emperor, see Wilson (2016: 26–9).

3 The Académie Francaise reflected this understanding precisely when it

stated in 1675 that the word *empire* denotes "all the countries which are governed by a great king." This was for them the meaning of "l'empire français," the "empire" of Louis XIV, similar to Henry VIII's "empire of England" (Koebner 1961: 277).

4 Even so, the spell of Rome always remained strong. "Remember always that you are Roman," the arch British imperialist Cecil Rhodes was fond of saying to his British compatriots (Lockhart and Woodhouse 1963: 31).

5 See, for these examples, Kumar (2017: 37–44, 89–93, 276–7, 340–7, 458–9).

6 In a personal communication to the author (December 28, 2016), the historian of China Timothy Brook remarks that "the subject of 'empire' has not been adequately addressed for China." Brook, the General Editor of the six-volume Harvard University Press *History of Imperial China* (2007–13), confesses that initially he had hoped to address that question in the series, but felt in the end that not enough had been done to enable him to do so, "so empire became a kind of residual category or label that we did not examine."

7 In thus interpreting the importation of the European term "empire" into China in the nineteenth century – as signifying backwardness – Wang Hui seriously misunderstands the place and discourse of empire in nineteenth-century Europe (Wang 2014: 39–60).

8 It is true that, in some of its earliest meanings, *Zhongguo* simply signified the middle or core states of a unified China, beyond which were peripheral or tributary states. But it was not a great extension of meaning to regard *Zhongguo* as the center of world civilization as such, beyond which there were, if not simply "barbarians," states or kingdoms of lesser significance. Certainly, by the time of the Qing (1644–1911), when the word *Zhongguo* came into general use as the name of the country that others called "China," this meaning had become established (Fairbank and Goldman 2006: 44; Wilkinson 2012: 19).

9 The fullest accounts of the history of the Chinese Empire are to be found in the 6-volume *History of Imperial China* published by Harvard University Press (General Editor Timothy Brook, 2007–13). These will be referred to by their individual volumes. There is also a wealth of material in the Cambridge University Press 15-volume *Cambridge History of China* (CHOC) (General Editors Dennis Twitchett and John K. Fairbank, 1978 –91). Individual listings of the *CHOC* are in Fairbank and Goldman (2006: 479). A good single-volume account covering much of the empire's history is Mote (2003); Keay (2009) is also good. There are helpful summaries in Ferguson and Mansbach (1996: 168–222) and in Davidson (2011: 68–71, 105–11).

10 Scholars in the Han dynasty attributed this violence and cruelty to the fact that the Qin were "barbarians," hailing from a marginal frontier region of China where they mixed with barbaric groups such as the Rong and Di (Lewis 2007: 39-46). This led them and many subsequent

commentators to regard the Qin as "un-Chinese," their rule based on a rigid Legalism abhorrent to the "Confucian Great Tradition." Frederick Mote argues that Legalism was in fact the primary basis of the Chinese Empire for most of its history, but because of the unpopularity of the Qin experience, and the veneration of the Great Tradition, the official ideology could not openly declare this. Terms such as "Imperial Confucianism" and "the Confucian state" therefore involve "limitations and contradictions"(Mote 1989: 102-3). For a robust rebuttal of this view, arguing that the imperial state managed successfully to accommodate both Confucianism and Legalism, see Zhao (2015).

11 For the growth of the Arab empires, see Lewis (1958); Hodgson (1977, I and II); Hourani (1992: part I); Kennedy (2006, 2008); Hoyland (2017). Good brief accounts are Ferguson and Mansbach (1996: 276–323); Farrington (2002: 66–71); Davidson (2011: 89–95).

12 It has always been unclear whether the caliph, as Muhammad's successor, also inherited his religious authority or was simply the political representative of all Muslims. If the latter, his legitimacy could be questioned by someone claiming greater religious purity, basing their claims on the Qur'an (Hourani 1992: 59–62; Ferguson and Mansbach 1996: 301–3).

13 For the Mughal Empire, see Mukhia (2004); Schimmel (2004); Robinson (2007: 112–79); Dale (2010). Good brief accounts are in Keay (2004: 289–382) and Davidson (2011: 112–18).

3 Rulers and Ruled

1 There are some helpful reflections on the distinction between land and overseas empires in Esherick et al. (2006: 9–13). See also Doyle (1986: 123–38, 162–79).

2 It would be fair to say that the great land empire of Alexander the Great, stretching from the Mediterranean to northern India, encompassed as many different cultures as most overseas empires. But, even there, Alexander's ability to move relatively easily across the Eurasian landmass, together with the administrative uniformity already put in place by the preceding Persian Empire, suggest a different pattern of rule from that of most overseas empires.

3 There were several mostly polytheistic local religions among the Siberian tribes conquered by the Russians, but they mostly ignored them or abolished them through "Russification."

4 Jennifer Pitts (2018) shows that the development of the "law of nations" – international law – in the eighteenth and nineteenth centuries was highly inflected by notions of European superiority on the "ladder of civilizations." While that was easy to apply in the case of tribal cultures such as those of Africans, American Indians, and Australian Aborigines, it was less easy to do so with the ancient civilizations of Asia. Here, Montesquieu's category of "Oriental Despotism" supplied the necessary

justification: Asian societies lacked the Enlightenment understanding of human rights, toleration, and the rule of law that was the shared heritage of European societies. Haskins (2018) argues that Montesquieu deliberately distorted his sources on China and India to warn Europeans against the slide to "despotism."

5 For the figures in this and preceding paragraphs, see Cipolla (1974: 115–16); Crosby (1986: 2–5); Livi-Bacci (1992: 123–4); Dalziel (2006: 68–9); Bellich (2009: 25–39); Bickers (2014: 2–3); Osterhammel (2014: 117–30). There are some variations, depending on the exact time period selected. For some writers, the settler communities – "plantations" – of Europeans were so distinctive as to separate them out from other expressions of empire – such as, e.g., rule by a small number of Europeans over millions of Indians. Moses Finley (1976) would wish to restrict the term "colonialism" to the former, leaving "empire" to the various other forms of rule by one people over another. This seems a step too far, but it does usefully draw attention to the historical novelty of the European colonization that began in the sixteenth and seventeenth centuries. For further discussion, see Kumar (forthcoming b).

6 Patrick Wolfe notes the interesting feature that "on the one hand, settler society required the practical elimination of the natives in order to establish itself on their territory. On the symbolic level, however, settler society subsequently sought to recuperate indigeneity in order to express its difference – and, accordingly, its independence – from the mother country" (Wolfe 2006: 389). In Latin America, after independence from Spain and Portugal, the white settlers began to recover and memorialize the indigenous cultures they had supplanted, for instance in the renaming of New Spain as Mexico, the land of the Mexica (Aztecs), while the great twentieth-century muralists – Diego Rivera, David Siqueiros, and Jose Orozco – painted the Indians as the innocent victims of cruel Spaniards, and sought to celebrate their lives and struggles (Rochfort 1998). In Australia, "public buildings and official symbolism, along with the national airlines, film industry, sports teams and the like, are distinguished by ostentatious borrowing of Aboriginal motifs. For nationalist purpose, it is hard to see an alternative to this contradictory reappropriation of a foundationally disavowed Aboriginality." It represents the "return of the native repressed, which continues to structure settler-colonial society" (Wolfe 2006: 389–90).

7 See, on the "British (or Britannic) world," Bridge and Fedorowich (2003); Buckner and Francis (2005); Darwin (2009: 144–79); Fedorowich and Thompson (2013).

8 As late as 1911, there were no more than 164,000 "Europeans" (mostly British) in India, a number that remained constant throughout the 1920s and 1930s. The native Indian population in 1911 was 300 million (Washbrook 2014: 192, 194). See further, on the British in India, Gilmour (2018).

4 Empires, Nations, and Nation-States

1 Some scholars have wished to distinguish between nations and ethnic groups or *ethnies*, regarding *ethnies* as the older formations on which nations are built. Anthony Smith has been the foremost exponent of this view – see, e.g., Smith (1986). For some of the many problems of defining "nation," see Connor (1994); see also the essays in Delanty and Kumar (2006). For the purposes of our discussion here, what is more important is the distinction between nations and nation-states.

2 A good account of the origins and development of nationalism is Hobsbawm (1992). Benedict Anderson's well-known claim (Anderson 2006), that nationalism started in the New World, among European creoles in the Americas, has been discounted by most scholars.

3 As Erez Manela points out, "contrary to popular perceptions both at the time and later, the term 'self-determination' itself was nowhere to be found in the text of the address" – what came to be known as the "Fourteen Points" – that Wilson delivered to the American Congress on January 8, 1918. But he agrees that the general principle is implicit in several of the points in that address; and, in another speech to Congress – known as the "Four Points" – made by Wilson within a few weeks of this address, the term "self-determination" makes a definite appearance (Manela 2009: 40–1).

4 In his posthumously published book, *Language and Solitude* (1998), Gellner, disturbed by what he thought had been the destructive effects of nationalism in the Soviet Union, somewhat revised his views, arguing now that something like a "global Habsburg Empire" might be the best framework for the future world order. See Kumar (2015).

5 For assessments of Gellner's theory of nationalism, see Hall (1998); Malešević and Haugaard (2007).

6 There is a fuller and more detailed account, with supporting references, of the argument that follows in Kumar (2010, 2017: 20–36). See also, with specific reference to empire and nationalism in Central Europe and the Balkans, Comisso (2006).

7 There is a clear, detailed, listing of "typological" differences between nation-states and empires – drawing mainly on Gellner and Anderson – in Osterhammel (2014: 422–8). These are, as Osterhammel stresses, "ideal types"; empirically, there are overlaps between them.

8 The president of the Catalan government, Jordi Pujol, expressed this sense of being a colony of Spain in a speech in 1988 commemorating Catalonia's millennium: "Catalonia is Carolingia. This has characterized Catalonia politically, culturally and mentally for centuries. In certain aspects it still characterizes us today" (Balfour 2004: 157). Catalonia – as the County of Barcelona – was originally a frontier region of the Carolingian Empire.

9 For Germany as a "land empire," similar in some respects to the other land empires in Central and Eastern Europe, see Ther (2004). Ther argues against the tendency among German historians to consider only

Germany's short-lived overseas empire, from the 1880s to the First World War, as relevant to German imperial experience. See also, similarly, Conrad (2012: 153–9, 177–85). The Nazi Empire, moreover, is always treated as a special case, and in any case is often seen more as an instance of extreme nationalism than of imperialism. For the imperial character of Nazi rule, and its continuation with earlier imperial traditions of German history, see Mazower (2009b); Baranowski (2011); Conrad (2012: 159–68). Ther suggests that it is this very experience of Nazi imperialism that has made German historians reluctant to treat the earlier German state as imperial (Ther 2004: 52).

10 As we will see in the next chapter, this concept of a homogeneous Chinese nation-state was severely qualified by the republican leaders themselves, from the very outset.

11 The exceptions were Tibet, which broke away until re-conquered by China in 1950; and Mongolia, which sought autonomy under Russian protection and, following the Bolshevik Revolution, was divided between an independent (communist) Outer Mongolia and a Chinese Inner Mongolia.

12 It is not always possible to identify clearly the ruling people in an empire. For instance, despite conventional usage, the "Turks" were not the ruling people of the Ottoman Empire for most of its history. The empire was ruled by the Ottoman dynasty which drew upon many ethnic groups – Greeks, Albanians, and others, as well as those of Turkish origin – in ruling the empire. Only toward the end of the nineteenth century did Turkish nationalism manage to associate the empire with Turkish national aspirations. Similarly, in neither the Spanish Habsburg nor the Austrian Habsburg empires were Spanish or Germans clearly the dominant ethnic groups, though over time Spanish and German culture generally came to predominate. See, further, Kumar (2010: 129; 2017: chs. 3 and 4).

13 One could also equally see this as the hijacking of nationalism by the European empires. For some good studies of this, see Berger and Miller (2015), though their use of the term "imperial nationalism" is different from mine. Nationalism could also occasionally make use of imperialism. See, on the imperial aspirations of, and use of imperial ideologies by, the new nation-states of Serbia and Bulgaria – recalling their imperial pasts – Malešević (2019: 90–110).

14 A similar view was put forward by Joseph Schumpeter ([1919] 1974), though in his case the archaic feature of empires was to be explained by the persistence of rule by a "feudal," militarist, aristocracy, destined to be replaced by the more peaceful bourgeois class and their nation-state.

15 Jane Burbank and Frederick Cooper have written more fully about this in Burbank and Cooper (2010: esp. 2–3, 219–21, 413–15).

16 While, says Edward Walker, "there are no self-described empires in existence today," "we should avoid a teleology that assumes an inevitable transition from anachronistically large and diverse 'empires' to small,

ethnically homogeneous, nationally unified, and 'modern' nation-states" (2006: 302). Post-Soviet Russia, China, and India, among a number of other examples, are large, multiethnic states with many of the features of the old empires.

17 On the nineteenth century – and beyond – as an "age of empire," see Hobsbawm (1987: 56–7); Ferguson (2005: xi–xiii); Cooper (2005: 171); Burbank and Cooper (2010: 219–50); Osterhammel (2014: 419–22).

18 As Darwin points out, such a fusion was not restricted to the non-Western native elites. It also happened at home, in the metropolis – for instance, in the way in which the British Empire produced new British identities, drawing on the local identities of Englishness, Scottishness, Welshness, and Irishness (2013: 156–60). See also on this, Colley (1994); Kumar (2003: 121–74). "Imperial ethnicities" was not just for the (non-European) natives. For the formation of imperial ethnicities – new forms of Britishness – in the "white dominions" of Canada, Australia, New Zealand, and South Africa, see Darwin (2013: 160–2). Darwin also mentions the way in which the experience of empire made the ruling Manchus of the Qing dynasty in China tighten up and cultivate more elaborately their ethnic identity, as a way of distinguishing themselves from the Han Chinese; so, too, imperial identities among the German "Baltic Barons" in the Russian Empire, and the many non-German groups – Polish, Slovenian, Ruthenian, Jewish – in the Habsburg Empire, were constructed (Darwin 2013: 166–7). In all these cases, empire decisively inflected the identities produced. As Osterhammel puts it, "empires generated willy-nilly the forces that would later turn against them" (2014: 465).

5 Decline and Fall

1 For the role of apocalyptic Christian thought in communicating the "sense of an ending" in a wide variety of contexts in European societies, see Kermode (2000). See also, for the European experience of decline in social and economic terms, Thompson (1998).

2 For edited collections and studies of the decline and fall of empires, ancient and modern, see Eisenstadt (1967); Cipolla (1970); Kennedy (1989); Barkey and von Hagen (1997); Dawisha and Parrott (1997); Brix et al. (2001).

3 "The collapse of Rome," says Michael Mann, "is the greatest tragic and moral story of Western culture" (Mann 1986: 283; and see 283–98 for his interesting account of the fall).

4 A clear statement of the inevitability thesis is Motyl (2001). See also Parsons (2010).

5 Further, as Alexander Motyl says, "if overreach gets empires into trouble after several hundred years of plenitude, surely it cannot be all that alarming" (Motyl 1999: 140).

6 For this research, see especially the essays in Wright (1971); see also Min

(1989). There are good syntheses in Rowe (2012: 253–83) and Spence (2013: 208–54).

7 The weakness of the revolutionary threat posed by the "Revolutionary Alliance" can be seen in the fact that they sponsored eight uprisings between 1907 and 1911, all of which failed – thus reprising the failures of the Canton plot of 1895 and the Waichow rising of 1900. It was only when the revolutionaries joined up with the young officers of the New Army that they had any chance of success – and it was the army that took the lead in the Wuchang army mutiny of 1911 which sparked the revolution. Moreover, the revolutionary movement in the army developed in relative independence from the student organizations and secret societies that formed the core of the Revolutionary Alliance (Dutt 1971; Schiffrin 1971: 466–7).

8 For accounts of nationalist thought and culture in China in the later nineteenth and early twentieth centuries, see Duara (1995: esp. part one); Harrison (2001); Esherlick (2006); Zhao (2006); Perdue (2007); Rowe (2012: 236–43). Karl (2002) interestingly argues that Chinese nationalism was influenced not just by Japanese and Western thought and experience, but also by contemporary nationalist struggles in the "Third World," in Hawai'i, the Philippines, and South Africa.

9 Anti-Manchuism had been a strong theme in the Taiping Rebellion, and this undoubtedly influenced a number of the revolutionaries, Sun Yat-Sen included (Schiffrin 1971: 445). There was a longer tradition that went back to the late seventeenth and early eighteenth centuries, in the popular writings especially of Zeng Jing and those who continued to be loyal to the Ming (Perdue 2007: 154–8).

10 William Rowe indeed argues that "the Sino-Japanese War was a major watershed in Chinese imperial history – far more so than the Opium War of 1839–1842, which is so often assigned this significance" (2012: 230).

11 Barkey (2006: 169–70, 194) lists a representative sample of accounts that blame nationalism for the fall of these empires.

12 For the Ottoman Empire, Reşat Kasaba, noting the indifference shown by the ordinary people to the nationalist ideologies being thought up mostly outside the boundaries of the empire, observes: "From Macedonia to Yemen, all across the imperial lands, people of different backgrounds were pursuing rewarding lives by participating in diverse networks and relationships. The idea that people should only live with and be ruled by people of their own kind would be alien to most of the subjects of the empire" (Kasaba 2006: 211). Kasaba notes that many of the most influential nationalist thinkers in the Greek, Arab, and Turkish national movements – Admantios Korais, Yusuf Akçura, Jamal-al-Din al-Afghani – spent much of their time outside the empire, especially in Paris (2006: 212).

13 I discuss this in more detail in the relevant chapters of Kumar (2017). See also, for skeptical assessments of the role of nationalism in bringing down the empires, Roshwald (2001: 7–33); Comisso (2006); Barkey

(2006); Kasaba (2006); Esherick et al. (2006: 19–28); Reynolds (2011); Osterhammel (2014: 466); Malešević (2019: 90–110).

14 One should note, though, that the French Revolution itself, with its abolition of slavery, was a spur to Haitian aspirations, not least in the person of Toussaint L'Ouverture; and that, in the subsequent war with Napoleonic France, the Haitians received valuable support from the British and the Spanish.

15 Sebastian Balfour comments that, with the loss of its remaining colonies, Spain lost the "overarching purpose" that had been provided by the empire: "The advantages of being Spanish were no greater now than the advantages of being Catalan or Basque" (Balfour 2004: 154; see also McCoy et al. 2012: 43–103). Something similar could be said about the United Kingdom after the loss of its empire after 1945 (Kumar 2003: 239–49).

16 As the German chancellor Otto von Bismarck told the Ottoman delegates at the 1878 Berlin Congress, "if you think the Congress has met for Turkey, disabuse yourselves. San Stefano would have remained unaltered, if it had not touched certain European interests" (in Todorova 1996: 54–5).

17 An earlier example, also in the Ottoman Empire, was, of course, that of Greece, which gained its independence in 1830 only after intervention by the British and French in the "Greek War of Independence," and their imposition of a settlement on the Ottoman government.

18 Erez Manela says that the First World War "dealt a severe blow to the power and prestige of the leading imperial powers," but then straightaway goes on to admit that "despite the war's drain on European power and prestige, there was surprisingly little agitation against empire during the war itself, when the imperial powers were militarily most vulnerable, neither did uprisings break out immediately after the war ended" (2009: 11–12).

19 See, on this, Osterhammel (2005: 36); Jansen and Osterhammel (2016: 54–62); Kumar (2017: 347–65, 450–8). See also August (1986), who argues that it is the interwar period, the 1920s and 1930s, rather than the more conventional dating of 1880–1914, that should be seen as "the age of imperialism," for it was then that imperial ideologies were actually realized in state policies and practices. Bayly (1998), on the contrary, wishes to argue for the key importance of the period 1760–1830, as the "first age of global imperialism."

20 There is now an enormous literature on post-1945, "Third World," decolonization. On the word and its history – which began in Europe – see Ward (2016). An invaluable survey is Rothermund (2006). Excellent brief accounts are Chamberlain (1999), Betts (2004), Kennedy (2016), and Jansen and Osterhammel (2017). There are authoritative essays in Thomas et al. (2015), and interesting "theoretical" analyses in Spruyt (2005) and Shipway (2008). See also the reflections in Hopkins (2008), the review article by Howe (2005), and the still useful survey by Holland

(1985). Also valuable is the special issue of the *Journal of Contemporary History*, "Colonialism and Decolonization" (1969). A stimulating exercise in comparative analysis – "imperial decline" in Europe and America – is McCoy et al. (2012).

21 As Stuart Ward (2016: esp. 258–60) has shown, "decolonization" was in any case a term with a "European provenance," with European concerns very much in mind. It did not in most of its European uses mean outright independence for the colonies, more a peaceful and negotiated settlement – a "décolonisation aimable" – in which Europeans kept close relationships with, and possible oversight of, their former colonies. That was why the term was rejected by many non-Western anti-colonial activists and thinkers, such as Kwame Nkrumah and Frantz Fanon. When, toward the end of his life, Fanon did adopt the term, it was with the intent to infuse it with new meaning – one that was "a calculated assault on the term itself," radically undermining its common European understanding (Ward 2016: 253–6).

22 Speech at the Lord Mayor's Luncheon, Mansion House, November 10, 1942.

23 Though some might think that responsibility for the bloody partition riots that accompanied Indian and Pakistani independence in 1948 might at least partly be laid at Britain's door. For less congratulatory accounts of Britain's exit from empire, see, e.g., Elkins (2005); Grob-Fitzgibbon (2011); Gildea (2019: 93–5).

24 Writing about the same time, the world historian Geoffrey Barraclough observed: "Between 1945 and 1960 no less than forty countries with a population of 800 million – more than a quarter of the world's inhabitants – revolted against colonialism and won their independence. Never before in the whole of human history had so revolutionary a reversal occurred with such rapidity" (Barraclough 1964: 164).

25 David Strang points out that, "beginning with Britain's continental colonies in 1783 and ending with the Caribbean islands of Saint Kitts and Nevis in 1983, 165 colonial dependencies have become new independent states or have been fully incorporated into existing sovereign states." This extended process of decolonization, rather than the recognition of existing non-Western states by Western powers, has been by far the commonest method by which new states were added to the international state system: "As a central feature of the expansion of the Western state system, decolonization finds a parallel only in the process of imperial conquest and colonization" (Strang 1991: 429).

6 Empire after Empire

1 See the remarkable tribute to Gandhi's influence on Indian society in Modi (2019).

2 There is, of course, also the question of the legacy of the Mongol Empire, of which Russia was a part for more than a century and a half, on the

Russian core itself. Russia may, in its imperial expansion, have projected itself on Central Eurasia, but, in part, it may have been reflecting Central Eurasia – the heartland of the Mongol Empire – back on itself. For a brief discussion of the possible "Asiatic" legacy in.Russian society and culture, see Kumar (2017: 216–17); see also, for a broader view of the Mongol inheritance, Neumann and Wigen (2015).

3 For invaluable historical considerations of the complexities of this "borderland" region of Europe, see Snyder (2003, 2010); see also Bartov and Weitz (2013). The revealing case of Galicia is discussed in Hann and Magocsi (2005); Ukraine in *Thesis Eleven* (2016). For further discussion of the legacies of Russian/Soviet, Habsburg, and Ottoman rule in the region, see Barkey and Hagen (1997); Ekiert and Hanson (2003); Kumar (forthcoming a).

4 The original name was the "One Belt, One Road" (OBOR) initiative. Under criticism, the Chinese came to feel that this had too strong a whiff of a controlling Chinese influence, and it was officially renamed the "Belt and Road Initiative" (BRI) in 2016.

5 On the extent to which the "Belt and Road Initiative" may be inspired by China's imperial past and its previously central place in the world economy, see Miller (2017), French (2018), Frankopan (2018), Goldstone (2018).

6 The global coronavirus pandemic of 2020, of course, makes all such previously conventional predictions problematic.

7 For postcolonial thought, see Moore-Gilbert (1997); R. Young (2001, 2015); Go (2016). Some of the key texts are in Ashcroft, Griffiths, and Tiffin (1995); key concepts are in Ashcroft, Griffiths and Tiffin (2000). All of these focus on societies of the "global South," though they acknowledge that aspects of the global South can also be found in the North – e.g. the black ghettoes of many American cities.

8 An excellent synthesis of recent work on the effect of empire on the erstwhile ruling societies of Europe is Buettner (2016). See also Garavani (2012). For a range of specific studies, see Thompson (2012); Halperin and Palan (2015); Nicolaïdis et al. (2015); Rothermund (2015); Ponzanesi and Colpani (2016). See also the special issue of the *Journal of Contemporary History*, "Imperial Hangovers" (1980).

9 It is striking that 40 percent of the length of all international borders in the world today were originally drawn by Britain and France (Jansen and Osterhammel 2016: 177).

10 A good brief account of post-imperial conflicts in Africa is Breuilly (1994: 257–68); see also C. Young (2001); Neuberger (2006).

11 A powerful statement of this view is Tully (2009). Much of the theorizing of this position has been done under the label of "dependency" theory, the classic account of which is Frank (1967); for his later thoughts, see Frank (1998). A good brief survey of theories of this kind – "neo-colonialism," "underdevelopment" – is in Mommsen (1982: 113–41). For the literary expression of these ideas, see Said (1994: 230–340). See also the essays in

Mommsen and Osterhammel (1986), especially those by Colin Leys and Anthony Brewer. More recently these views have tended to be absorbed in theories of capitalism as a new kind of global "empire" – see, e.g., Hardt and Negri (2000); Gildea (2019: 117–21). The common theme remains the persisting inability of the postcolonial societies of the "global South" to throw off the hegemony of Western capitalism – the more so with the fall of its main rival, the Soviet Union, in 1991. In all these accounts, moreover, the United States is seen as having taken the leading role at least since 1945, if not earlier.

12 For France, Elizabeth Buettner has argued that "presided over by loyal Francophone elites, sub-Saharan Africa's relationship with its former colonial ruler remained one strongly marked by political subservience and economic dependency" (2016: 160). On *francophonie* – revived by President Macron – see Alexandre (1969) and Gildea (2019: 251–2); on the concept of *Françafrique*, Lorcin (2013: 100–1); Gildea (2019: 99–103). With Britain's imminent departure from the European Union ("Brexit"), Britain's relationship with the Commonwealth has moved from a somewhat tepid commitment to a more urgent sense of the need to strengthen ties, as a substitute for European partners. See Gildea (2019: 234–7, 243–7); Bell and Vucetic (forthcoming).

13 In a speech to Harvard graduates in 1943, Winston Churchill declared that the "empires of the future would be the empires of the mind." He meant by this that he hoped the warring empires of the past would be replaced by a peaceful and harmonious world community (Gildea 2019: 2). But many have chosen to employ the phrase in a wider context, to mean psychological or spiritual control.

14 As Fanon himself noted, in an extended quotation from Césaire's play, *Les Armes miraculeuses (et les chiens se taisaient)*, Césaire had already anticipated this espousal of violence as necessary to free the colonized mind (Fanon [1961] 1967: 68–9). A radical extension of Fanon, which argues that violence must not just mark the beginning of the decoloniza-tion process, but must continue more or less without end – such is the weight of the colonial heritage – is Ciccariello-Maher (2017).

15 For a good brief account of "the rise of global Islam," see Gildea (2019: 158–81, 213–31). Gildea dates this from the Iranian Revolution of 1979 that deposed the Shah and installed the Islamic Republic of Ayatollah Khomeini; also the war, begun in 1979, against the Soviets in Afghanistan, conducted by the *mujahideen* and their international sup-porters (one of whom was the Saudi Osama bin Laden).

16 The literature on this is voluminous, but often restricted to particular societies, lacking a comparative dimension. Such a dimension is valu-ably present in Buettner (2016: 250–321), which focuses particularly on immigrants from the former European empires. See also Gildea (2019: 122–43, 195–203). Both accounts contain extensive references to the relevant studies.

17 Nevertheless, spirited proposals for a different kind of multiculturalism

– "convivial," "demotic" – already evident in the everyday life of many major European cities, have been proposed by a number of commentators – e.g. Gilroy (2004); Valluvan (2019). See also Modood (2019) for a powerful restatement of the theory and practice of multiculturalism.

18 See, e.g. for Britain, Ward (2001); for France, in which Algeria dominates, see Saverese (2015); for Holland, in which Indonesia is the main concern, Baudet (1969) and Wesseling (1980). One of the best sources for the cultural impact of empire, during and after its existence, is the hundred or so volumes in the series "Studies in Imperialism," edited by John Mackenzie and published by Manchester University Press. See, for a complete listing to date, Thompson (2014: vii–xi).

19 There was a strong echo of this view in a remarkable paper of 2002 by a British diplomat, Robert Cooper, in which he argued that, in the dangerous state in which the world found itself post 9/11, the best solution was "a defensive imperialism": "The most logical way to deal with chaos, and the one most employed in the past, is colonization" (in Ferguson 2004: 375–6). Unlike many others, however, the entity that Cooper looked to for this new "post-modern imperialism" was not America, but the European Union.

20 The relation between European decolonization and the construction of the European Union is an understudied subject. For some helpful thoughts, see Garavani (2012); Hansen and Jonsson (2015); Buettner (2016: 498–504).

21 For other views on "Europe" – i.e., the EU – as empire, see Böröcz and Kovács (2001); Foster (2015); Behr and Stivachtis (2016).

22 That America was – and perhaps had always been – an empire was declared by a number of prominent scholars and commentators at the time, among them Bacevich (2002), Ignatieff (2003), Mann (2003, 2008), Johnson (2004), Ferguson (2005). See Chibber (2004) for a good review of this literature. This reprised similar, mostly left-wing, views from the 1960s and 1970s, at the time of the Vietnam War (e.g. Williams 1969, Kiernan [1978] 2005), but with the added impetus given by post-9/11 developments, and often with a more positive gloss. More recent statements are Bulmer-Thomas (2018), Fradera (2018: 154–84), Hopkins (2018). For helpful discussions of this view, and comparisons with other empires, see Steinmetz (2005), Calhoun et al. (2006), Maier (2007), Münkler (2007: 139–67), McCoy and Scarano (2009), McCoy et al. (2012).

23 On Wilson and Roosevelt's attitudes to empire, see Ferguson (2005: 172). However, it is the argument of Erez Manela's well-received book *The Wilsonian Moment* (2009) that Wilson did not expect his principle of "self-determination" to be applied to the European colonies in the non-Western world, which were not thought ready for self-rule, and that he was somewhat nonplussed when Asian and other nationalists took his message to heart.

24 America occupied the Philippines for nearly 50 years, and the Panama

Canal Zone for 75 years. That, plus the existing overseas territories, have led some to speak of the "Greater United States," on the analogy of "Greater Britain" and "Greater France" (see Immerwahr 2019). Immerwahr (2019: 17) shows that, by 1940, 23 million subjects worldwide fell under American colonial rule, and that US territories made up nearly a fifth of the land area of the "Greater United States" (see also Hopkins 2018). David Armitage argues that American possessions, together with its nearly 800 military bases around the world, "comprise perhaps the largest imperial assemblage in the world today" (2018: 25).

25 The Mexican provinces of "New Mexico" and "Upper California," ceded to the US by the Treaty of Guadalupe Hidalgo (1848), included lands that now comprise most of the current states of New Mexico, Arizona, Colorado, Utah, Nevada, and California. Good recent accounts of the Mexican–American war of 1848 are Greenberg (2013) and Guardino (2017).

Select Bibliography

This brief bibliography is meant to suggest further reading – in English – on the subject of empires in general, together with some specific topics that are of importance for a general and comparative view. More detailed references are in the endnotes and list of references.

General, Comparative, and Theoretical Works

The most comprehensive account is Jane Burbank and Frederic Cooper, *Empires in World History: Power and the Politics of Difference* (Princeton University Press, 2010). See also John Darwin, *After Tamerlane: The Rise and Fall of Global Empires, 1400–2000* (Penguin Books, 2008); Herfried Münkler, *Empires: The Logic of World Domination from Ancient Rome to the United States* (Polity, 2007); Peter Fibiger Bang and C. A. Bayly (eds.), *Tributary Empires in Global History* (Palgrave Macmillan, 2011); Peter Fibiger Bang and Dariusz Kołodziejczyk (eds.), *Universal Empire: A Comparative Approach to Imperial Culture and Representation in Eurasian History* (Cambridge University Press, 2015).

Good conceptual and theoretical studies are Richard Koebner, *Empire* (Cambridge University Press, 1961); Richard Koebner and Helmut Dan Schmidt, *Imperialism: The Story and Significance of a Political Word, 1840–1960* (Cambridge University Press, 1964); Roger Owen and Bob Sutcliffe (eds.), *Studies in the Theory of Imperialism* (Longman, 1972); Michael W. Doyle, *Empires* (Cornell University Press, 1986); Wolfgang J. Mommsen, *Theories of Imperialism* (University of Chicago Press, 1982); Anthony Pagden, *Lords of All the World: Ideologies of Empire in Spain, Britain and France, c. 1500 – c. 1800* (Yale University Press, 1995); Alejandro Colás, *Empire* (Polity, 2007); Sankar Muthu (ed.), *Empire and Modern Political Thought* (Cambridge University Press, 2014). Two excellent short introductions are Stephen Howe, *Empire: A Very Short Introduction* (Oxford University Press, 2002); Anthony Pagden, *Peoples and Empire* (Modern Library, 2003).

Ancient and Non-Western Empires

Thomas Harrison (ed.), *The Great Empires of the Ancient World* (The J. Paul Getty Museum, Los Angeles, 2009); Susan E. Alcock, Terence N. D'Altroy, Kathleen D. Morrison, and Carlo M. Sinopoli (eds.), *Empires: Perspectives from Archaeology and History* (Cambridge University Press, 2001); Walter Scheidel (ed.), *Rome and China: Comparative Perspectives on Ancient World Empires* (Oxford University Press, 2009); Ian Morris and Walter Scheidel (eds.), *The Dynamics of Ancient Empires: State Power from Assyria to Byzantium* (Oxford University Press, 2010); P. D. A. Garnsey and C. R. Whittaker (eds.), *Imperialism in the Ancient World* (Cambridge University Press, 1978); Mogens Trolle Larsen (ed.), *Power and Propaganda: A Symposium on Ancient Empires* (Akademisk Forlag, 1979); Michael Mann, *The Sources of Social Power*, Vol. I: *A History of Power from the Beginning to A. D. 1760* (Cambridge University Press, 1986).

Specifically on the Muslim empires, there are Robert G. Hoyland, *In God's Path: The Arab Conquests and the Creation of An Islamic Empire* (Oxford University Press, 2017); Stephen F. Dale, *The Muslim Empires of the Ottomans, Safavids, and Mughals* (Cambridge University Press, 2010); and the gorgeously illustrated Francis Robinson, *The Mughal Emperors, and the Islamic Dynasties of India, Iran and Central Asia, 1206–1925* (Thames and Hudson, 2007). For the steppe empires, Thomas J. Barfield, *The Perilous Frontier: Nomadic Empires and China, 221 BC–AD 1757* (Blackwell, 1992); David Morgan, *The Mongols*, 2nd edition (Blackwell, 2007).

For the Chinese Empire, Yuri Pines, *The Everlasting Empire: The Political Culture of Ancient China and Its Imperial Legacy* (Princeton University Press, 2012); Wang Hui, *China from Empire to Nation-State* (Harvard University Press, 2014); Dingxin Zhao, *The Confucian Legalist State: A New Theory of Chinese History* (Oxford University Press, 2015). An engaging inquiry, drawing on China's imperial past, is Ge Zhaoguang, *What is China? Territory, Ethnicity, Culture, and History* (Harvard University Press, 2008).

European Empires and European Colonialism

Excellent essays are in Robert Aldrich (ed.), *The Age of Empires* (Thames and Hudson, 2007), and Robert Aldrich and Kirsten McKenzie (eds.), *The Routledge History of Western Empires* (Routledge, 2014). Similarly wide coverage is in Krishan Kumar, *Visions of Empire: How Five Imperial Regimes Shaped the World* (Princeton University Press, 2017). See also Wolfgang J. Mommsen and Jürgen Osterhammel (eds.), *Imperialism and After: Continuities and Discontinuities* (Allen and Unwin, 1986); Dominic Lieven, *Empire: The Russian Empire and Its Rivals* (Yale University Press, 2001); Alexei Miller and Alfred J. Rieber (eds.), *Imperial Rule* (Central European University Press, 2004).

Broad surveys of European colonialism are D. K. Fieldhouse, *The Colonial Empires: A Comparative Survey from the Eighteenth Century*, 2nd edition (Macmillan, 1982); David B. Abernethy, *The Dynamics of Global Dominance: European Overseas Empires 1415–1980* (Yale University Press, 2000); H. L. Wesseling, *The European Colonial Empires 1815–1919* (Pearson, 2004); Jonathan Hart, *Empires and Colonies* (Polity, 2008); Heather Streets-Salter and Trevor R. Getz, *Empires and Colonies in the Modern World* (Oxford University Press, 2016). Specifically on European settlements overseas, L. Veracini, *Settler Colonialism: A Theoretical Overview* (Cambridge University Press, 2010). See also Marco Ferro's lively *Colonization: A Global History* (Routledge, 1997).

Penetrating questions are raised in Frederick Cooper, *Colonialism in Question: Theory, Knowledge, History* (University of California Press, 2005); see also Jürgen Osterhammel, *Colonialism: A Theoretical Overview*, 2nd edition (Markus Wiener, 2005). A good case study of one discipline's involvement with empire is George Steinmetz (ed.), *Sociology and Empire: The Imperial Entanglements of a Discipline* (Duke University Press, 2013).

On the cultural dimensions of European colonialism, Edward W. Said, *Culture and Imperialism* (Vintage, 1994); Frederick Cooper and Ann Laura Stoler (eds.), *Tensions of Empire: Colonial Cultures in a Bourgeois World* (University of California Press, 1997). On rulers and ruled, Timothy H. Parsons, *The Rule of Empires: Those Who Built Them, Those Who Endured Them, and Why They Always Fall* (Oxford University Press, 2010); Tony Ballantyne and Antoinette Burton, *Empires and the Reach of the Global 1870–1945* (Harvard University Press, 2012).

On the relation between empires and nation-states, Harry G. Gelber, *Nations Out of Empires: European Nationalism and the Transformation of Asia* (Palgrave, 2001); Joseph W. Esherick, Hasan Kayali, and Eric van Young (eds.), *Empire to Nation: Historical Perspectives on the Making of the Modern World* (Rowman and Littlefield, 2006); Krishan Kumar, "Nation-States as Empires, Empires as Nation-States: Two Principles, One Practice?" *Theory and Society* 39 (2), 2010: 119–43; Stefan Berger and Alexei Miller (eds.), *Nationalizing Empires* (Central European University Press, 2015); *Thesis Eleven*, "Empires and Nation-States: Beyond the Dichotomy," no. 139, 2017.

Decolonization and the End of Empire

Comprehensive coverage in Dietmar Rothermund (ed.), *The Routledge Companion to Decolonization* (Routledge, 2006); see also R. F. Holland, *European Decolonization 1918–1981: An Introductory Survey* (Macmillan, 1985); Martin Shipway, *Decolonization and Its Impact: A Comparative Approach to the End of the Colonial Empires* (Blackwell, 2008); Martin Thomas, Bob Moore, and L. J. Butler (eds.), *Crises of Empire: Decolonization and Europe's Imperial States*, 2nd edition (Bloomsbury, 2015). An excellent short introduction is Dane Kennedy, *Decolonization: A Very Short Introduction* (Oxford University Press, 2016); see also Jan C. Jansen and Jürgen Osterhammel, *Decolonization: A Short History* (Princeton University

Press, 2017). Rupert Emerson, *From Empire to Nation: The Rise to Self-Assertion of Asian and African Peoples* (Beacon Press, 1962), is an incisive account written in the midst of the process. The intellectual background in the Asian case is vividly told by Pankaj Mishra, *From the Ruins of Empire: The Revolt against the West and the Remaking of Asia* (Penguin Books, 2013). Key texts and commentaries are in Prasenjit Duara (ed.), *Decolonization: Perspectives from Now and Then* (Routledge, 2004). Frantz Fanon and others are discussed in George Ciccariello-Maher, *Decolonizing Dialectics* (Duke University Press, 2017).

On the general causes of the decline and fall of empires, S. N. Eisenstadt (ed.), *The Decline of Empires* (Prentice-Hall, 1967); Paul Kennedy, *The Rise and Fall of the Great Powers: Economic Change and Military Conflict from 1500 to 2000* (Fontana Press, 1989); Alexander J. Motyl, *Imperial Ends: The Decay, Collapse, and Revival of Empires* (Columbia University Press, 2001).

Empire after Empire

On imperial legacies generally, and what comes after empire, Karen Barkey and Mark von Hagen (eds.), *After Empire: Multiethnic Societies and Nation-Building. The Soviet Union and the Russian, Ottoman, and Habsburg Empires* (Westview Press, 1997); Kalypso Nicolaïdis, Berny Sèbe, and Gabrielle Maas (eds.), *Echoes of Empire: Memory, Identity and Colonial Legacies* (I. B. Tauris, 2015); Sandra Halperin and Ronen Palan (eds.), *Legacies of Empire: Imperial Roots of the Contemporary Global Order* (Cambridge University Press, 2015); Robert Gildea, *Empires of the Mind: The Colonial Past and the Politics of the Present* (Cambridge University Press, 2019).

For Europe, Elizabeth Buettner, *Europe after Empire: Decolonization, Society, and Culture* (Cambridge University Press, 2016), is outstanding. Also with the focus on Europe are Giuliano Garavini, *After Empires: European Integration, Decolonization, and the Challenge from the Global South 1957–1986* (Oxford University Press, 2012); Sandra Ponzanesi and Gianmaria Colpani (eds.), *Postcolonial Transition in Europe* (Rowman and Littlefield, 2016). Jordanna Bailkin, *The Afterlife of Empire* (University of California Press, 2012), is a fascinating attempt, with implications for other European countries, to link the post-1945 welfare state in Britain with the loss of empire. L. Carl Brown (ed.), *Imperial Legacy: The Ottoman Imprint on the Balkans and the Middle East* (Columbia University Press, 1996), is also exemplary in tracing the effects of empire in Europe and beyond.

The "American Empire" can also be seen as a case of empire persisting beyond the era of empire: see, for a comparative approach, Charles S. Maier, *Among Empires: American Ascendancy and Its Predecessors* (Harvard University Press, 2007); Craig Calhoun, Frederick Cooper, and Kevin W. Moore (eds.), *Lessons of Empire: Imperial Histories and American Power* (The New Press, 2006); A. G. Hopkins, *American Empire: A Global History* (Princeton University Press, 2018).

On postcolonial approaches, see Patrick Williams and Laura Chrisman (eds.), *Colonial Discourse and Post-Colonial Theory* (Harvester Wheatsheaf, 1993); Gyan Prakash (ed.), *After Colonialism: Imperial Histories and Postcolonial Displacements* (Princeton University Press, 1995); Bill Ashcroft, Gareth Griffiths, and Helen Tiffin (eds.), *Post-Colonial Studies: The Key Concepts* (Routledge, 2000); Robert J. C. Young, *Postcolonialism: An Historical Introduction* (Blackwell, 2001); Robert J. C. Young, *Empire, Colony, Postcolony* (Wiley-Blackwell, 2015); Julian Go, *Postcolonial Thought and Social Theory* (Oxford University Press, 2016).

References

Abernethy, David B. (2000) *The Dynamics of Global Dominance: European Overseas Empires 1415–1980.* New Haven, CT: Yale University Press.

Adams, William Y. (1984) "The First Colonial Empire: Egypt in Nubia, 3200–1200 B.C.," *Comparative Studies in Society and History* 26 (1): 36–71.

Adil, Alev (2019) "Legacy of Empire," *Times Literary Supplement* January 11: 12.

Albertini, Rudolf von (1969) "The Impact of Two World Wars on the Decline of Colonialism," *Journal of Contemporary History* 4 (1): 17–35.

Alcock, Susan E., Terence N. D'Altroy, Kathleen D. Morrison, and Carlo M. Sinopoli (eds.) (2001) *Empires: Perspectives from Archaeology and History.* Cambridge University Press.

Aldrich, Robert (ed.) (2007) *The Age of Empires.* London: Thames and Hudson.

Alexandre, Pierre (1969) "Francophonie: The French and Africa," *Journal of Contemporary History* 4 (1): 117–25.

Anderson, Benedict (2006) *Imagined Communities: Reflection on the Origin and Spread of Nationalism,* revised edition. London: Verso.

Annan, Noel (1991) *Our Age: The Generation that Made Post-War Britain.* London: Fontana.

Arendt, Hannah (1958) *The Origins of Modern Totalitarianism,* 2nd edition. New York: Meridian Books.

Armitage, David (2017) *Civil Wars.* New York: Alfred A. Knopf.

Armitage, David (2018) "The Anti-imperial Empire?" *Times Literary Supplement* August 3: 25.

Armstrong, John (1982) *Nations before Nationalism.* Chapel Hill: University of North Carolina Press.

Arnason, Johann P., Shmuel N. Eisenstadt, and Bjorn Wittrock (eds.) (2004) *Axial Civilizations and World History.* Leiden: Brill Academic Publishers.

Ashcroft, Bill, Gareth Griffiths, and Helen Tiffin (eds.) (1995) *The Post-Colonial Studies Reader*. London and New York: Routledge.

Ashcroft, Bill, Gareth Griffiths, and Helen Tiffin (eds.) (2000) *Post-Colonial Studies: The Key Concepts*. London and New York: Routledge.

August, Thomas (1986) "Locating the Age of Imperialism," *Itinerario* 10 (2): 85–97.

Aydin, Cemil (2017) *The Idea of the Muslim World: A Global Intellectual History*. Cambridge, MA: Harvard University Press.

Bacevich, Andrew J. (2002) *American Empire: The Realities and Consequences of U.S. Diplomacy*. Cambridge, MA: Harvard University Press.

Balfour, Sebastian (2004) "The Spanish Empire and its End: A Comparative View in Nineteenth and Twentieth Century Europe." In Miller and Rieber (2004: 151–60).

Bang, Peter Fibiger, and Darius Kołodziejczyk (eds.) (2015) *Universal Empire: A Comparative Approach to Imperial Culture and Representation in Eurasian History*. Cambridge University Press.

Baranowski, Shelley (2011) *Nazi Empire: German Colonialism and Imperialism from Bismarck to Hitler*. Cambridge University Press.

Barbir, Karl K. (1996) "Memory, Heritage, and History: The Ottomans and the Arabs." In Brown (1996: 100–14).

Barkey, Karen (2006) "Changing Modalities of Empire: A Comparative Study of Ottoman and Habsburg Decline." In Esherick et al. (2006: 167–97).

Barkey, Karen, and Mark von Hagen (eds.) (1997) *After Empire: Multiethnic Societies and Nation-Building: The Soviet Union and the Russian, Ottoman, and Habsburg Empires*. Boulder, CO: Westview Press.

Barraclough, Geoffrey (1964) *An Introduction to Contemporary History*. London: C. A. Watts.

Bartov, Omer, and Eric D. Weitz (eds.) (2013) *Shatterzone of Empires: Coexistence and Violence in the German, Habsburg, Russian, and Ottoman Borderlands*. Bloomington and Indianopolis: Indiana University Press.

Baudet, Henri (1969) "The Netherlands after the Loss of Empire," *Journal of Contemporary History* 4 (1): 127–39.

Bayly, C. A. (1998) "The First Age of Global Imperialism, c. 1760–1830," *Journal of Imperial and Commonwealth History* 26 (2): 28–47.

Bayly, C. A. (2004) *The Birth of the Modern World 1780–1914: Global Connections and Comparisons*. Oxford: Blackwell.

Beazley, C. Raymond (1910) "Prince Henry of Portugal and the African Crusade of the Fifteenth Century," *American Historical Review* 16 (1): 11–23.

Bedford, Peter R. (2010) "The Neo-Assyrian Empire." In Morris and Scheidel (2010: 30–65).

Behr, Hartmut, and Yannis A. Stivachtis (eds.) (2016) *Revisiting the European Union as Empire*. London and New York: Routledge.

Beissinger, Mark (2006) "Soviet Empire as 'Family Resemblance,'" *Slavic Review* 65 (2): 294–303.

Bell, Duncan, and Srdjan Vucetic (forthcoming) "Brexit, CANZUK, and the Legacy of Empire," *British Journal of Politics and International Relations*.

Bellah, Robert N., and Hans Joas (eds.) (2012) *The Axial Age and Its Consequences*. Cambridge, MA: Harvard University Press.

Beller, Steven (2011) *A Concise History of Austria*. Cambridge University Press.

Bellich, James (2009) *Replenishing the Earth: The Settler Revolution and the Rise of the Anglo-World, 1783–1939*. Oxford University Press.

Benjamin, Craig (2018) *Empires of Ancient Eurasia: The First Silk Roads Era, 100 BCE – 250 CE*. Cambridge University Press.

Bentley, Jerry H. (1996) "Cross-Cultural Interaction and Periodization in World History," *American Historical Review* 101 (3): 749–70.

Berger, Stefan (2004) *Germany*. London: Hodder Arnold.

Berger, Stefan, and Alexei Miller (eds.) (2015) *Nationalizing Empires*. Budapest and New York: Central European University Press.

Betts, Raymond F. (2004) *Decolonization*, 2nd edition. New York: Routledge.

Bickers, Robert (ed.) (2014) *Settlers and Expatriates: Britons over the Seas*. Oxford University Press.

Blackburn, Robin (2005) "Emancipation and Empire, from Cromwell to Karl Rove," *Daedalus* 134 (2): 72–87.

Blanshard, Alastair (2009) "The Athenian Empire 478–404, 378–338." In Harrison (2009: 122–46).

Böröcz, József and Melinda Kovács (eds.) (2001) "Empire's New Clothes: Unveiling EU Enlargement," *Central Europe Review*: 1–305.

Boxer, C. R. (1969) *Four Centuries of Portuguese Expansion, 1415–1825*. Berkeley: University of California Press.

Boxer, C. R. (1977) *The Portuguese Seaborne Empire 1415–1825*. London: Hutchinson.

Boxer, C. R. (1990) *The Dutch Seaborne Empire 1600–1800*. London: Penguin Books.

Brendon, Piers (2007) *The Decline and Fall of the British Empire 1781–1997*. New York: Vintage Books.

Breuilly, John (1994) *Nationalism and the State*, 2nd edition. University of Chicago Press.

Briant, Pierre (2002) *From Cyrus to Alexander: A History of the Persian Empire*, trans. Peter D. Daniels. Winona Lake, IN: Eisenbrauns.

Bridge, Carl, and Kent Fedorowich (eds.) (2003) *The British World: Diaspora, Culture and Identity*. London: Frank Cass.

Brix, Emil, Klaus Koch, and Elizabeth Vyslonzil (eds.) (2001) *The Decline of Empires*. Vienna: Verlag für Geschichte und Politik; Munich: Oldenburg.

Brook, Timothy (2013) *The Troubled Empire: China in the Yuan and Ming Dynasties*. Cambridge, MA: Harvard University Press.

Brook, Timothy (2016) "Great States," *Journal of Asian Studies* 75 (4): 957–72.

Brown, L. Carl (ed.) (1996) *Imperial Legacy: The Ottoman Imprint on the Balkans and the Middle East*. New York: Columbia University Press.

Brubaker, Rogers (2015) *Grounds for Difference*. Cambridge, MA: Harvard University Press.

Buckner, Phillip, and R. Douglas Francis (eds.) (2005) *Rediscovering the British World*. University of Calgary Press.

Buettner, Elizabeth (2016) *Europe after Empire: Decolonization, Society, and Culture*. Cambridge University Press.

Bulmer-Thomas, Victor (2018) *Empire in Retreat: The Past, Present, and Future of the United States*. New Haven, CT: Yale University Press.

Burbank, Jane, and Frederick Cooper (2010) *Empires in World History: Power and the Politics of Difference*. Princeton University Press.

Calhoun, Craig, Frederick Cooper, and Kevin W. Moore (eds.) (2006) *Lessons of Empire: Imperial Histories and American Power*. New York: The New Press.

Camões, Luís Vaz de ([1572] 1997) *The Lusíads*, trans. with an Introduction by Landeg White. Oxford University Press.

Césaire, Aimé ([1950] (2000) *Discourse on Colonialism*, trans. Jon Pinkham. New York: Monthly Review Press.

Chamberlain, M. E. (1999) *Decolonization: The Fall of the European Empires*, 2nd edition. Malden, MA: Blackwell.

Chatterjee, Partha (1993) *The Nation and Its Fragments: Colonial and Postcolonial Histories*. Princeton University Press.

Chibber, Vivek (2004) "The Return of Imperialism to Social Science," *European Journal of Sociology* 45 (3): 427–41.

Ciccariello-Maher, George (2017) *Decolonizing Dialectics*. Durham, NC: Duke University Press.

Cipolla, Carlo M (ed.) (1970) *The Economic Decline of Empires*. London: Methuen.

Cipolla, Carlo M. (1974) *The Economic History of World Population*, 6th edition. Harmondsworth: Penguin Books.

Clarke, Peter (2008) *The Last Thousand Days of the British Empire: Churchill, Roosevelt, and the Birth of the Pax Americana*. New York: Bloomsbury Press.

Colley, Linda (1994) *Britons: Forging the Nation 1707–1837*. London: Pimlico.

Comisso, Ellen (2006) "Empires as Prisons of Nations versus Empires as Political Opportunity Structures: An Exploration of the Role of Nationalism in Imperial Dissolutions in Europe." In Esherick et al. (2006: 138–66).

Connor, Walker (1994) *Ethnonationalism: The Quest for Understanding*. Princeton University Press.

Conrad, Joseph ([1902] 1995) *Heart of Darkness*. London: Penguin Books.

Conrad, Sebastian (2012) *German Colonialism: A Short History*. Cambridge University Press.

Cooper, Frederick (2005) *Colonialism in Question: Theory, Knowledge, History*. Berkeley: University of California Press.

Crosby, Alfred (1972) *The Columbian Exchange: Biological and Cultural Consequences of 1492*. Westport, CT: Greenwood Press.

Crosby, Alfred W. (1986) *Ecological Imperialism: The Biological Expansion of Europe, 900–1900*. Cambridge University Press.

Crowley, Roger (2015) *Conquerors: How Portugal Forged the First Global Empire*. New York: Random House.

Dale, Stephen F. (2010) *The Muslim Empires of the Ottomans, Safavids, and Mughals*. Cambridge University Press.

Dalziel, Nigel (2006) *The Penguin Historical Atlas of the British Empire*. London: Penguin Books.

Dante, Alighieri ([1314] 1996) *Monarchy [De Monarchia]*, trans. and ed. Prue Shaw. Cambridge University Press.

Darwin, John (1988) *Britain and Decolonisation: The Retreat from Empire in the Post-War World*. Houndmills: Macmillan.

Darwin, John (2008) *After Tamerlane: The Rise and Fall of Global Empires, 1400–2000*. London: Penguin Books.

Darwin, John (2009) *The Empire Project: The Rise and Fall of the British World-System, 1830–1970*. Cambridge University Press.

Darwin, John (2013) "Empire and Ethnicity." In Hall and Malešević (2013: 147–71).

Davidson, Peter (2011) *Atlas of Empires*. London: New Holland Publishers.

Davies, R. R. (2000) *The First English Empire: Power and Identities in the British Isles 1093–1343*. Oxford University Press.

Dawisha, Karen, and Bruce Parrott (eds.) (1997) *The End of Empire? The Transformation of the USSR in Comparative Perspective*. Armonk, NY: M. E. Sharpe.

Delanty, Gerard, and Krishan Kumar (eds.) (2006) *The Sage Handbook of Nations and Nationalism*. London: Sage Publications.

Di Cosmo, Nicola (1998) "Qing Colonial Administration in Inner China," *The International History Review* 20 (2): 287–309.

Dias, Jill (2007) "Portugal: Empire-building in the Old World and the New." In Aldrich (2007: 68–91).

Dikötter, Frank (2015) *The Discourse of Race in Modern China*, 2nd edition. New York: Oxford University Press.

Disney, A. R. (2009) *A History of Portugal and the Portuguese Empire: From Beginnings to 1807*, 2 vols. Cambridge University Press.

Doyle, Michael W. (1986) *Empires*. Ithaca and London: Cornell University Press.

Dreyer, Edmund I. (2007) *Zheng He: China and the Oceans in the Early Ming Dynasty, 1405–1433*. New York: Pearson Longman.

Duara, Prasenjit (1995) *Rescuing History from the Nation: Questioning Narratives of Modern China*. University of Chicago Press.

Dutt, Vidya Prakash (1971) "The First Week of the Revolution: The Wuchang Uprising." In Wright (1971: 383–416).

Eade, John, Martyn Barrett, Chris Flood, and Richard Race (eds.) (2008) *Advancing Multiculturalism Post 7/7*. Newcastle, UK: Cambridge Scholars Publishing.

Eisenstadt, S. N. (ed.) (1967) *The Decline of Empires*. Englewood Cliffs, NJ: Prentice-Hall.

Eisenstadt, S. N. (ed.) (1986) *The Origins and Diversity of Axial Age Civilizations*. Albany: State University of New York Press.

Ekiert, Grzegorz, and Stephen E. Hanson (eds.) (2003) *Capitalism and Democracy in Central and Eastern Europe: Assessing the Legacy of Communist Rule*. Cambridge University Press.

Elliott, J. H (1970) *Imperial Spain 1469–1716*. London: Penguin Books.

Elliott, J. H. (1989) *Spain and Its World 1500–1700: Selected Essays*. New Haven, CT: Yale University Press.

Elliott, J. H. (1992) *The Old World and the New 1492–1650*. Cambridge University Press.

Elliott, J. H. (2007) *Empires of the Atlantic World: Britain and Spain in America, 1492–1830*. New Haven, CT: Yale University Press.

Elliott, J. H. (2016) "Portugal's Empire: Ruthless and Intermingling," *New York Review of Books* June 23: 76–80.

Elkins, Caroline (2005) *Imperial Reckoning: The Untold Story of Britain's Gulag in Kenya*. New York: Henry Holt and Company.

Elvin, Mark (1973) *The Pattern of the Chinese Past*. Stanford University Press.

Emerson, Rupert (1962) *From Empire to Nation: The Rise to Self-Assertion of Asian and African Peoples*. Boston: Beacon Press.

Emerson, Rupert (1969) "Colonialism," *Journal of Contemporary History* 4 (1): 3–16.

Esherick, Joseph W. (2006) "How the Qing Became China." In Esherick et al. (2006: 229–59).

Esherick, Joseph W., Hasan Kayali, and Eric Van Young (eds.) (2006) *Empire to Nation: Historical Perspectives on the Making of the Modern World*. Lanham, MD: Rowman and Littlefield.

Fairbank, John King, and Merle Goldman (2006) *China: A New History*, 2nd enlarged edition. Cambridge, MA: Harvard University Press.

Fanon, Frantz ([1961] 1967) *The Wretched of the Earth*, trans. Constance Farrington, preface by Jean-Paul Sartre. Harmondsworth: Penguin Books.

Farrington, Karen (2002) *Historical Atlas of Empires*. New York: Checkmark Books.

Fearon, James T. and David D. Laitin (2003) "Ethnicity, Insurgency, and Civil War," *American Political Science Review* 97 (1): 75–90.

Fedorowich, Kent, and Andrew S. Thompson (eds.) (2013) *Empire, Migration, and Identity in the British World*. Manchester University Press.

Ferguson, Niall (2004) *Empire: How Britain Made the Modern World*. London: Penguin Books.

Ferguson, Niall (2005) *Colossus: The Rise and Fall of the American Empire*. New York: Penguin Books.

Ferguson, Niall (2010) "Complexity and Collapse: Empires on the Edge of Chaos," *Foreign Affairs* March–April: 18–32.

Ferguson, Yale H., and Richard W. Mansbach (1996) *Polities: Authority, Identities, and Change.* Columbia: University of South Carolina Press.

Fieldhouse, D. K (1981) *Colonialism 1870–1945: An Introduction.* London: Weidenfeld and Nicolson.

Finley, M. I. (1976) "Colonies – An Attempt at a Typology," *Transactions of the Royal Historical Society* 5th ser., 26: 167–88.

Finley, M. I. (1978) "The Fifth-Century Athenian Empire: A Balance Sheet." In Garnsey and Whittaker (1978: 103–26).

Folz, Robert (1969) *The Concept of Empire in Western Europe, from the Fifth to the Fourteenth Century*, trans. Sheila Ann Ogilvie. London: Edward Arnold.

Foster, Russell (2015) *Mapping European Empire: Tabulae imperii Europaei.* London and New York: Routledge.

Fradera, Josep (2007) "Spain: The Genealogy of Modern Colonialism." In Aldrich (2007: 44–67).

Fradera, Josep M. (2018) *The Imperial Nation: Citizens and Subjects in the British, French, Spanish, and American Empires.* Princeton University Press.

Frank, Andre Gunder (1967) *Capitalism and Underdevelopment in Latin America.* New York: Monthly Review Press.

Frank, Andre Gunder (1998) *ReOrient: Global Economy in the Asian Age.* Berkeley: University of California Press.

Frankopan, Peter (2018) *The New Silk Roads: The Present and Future of the World.* London: Bloomsbury.

French, Howard W. (2018) *Everything Under the Heavens: How the Past Helps Shape China's Push for Global Power.* New York: Vintage Books.

Gallagher, John, and Ronald Robinson (1953) "The Imperialism of Free Trade," *Economic History Review* new ser., 6 (1): 1–15.

Garavani, Giuliano (2012) *After Empires: European Integration, Decolonization, and the Challenge from the Global South 1957–1986.* Oxford University Press.

Garnsey, P. D. A., and C. R. Whittaker (eds.) (1978) *Imperialism in the Ancient World.* Cambridge University Press.

Gellner, Ernest (1998) *Language and Solitude: Wittgenstein, Malinowski, and the Habsburg Dilemma.* Cambridge University Press.

Gellner, Ernest (2006) *Nations and Nationalism*, 2nd edition. Oxford: Blackwell Publishing.

Gibbon, Edward ([1776–88] 1995) *The History of the Decline and Fall of the Roman Empire*, 3 vols., ed. David Womersley. London: Penguin Books.

Gildea, Robert (2019) *Empires of the Mind: The Colonial Past and the Politics of the Present.* Cambridge University Press.

Gilmour, David (2018) *The British in India: Three Centuries of Ambition and Experience.* London: Allen Lane.

Gilroy, Paul (2004) *After Empire: Melancholia or Convivial Culture?* Abingdon: Routledge.

Go, Julian (2016) *Postcolonial Thought and Social Theory.* Oxford University Press.

Goldstone, Jack A. ([1991] 2016) *Revolution and Rebellion in the Early Modern World,* new edition. London and New York: Routledge.

Goldstone, Jack A. (2018) "The Once and Future Middle Kingdom: China's Return to Dominance in the World Economy," *Comparativ* 28 (4): 120–39.

Goldstone, Jack A., and John F. Haldon (2010) "Ancient States, Empires, and Exploitation." In Morris and Scheidel (2010: 3–29).

Green, William A. (1992) "Periodization in European and World History," *Journal of World History* 3 (1): 13–53.

Green, William A. (1995) "Periodizing World History," *History and Theory* 34 (2): 99–111.

Greenberg, Amy S. (2013) *A Wicked War: Polk, Clay, Lincoln and the 1846 US Invasion of Mexico.* New York: Knopf.

Greenblatt, Stephen (1992) *Marvelous Possessions: The Wonder of the New World.* Oxford University Press.

Griffiths, G. T. (1978) "Athens in the Fourth Century." In Garnsey and Whittaker (1978: 127–44).

Grob-Fitzgibbon, Benjamin (2011) *Imperial Endgame: Britain's Dirty Wars and the End of Empire.* Houndmills: Palgrave Macmillan.

Guardino, Peter (2017) *The Dead March: A History of the Mexican–American War.* Cambridge, MA: Harvard University Press.

Hall, Catherine (2005) "What Did a British World Mean to the British? Reflections on the Nineteenth Century." In Buckner and Francis (2005: 21–37).

Hall, John A. (1998) *The State of the Nation: Ernest Gellner and the Theory of Nationalism.* Cambridge University Press.

Hall, John A., and Siniša Malešević (eds.) (2013) *Nationalism and War.* Cambridge University Press.

Halperin, Sandra, and Ronen Palan (eds.) (2015) *Legacies of Empire: Imperial Roots of the Contemporary Global Order.* Cambridge University Press.

Hann, Christopher, and Paul Robert Magocsi (eds.) (2005) *Galicia: A Multicultured Land.* University of Toronto Press.

Hansen, Per, and Stefan Jonsson (2015) "Building Eurafrica: Reviving Colonialism through European Integration." In Nicolaïdis et al. (2015: 209–26).

Hardt, Michael, and Antonio Negri (2000). *Empire.* Cambridge, MA: Harvard University Press.

Harrison, Henrietta (2001) *Inventing the Nation: China.* London: Arnold.

Harrison, Thomas (ed.) (2009) *The Great Empires of the Ancient World.* Los Angeles, CA: The J. Paul Getty Museum.

Hart, Jonathan (2008) *Empires and Colonies.* Cambridge: Polity.

Haskins, Alex (2018) "Montesquieu's Paradoxical Spirit of Moderation: On the Making of Asian Despotism in *De l'esprit des lois*," *Political Theory* 46 (6): 915–37.

Haywood, John (2005) *Historical Atlas of Ancient Civilizations*. London: Penguin Books.

Hechter, Michael (1999) *Internal Colonialism: The Celtic Fringe in British National Development*, 2nd edition. New Brunswick, NJ: Transaction Books.

Heer, Friedrich (2002) *The Holy Roman Empire*, trans. Janet Sondheimer. London: Phoenix Press.

Herodotus (2003) *The Histories*, trans. Aubrey de Sélincourt. London: Penguin Books.

Hewitt, Martin (ed.) (2012) *The Victorian World*. London: Routledge.

Hiers, Wesley, and Andreas Wimmer (2013) "Is Nationalism the Cause or Consequence of the End of Empire?" In Hall and Malešević (2013: 212–54).

Hind, Robert J. (1984) "The Internal Colonial Concept," *Comparative Studies in Society and History* 26 (3): 543–68.

Hobsbawm, E. J. (1987) *The Age of Empire: 1875–1914*. London: Weidenfeld and Nicolson.

Hobsbawm, E. J. (1992) *Nations and Nationalism since 1780: Programme, Myth, Reality*, 2nd edition. Cambridge University Press.

Hobson, J. A. ([1902] 1938) *Imperialism: A Study*, 3rd edition. London: Unwin Hyman.

Hodgson, Marshall G. S. (1977) *The Venture of Islam: Conscience and History in a World Civilization*, 3 vols. University of Chicago Press.

Hoffman, Philip T. (2015) *Why Did Europe Conquer the World?* Princeton University Press.

Hofstadter, Richard (1965) "Cuba, the Philippines, and Manifest Destiny," in *The Paranoid Style in American Politics, and Other Essays*. New York: Alfred A. Knopf, pp. 145–87.

Holland, R. F. (1985) *European Decolonization 1918–1981: An Introductory Survey*. London: Macmillan.

Hopkins, A. G. (2008) "Re-thinking Decolonization," *Past and Present* 200: 211–47.

Hopkins, A. G. (2018) *American Empire: A Global History*. Princeton University Press.

Hosking, Geoffrey (2012) *Russia and the Russians: From Earliest Times to the Present*, 2nd edition. London: Penguin Books.

Hourani, Albert (1992) *A History of the Arab Peoples*. New York: Warner Books.

Howard, Michael, and W. Roger Louis (eds.) (1998) *The Oxford History of the Twentieth Century*. Oxford University Press.

Howe, Stephen (2002) *Empire: A Very Short Introduction*. Oxford University Press.

Howe, Stephen (2005) "When – If Ever – Did Empire End? Recent Studies of Imperialism and Decolonization," *Journal of Contemporary History* 40 (3): 585–99.

Hoyland, Robert G. (2017) *In God's Path: The Arab Conquests and the Creation of an Islamic Empire*. Oxford University Press.

Ignatieff, Michael (2003) *Empire Lite: Nation-Building in Bosnia, Kosovo and Afghanistan*. London: Verso.

Immerwahr, Daniel (2019) *How to Hide an Empire: A History of the Greater United States*. New York: Farrar, Straus, and Giroux.

Jansen, Jan C., and Jürgen Osterhammel (2016) *Decolonization: A Short History*, trans. Jeremiah Riemer. Princeton University Press.

Jaspers, Karl (2010) *The Origin and Goal of History*, trans. Michael Bullock. Abingdon: Routledge.

Jenner, W. J. F. (2009) "The Early Empires of China, 221 BC – AD 220." In Harrison (2009: 250–75).

Johnson, Chalmers (2004) *The Sorrows of Empire: Militarism, Secrecy, and the End of the Republic*. New York: Henry Holt.

Journal of Contemporary History (1969) Special issue, "Colonialism and Decolonization." 4 (1).

Journal of Contemporary History (1980). Special issue, "Imperial Hangovers." 15 (1).

Judson, Pieter M. (2016) *The Habsburg Empire: A New History*. Cambridge, MA: Harvard University Press.

Kamen, Henry (2003). *Empire: How Spain Became a World Power 1492–1763*. New York: Harper Perennial.

Karl, Rebecca E. (2002) *Staging the World: Chinese Nationalism at the Turn of the Twentieth Century*. Durham, NC: Duke University Press.

Kasaba, Reşat (2006) "Dreams of Empire, Dreams of Nations." In Esherick et al. (2006: 198–225).

Kaufmann, Eric P. (ed.) (2004) *Rethinking Ethnicity: Majority Groups and Dominant Minorities*. London: Routledge.

Keay, John (2004) *India: A History*. Uttar Pradesh, India: Harper Perennial.

Keay, John (2009) *China: A History*. London: Harper Press.

Kelly, Duncan (ed.) (2009) *Lineages of Empire: The Historical Roots of British Imperial Thought*. Oxford University Press.

Kemp, B. J. (1978) "Imperialism and Empire in the New Kingdom (c. 1575–1087 B.C.)." In Garnsey and Whittaker (1978: 7–57).

Kennedy, Dane (2016) *Decolonization: A Very Short Introduction*. Oxford University Press.

Kennedy, Hugh (2006) *When Baghdad Ruled the Muslim World*. Cambridge, MA: Da Capo Press.

Kennedy, Hugh (2008) *The Great Arab Conquests: How the Spread of Islam Changed the World We Live In*. Philadelphia, PA: Da Capo Press.

Kennedy, Paul (1989) *The Rise and Fall of the Great Powers: Economic Change and Military Conflict from 1500 to 2000*. London: Fontana Press.

Kermode, Frank (2000) *The Sense of an Ending: Studies in the Theory of Fiction*, new edition. Oxford University Press.

Khalid, Adeeb (2007) "The Soviet Union as an Imperial Formation." In Stoler et al. (2007: 113–39).

Kiernan, V. G. (1974) *Marxism and Imperialism*. London: Edward Arnold.

Kiernan, V. G. ([1978] 2005) *America: The New Imperialism. From White Settlement to World Hegemony*, new edition. London: Verso.

King, Desmond (2006) "When an Empire is Not an Empire: The US Case," *Government and Opposition* 41 (2): 163–96.

Koebner, Richard (1961) *Empire*. Cambridge University Press.

Koebner, Richard, and Helmut Dan Schmidt (1964) *Imperialism: The Story and Significance of a Political Word, 1840–1960*. Cambridge University Press.

Kozuchowski, Adam (2013) *The After-Life of Austria-Hungary: The Image of the Habsburg Monarchy in Interwar Europe*. Pittsburgh University Press.

Kuhrt, Amélie (2001) "The Achaemenid Persian Empire (c.550 – c.330 BCE)." In Alcock et al. (2001: 93–123).

Kumar, Krishan (2000) "Nation and Empire: English and British National Identity in Comparative Perspective," *Theory and Society* 29 (5): 578–608.

Kumar, Krishan (2003) *The Making of English National Identity*. Cambridge University Press.

Kumar, Krishan (2008) "Core Ethnicities and the Problem of Multiculturalism: The British Case," in Eade et al. (2008: 116–34).

Kumar, Krishan (2010) "Nation-States as Empires, Empires as Nation-States: Two Principles, One Practice?" *Theory and Society* 39 (2): 119–43.

Kumar, Krishan (2012) "Varieties of Nationalism." In Hewitt (2012: 160–74).

Kumar, Krishan (2015) "Once More and For the Last Time: Ernest Gellner's Later Thoughts on Nations and Empires," *Thesis Eleven* 128: 72–84.

Kumar, Krishan (2017) *Visions of Empire: How Five Imperial Regimes Shaped the World*. Princeton University Press.

Kumar, Krishan (forthcoming a) "The Legacy of Empire in East-Central Europe: Fractured Nations and Divided Loyalties," in Simon Lewis, Jeffrey K. Olick, Malgorzata Pakier, and Joanna Wawrzyniak (eds.), *Regions of Memory*. New York: Palgrave Macmillan.

Kumar, Krishan (forthcoming b) "Colony and Empire, Colonialism and Imperialism: A Meaningful Distinction?" *Comparative Studies in Society and History*.

Kwarteng, Kwasi (2012) *Ghosts of Empire: Britain's Legacies in the Modern World*. London: Bloomsbury.

Lanfranchi, Giovanni B., Michael Roaf, and Robert Rollinger (eds.) (2003) *Continuity of Empire (?): Assyria, Media, Persia*. Padova: S.a.r.g.o.n. Editrice e Libreria.

Larsen, Mogens Trolle (ed.) (1979) *Power and Propaganda: A Symposium on Ancient Empires*. Copenhagen: Akademisk Forlag.

Le Goff, Jacques (1990) *Medieval Civilization 400–1500*, trans. Julia Barrow. Oxford: Blackwell Publishers.

Le Rider, Jacques (1994) "Hugo von Hofmannsthal and the Austrian Idea of Central Europe." In Robertson and Timms (1994: 121–35).

Leigh, James (2005) "Ever Buoyant Roman Empire: Re-emerging Europe in Post-Globalization," *Globalization* 5 (1): 1–21.

Lewis, Bernard (1958) *The Arabs in History*. London: Arrow Books.

Lewis, Bernard (1962) "Ottoman Observers of Ottoman Decline," *Islamic Studies* 1: 71–87.

Lewis, Mark Edward (2007) *The Early Chinese Empires: Qin and Han*. Cambridge, MA: Harvard University Press.

Lewis, Mark Edward (2009) *China's Cosmopolitan Empire: The Tang Dynasty*. Cambridge, MA: Harvard University Press.

Liverani, Mario (1979) "The Ideology of the Assyrian Empire." In Larsen (1979: 297–317).

Livi-Bacci, Massimo (1992) *A Concise History of World Population*, trans. Carl Ipsen. Cambridge, MA: Blackwell.

Llewellyn-Jones, Lloyd (2009) "The First Persian Empire." In Harrison (2009: 98–121).

Lockhart, J. G., and C. M. Woodhouse (1963) *Cecil Rhodes: The Colossus of Southern Africa*. New York: Macmillan.

Lonsdale, John (2014) "Kenya: Home County and African Frontier." In Bickers (2014: 74–111).

Lorcin, Patricia M. E. (2013) "Imperial Nostalgia: Differences of Theory, Similarities of Practice?" *Historical Reflections / Réflexions Historiques* 39 (3): 97–111.

Lorimer, Douglas (2005) "From Victorian Values to White Virtues: Assimilation and Exclusion in British Racial Discourse, c. 1870–1914." In Buckner and Francis (2005: 109–34).

Louis, W. Roger (1998) "The European Colonial Empires." In Howard and Louis (1998: 91–102).

Louis, W. Roger, and Ronald Robinson (1994) "The Imperialism of Decolonization," *Journal of Imperial and Commonwealth History* 22 (3): 462–511.

Lowry, Donal (2014) "Rhodesia 1890–1980: 'The Lost Dominion.'" In Bickers (2014: 112–49).

Lüthy, Herbert (1961) "Colonization and the Making of Mankind," *Journal of Economic History* 21 (4): 483–95.

Macartney, C. A. ([1937] 1965) *Hungary and Her Successors: The Treaty of Trianon and Its Consequences*. London: Oxford University Press.

Maier, Charles S. (2002) "Empires or Nations? 1918, 1945, 1989 . . .," in C. Levy and M. Roseman (eds.), *Three Postwar Eras in Comparison: Western Europe 1918–1945–1989*. Houndmills, UK: Macmillan, pp. 41–66.

Maier, Charles S. (2007) *Among Empires: American Ascendancy and Its Predecessors*. Cambridge, MA: Harvard University Press.

Malešević, Siniša (2019) *Grounded Nationalisms*. Cambridge University Press.

Malešević, Siniša, and Mark Haugaard (eds.) (2007) *Ernest Gellner and Contemporary Social Thought*. Cambridge University Press.

Manela, Erez (2009) *The Wilsonian Moment: Self-Determination and the International Origins of Anti-Colonial Nationalism*. New York: Oxford University Press.

Manley, Bill (2009) "The Empire of the New Kingdom." In Harrison (2009: 18–43).

Mann, Michael (1986) *The Sources of Social Power*, Vol. I: *A History of Power from the Beginning to A. D. 1760*. Cambridge University Press.

Mann, Michael (2003) *Incoherent Empire*. London: Verso.

Mann, Michael (2005) *The Dark Side of Democracy: Explaining Ethnic Cleansing*. Cambridge University Press.

Mann, Michael (2008) "American Empires: Past and Present," *CRSA/RCSA* 45 (1): 7–50.

Marx, Karl, and Friedrich Engels (1963) *The German Ideology*, Parts I and III, ed. R. Pascal. New York: International Publishers.

Marx, Karl, and Friedrich Engels ([1848] 1977) "The Communist Manifesto," in David McLellan (ed.) *Karl Marx: Selected Writings*. Oxford University Press, pp. 221–47.

Mazower, Mark (2009a) *No Enchanted Palace: The End of Empire and the Ideological Origins of the United Nations*. Princeton University Press.

Mazower, Mark (2009b) *Hitler's Empire: Nazi Rule in Occupied Europe*. London: Penguin Books.

Mazower, Mark (2013) *Governing the World: The History of an Idea*. London: Penguin Books.

McCoy, Alfred W., and Francisco Scarano (eds.) (2009) *Colonial Crucible: Empire in the Making of the Modern American State*. Madison: University of Wisconsin Press.

McCoy, Alfred W., Josep M. Fradera, and Stephen Jacobson (eds.) (2012) *Endless Empire: Spain's Retreat, Europe's Eclipse, America's Decline*. Madison: University of Wisconsin Press.

McNeill, William H. (1991) *The Rise of the West: A History of the Human Community, with a Retrospective Essay*. University of Chicago Press.

McPherson, James M. (2013) "America's 'Wicked War,'" *New York Review of Books* February 7: 32–3.

Mieroop, Marc van de (2009) "The Empires of Assyria and Babylonia 900–539 BC." In Harrison (2009: 70–97).

Miller, Alexei, and Alfred J. Rieber (eds.) (2004) *Imperial Rule*. Budapest and New York: Central European University Press.

Miller, Tom (2017) *China's Asian Dream: Empire Building along the New Silk Road*. London: Zed Books.

Miller-Melamed, Paul, and Claire Moreton (2019) "What the Habsburg Empire Got Right," *New York Times* September 10: A 19.

Millward, James A. (2019) "What Xi Jinping Hasn't Learned from China's Emperors," *New York Times* October 1: A16.

Min, Tu-Ki (1989) *National Polity and Local Power: The Transformation of*

Late Imperial China, ed. Philip A. Kuhn and Timothy Brook. Cambridge, MA: Harvard University Press.

Modi, Narendra (2019) "Why India and the World Need Gandhi," *New York Times* October 2: A 14.

Modood, Tariq (2019) *Essays on Secularism and Multiculturalism*. London and New York: Rowman and Littlefield.

Mommsen, Wolfgang J. (1982) *Theories of Imperialism*, trans. P. S. Falla. University of Chicago Press.

Mommsen, Wolfgang J., and Jürgen Osterhammel (eds.) (1986) *Imperialism and After: Continuities and Discontinuities*. London: Allen and Unwin.

Montaigne, Michel de ([1580] 1958) *Essays*, trans. J. M. Cohen. London: Penguin Books.

Montesquieu, Baron de ([1748] 1962). *The Spirit of the Laws*, 2 vols., trans. Thomas Nugent. New York: Hafner Publishing Company.

Moore-Gilbert, Bart (1997) *Postcolonial Theory: Contexts, Practices, Politics*. London: Verso.

Morkot, Robert (1996) *The Penguin Historical Atlas of Ancient Greece*. London: Penguin Books.

Morkot, Robert (2001) "Egypt and Nubia." In Alcock et al. (2001: 227–51).

Morris, Ian (2010) "The Greater Athenian State." In Morris amd Scheidel (2010: 99–177).

Morris, Ian, and Walter Scheidel (eds.) (2010) *The Dynamics of Ancient Empires: State Power from Assyria to Byzantium*. Oxford University Press.

Morrison, Alexander (2015) "The Russian Empire and the Soviet Union: Too Soon to Talk of Echoes?" In Nicolaïdis et al. (2015: 155–73).

Moses, A. Dirk (ed.) (2010) *Empire, Colony, Genocide: Conquest, Occupation, and Subaltern Resistance in World History*. New York and Oxford: Berghahn Books.

Mote, Frederick W. (1989) *Intellectual Foundations of China*, 2nd edition. New York: McGraw-Hill.

Mote, F. W. (2003) *Imperial China 900–1800*. Cambridge, MA: Harvard University Press.

Motyl, Alexander J. (1999) *Revolutions, Nations, Empires: Conceptual Limits and Theoretical Possibilities*. New York: Columbia University Press.

Motyl, Alexander J. (2001) *Imperial Ends: The Decay, Collapse, and Revival of Empires*. New York: Columbia University Press.

Mukhia, Harbans (2004) *The Mughals of India*. Oxford: Blackwell.

Muldoon, James (1999) *Empire and Order: The Concept of Empire, 800–1800*. Houndmills: Macmillan.

Münkler, Herfried (2007) *Empires: The Logic of World Domination from Ancient Rome to the United States*, trans. Patrick Camiller. Cambridge: Polity.

Murphy, Philip (2018) *The Empire's New Clothes: The Myth of the Commonwealth*. London: Hurst.

Naipaul, V. S. ([1967] 1985) *The Mimic Men*. New York: Vintage.

Neuberger, Benjamin (2006) "African Nationalism." In Delanty and Kumar (2006: 513–26).

Neumann, Iver B., and Einar Wigen (2015) "The Legacy of Eurasian Nomadic Empires: Remnants of the Mongol Imperial Tradition." In Halperin and Palan (2015: 99–127).

Newitt, Malyn (2005) A History of Portuguese Overseas Expansion, 1400–1668. London: Routledge.

Nicolaïdis, Kalypso, Berny Sèbe, and Gabrielle Maas (eds.) (2015) Echoes of Empire: Memory, Identity and Colonial Legacies. London and New York: I. B. Tauris.

Nietzsche, Friedrich (1956) The Birth of Tragedy and The Genealogy of Morals, trans. Francis Golfing. New York: Doubleday.

Nkrumah, Kwame (1965) Neo-Colonialism: The Last Stage of Imperialism. London: Nelson.

Onar, Nora Fisher (2015) "Between Memory, History and Historiography: Contesting Ottoman Legacies in Turkey, 1923–2012." In Nicolaïdis et al. (2015: 141–54).

Osterhammel, Jürgen (2005) Colonialism: A Theoretical Overview, 2nd edition, trans. from the German by Shelley L. Frisch. Princeton, NJ: Markus Wiener Publishers.

Osterhammel, Jürgen (2014) The Transformation of the World: A Global History of the Nineteenth Century, trans. Patrick Camiller. Princeton University Press.

Owen, Roger, and Bob Sutcliffe (eds.) (1972) Studies in the Theory of Imperialism. London: Longman.

Pagden, Anthony (1993) European Encounters with the New World. New Haven, CT: Yale University Press.

Pagden, Anthony (1995) Lords of All the World: Ideologies of Empire in Spain, Britain and France, c. 1500 – c. 1800. New Haven, CT: Yale University Press.

Pálffy, Géza (2001) "The Impact of Ottoman Rule on Hungary," Hungarian Studies Review 28 (1–2): 109–32.

Parker, Geoffrey (2013) Global Crisis: War, Climate Change, and Catastrophe in the Seventeenth Century. New Haven, CT: Yale University Press.

Parry, J. H. (1990) The Spanish Seaborne Empire. Berkeley: University of California Press.

Parsons, Timothy H. (2010) The Rule of Empires: Those Who Built Them, Those Who Endured Them, and Why They Always Fall. Oxford University Press.

Pedersen, Susan (2015) The Guardians: The League of Nations and the Crisis of Empire. Oxford University Press.

Perdue, Peter C. (2005) China Marches West: The Qing Conquest of Central Eurasia. Cambridge, MA: Harvard University Press.

Perdue, Peter C. (2007) "Erasing the Empire, Re-racing the Nation: Racialism and Culturalism in Imperial China." In Stoler et al. (2007: 141–69).

Pitts, Jennifer (2018) *Boundaries of the International: Law and Empire.* Cambridge, MA: Harvard University Press.

Pollock, Sheldon (2004) "Axialism and Empire." In Arnason et al. (2004: 397–450).

Pomeranz, Kenneth (2000) *The Great Divergence: China, Europe, and the Making of the Modern World Economy.* Princeton University Press.

Ponzanesi, Sandra, and Gianmaria Colpani (eds.) (2016). *Postcolonial Transitions in Europe: Contexts, Practices and Politics.* London: Rowman and Littlefield.

Porter, Bernard (2004a) *The Lion's Share: A Short History of British Imperialism 1850–2004*, 4th edition. Harlow: Pearson-Longman.

Porter, Bernard (2004b) *The Absent-Minded Imperialists: Empire, Society, and Culture in Britain.* Oxford University Press.

Quinn, Frederick (2002) *The French Overseas Empire.* London and Westport, CT: Praeger.

Quinn, Josephine (2017) *In Search of the Phoenicians.* Princeton University Press.

Renan, Ernest ([1882] 2001) "What is a Nation?" In Vincent P. Pecora (ed.), *Nations and Identities: Classic Readings.* Malden, MA: Blackwell, pp. 162–76.

Reynolds, Michael A. (2011) *Shattering Empires: The Clash and Collapse of the Ottoman and Russian Empires 1908–1918.* Cambridge University Press.

Rich, Paul B. (1990) *Race and Empire in British Politics*, 2nd edition. Cambridge University Press.

Robertson, Richie, and Edward Timms (eds.) (1994) *The Habsburg Legacy: National Identity in Historical Legacy.* Edinburgh University Press.

Robinson, Francis (2007) *The Mughal Emperors, and the Islamic Dynasties of India, Iran and Central Asia, 1206–1925.* London: Thames and Hudson.

Robinson, Ronald (1972) "Non-European Foundations of European Imperialism: Sketch for a Theory of Collaboration." In Owen and Sutcliffe (1972: 117–42).

Robinson, Ronald (1986) "The Excentric Idea of Imperialism, With or Without Empire." In Mommsen and Osterhammel (1986: 267–89).

Rochfort, Desmond (1998) *Mexican Muralists: Orozco, Rivera, Siqueiros.* San Francisco, CA: Chronicle Books.

Roshwald, Aviel (2001) *Ethnic Nationalism and the Fall of Empires: Central Europe, Russia and the Middle East, 1914–1923.* London and New York: Routledge.

Rothermund, Dietmar (2006) *The Routledge Companion to Decolonization.* London and New York: Routledge.

Rothermund, Dietmar (2013) *Empires in Indian History and Other Essays.* New Delhi: Manohar Publishers.

Rothermund, Dietmar (ed.) (2015) *Memories of Post-Imperial Nations: The*

Aftermath of Decolonization, 1945–2013. Delhi: Cambridge University Press.

Rowe, William T. (2012). *China's Last Empire: The Great Qing.* Cambridge, MA: Harvard University Press.

Rusinow, Dennison (1996) "The Ottoman Legacy in Yugoslavia's Disintegration and Civil War." In Brown (1996: 79–99).

Said, Edward W. (1979) *Orientalism.* New York: Vintage Books.

Said, Edward W. (1994) *Culture and Imperialism.* London: Vintage.

Saverese, Eric (2015) "The Post-colonial Encounter in France." In Rothermund (2015: 76–96).

Scarisbrick, J. J. (1970) *Henry VIII.* Berkeley: University of California Press.

Schiffrin, Harold Z. (1971) "The Enigma of Sun Yat-Sen." In Wright (1971: 443–74).

Schimmel, Annemarie (2004) *The Empire of the Great Mughals: History, Art and Culture,* trans. Corinne Attwood. London: Reaktion Books.

Schivelbusch, Wolfgang (2004) *The Culture of Defeat: On National Trauma, Mourning, and Recovery,* trans. Jefferson Chase. London: Granta Books.

Schumpeter, Joseph ([1919] 1974) "The Sociology of Imperialisms," in *Imperialism and Social Classes: Two Essays,* trans. H. Norden. New York: Meridian Books, pp. 3–98.

Schwartz, Benjamin I. (1985) *The World of Thought in Ancient China.* Cambridge, MA: Harvard University Press.

Schwarz, Bill (2013) *Memories of Empire,* Vol. I: *The White Man's World* (Oxford University Press).

Schwarz, Vera (1984) *The Chinese Enlightenment: Intellectuals and the Legacy of the May Fourth Movement of 1919.* Berkeley: University of California Press.

Seeley, J. R. ([1883] 1971) *The Expansion of England.* University of Chicago Press.

Sengupta, Indra (2013) "Monument Preservation and the Vexing Question of Religious Structures in Colonial India." In Swenson and Mandler (2013: 171–85).

Shawcross, Teresa (2016) "At Empire's End: Theories of Decline from Metochites to Ibn Khaldun." Paper given at the Shelby Cullom Davis Center for Historical Studies, Princeton University, February 12.

Shipway, Martin (2008) *Decolonization and Its Impact: A Comparative Approach to the End of the Colonial Empires.* Oxford: Blackwell.

Smith, Adam ([1776] 1910) *The Wealth of Nations,* 2 vols., ed. Edwin R. A. Seligman. London: J. M. Dent and Sons Ltd.

Smith, Anthony D. (1986) *The Ethnic Origins of Nations.* Oxford: Basil Blackwell.

Smith, Anthony D. (2003) *Chosen Peoples: Sacred Sources of National Identity.* Oxford University Press.

Snyder, Timothy (2003) *The Reconstruction of Nations: Poland, Ukraine, Lithuania, Belarus, 1569–1999.* New Haven, CT: Yale University Press.

Snyder, Timothy (2010) *Bloodlands: Europe Between Hitler and Stalin*. New York: Basic Books.

Spence, Jonathan D. (2013) *The Search for Modern China*, 3rd edition. New York: W. W. Norton and Company.

Spruyt, Hendrik (2001) "Empires and Imperialism." In Alexander J. Motyl (ed.), *Encyclopedia of Nationalism*, 2 vols. San Diego, CA: Academic Press, Vol. I: 237–49.

Spruyt, Hendrik (2005) *Ending Empire: Contested Sovereignty and Territorial Partition*. Ithaca, NY: Cornell University Press.

Stearns, Peter N., Michael Adas, Stuart B. Schwartz, and Marc Jason Gilbert (2015) *World Civilizations: The Global Experience*, 7th edition. Upper Saddle River, NJ: Pearson Education.

Steinmetz, George (2005) "Return to Empire: The New U. S. Imperialism in Comparative Historical Perspective," *Sociological Theory* 23 (4): 339–67.

Stoler, Ann Laura, Carole McGranahan, and Peter C. Perdue (eds.) (2007) *Imperial Formations*. Sante Fe, NM: School for Advanced Research Press.

Strang, David (1991) "Global Patterns of Decolonization, 1500–1987," *International Studies Quarterly* 35 (4): 429–54.

Streets-Salter, Heather, and Trevor R. Getz (2016) *Empires and Colonies in the Modern World*. Oxford University Press.

Suskind, Ron (2004) "Without a Doubt," *New York Times Magazine* October 17: 42–51.

Swenson, Astrid (2013) "The Heritage of Empire." In Swenson and Mandler 2013: 3–28.

Swenson, Astrid, and Peter Mandler (eds.) (2013) *From Plunder to Preservation: Britain and the Heritage of Empire c. 1800–1940*. Oxford University Press.

Taylor, Alan (2016) *American Revolutions: A Continental History, 1750–1804*. New York: Norton.

Ther, Philipp (2004) "Imperial instead of National History: Positioning Modern German History on the Map of European Empires." In Miller and Rieber (2004: 47–66).

Thesis Eleven (2016) "Nations on the Edge: Special Section on Ukraine," no. 136: 49–106.

Thomas, Martin, Bob Moore, and L. J. Butler (2015) *Crises of Empire: Decolonization and Europe's Imperial States*, 2nd edition. London: Bloomsbury.

Thompson, Andrew (ed.) (2012) *Britain's Experience of Empire in the Twentieth Century*. Oxford University Press.

Thompson, Andrew S. (ed.) (2014) *Writing Imperial Histories*. Manchester University Press.

Thompson, J. K. J. (1998). *Decline in History: The European Experience*. Cambridge: Polity.

Todorov, Tzvetan (1992) *The Conquest of America: The Question of the Other*, trans. Richard Howard. New York: HarperPerennial.

Todorova, Maria (1996) "The Ottoman Legacy in the Balkans." In Brown (1996: 45–77).
Tully, James (2009) "Lineages of Contemporary Imperialism." In Kelly (2009: 3–29).
Turner, Frederick Jackson ([1920] 1962) *The Frontier in American History*. New York: Holt, Rinehart, and Winston.
Ullmann, Walter (1979) "'This Realm of England is an Empire,'" *Journal of Ecclesiastical History* 30 (2): 175–203.
Uribe-Uran, Victor (2006) "The Great Transformation of Law and Legal Culture: 'The Public' and 'The Private' in the Transition from Empire to Nation in Mexico, Colombia, and Brazil, 1750–1850." In Esherick et al. (2006: 68–105).
Valluvan, Sivamohan (2019) *The Clamour of Nationalism: Race and Nation in Twenty-First-Century Britain*. Manchester University Press.
Van Young, Eric (2006) "The Limits of Atlantic-World Nationalism in a Revolutionary Age: Imagined Communities and Lived Communities in Mexico, 1810–1821." In Esherick et al. (2006: 35–67).
Voegelin, Eric (1962) "World-Empire and the Unity of Mankind," *International Affairs* 38 (2): 170–88.
Walker, Edward W. (2006) "The Long Road from Empire: Legacies of Nation Building in the Soviet Successor States." In Esherick et al. (2006: 299–339).
Wang Hui (2014) *China from Empire to Nation-State*, trans. Michael Gibbs Hill. Cambridge, MA: Harvard University Press.
Ward, Stuart (ed.) (2001) *British Culture and the End of Empire*. Manchester University Press.
Ward, Stuart (2016) "The European Provenance of Decolonization," *Past and Present* 230 (1): 227–60.
Washbrook, David (2014) "Avatars of Identity: The British Community in India." In Bickers (2014: 178–204).
Weber, Eugen (1976) *Peasants into Frenchmen: The Modernization of Rural France, 1870–1914*. Stanford University Press.
Weber, Max (1978) *Economy and Society*, 2 vols., ed. Guenther Roth and Claus Wittich. Berkeley: University of California Press.
Weeks, Theodore R. (2001) "Russification and the Lithuanians, 1863–1905," *Slavic Review* 60 (1): 96–114.
Weitz, Eric D. (2019) *A World Divided: The Global Struggle for Human Rights in the Age of Nation-States*. Princeton University Press.
Wesseling, H. L. (1980) "Post-Imperial Holland," *Journal of Contemporary History* 15 (1): 125–42.
Wheatcroft, Andrew (1996) *The Habsburgs: Embodying Empire*. London: Penguin Books.
Whittaker, C. R. (1978) "Carthaginian Imperialism in the Fifth and Fourth Centuries." In Garnsey and Whittaker (1978: 59–90).
Wiesehöfer, Josef (2003) "The Medes and the Idea of the Succession of Empires in Antiquity." In Lanfranchi et al. (2003: 391–6).

Wiesehöfer, Josef (2010) "The Achaemenid Empire." In Morris and Scheidel (2010: 66–98).

Wilkinson, Endymion (2012) *Chinese History: A New Manual*. Cambridge, MA: Harvard University Press.

Williams, William Appleman (1969) *The Roots of the Modern American Empire*. New York: Random House.

Wilson, Peter H. (2016) *Heart of Europe: A History of the Holy Roman Empire*. Cambridge, MA: Harvard University Press.

Wolfe, Patrick (2006) "Settler Colonialism and the Elimination of the Native," *Journal of Genocide Research* 8 (4): 387–409.

Wright, Mary Clabaugh (ed.) (1971) *China in Revolution: The First Phase, 1900–1913*. New Haven, CT: Yale University Press.

Young, Crawford (2001) "Nationalism and Ethnic Conflict in Africa," in Montserrat Guibernau and John Hutchinson (eds.), *Understanding Nationalism*. Cambridge: Polity, pp. 164–81.

Young, Ernest P. (1971) "Yuan Shih-k'ai's Rise to the Presidency." In Wright (1971: 419–42).

Young, Robert J. C. (2001) *Postcolonialism: An Historical Introduction*. Oxford: Blackwell.

Young, Robert J. C. (2015) *Empire, Colony, Postcolony*. Malden, MA, and Oxford: Wiley-Blackwell.

Zhao, Dingxin (2015) *The Confucian-Legalist State: A New Theory of Chinese History*. Oxford University Press.

Zhao, Gang (2006) "Reinventing China: Imperial Qing Ideology and the Rise of Modern Chinese National Identity in the Early Twentieth Century," *Modern China* 32 (1): 3–30.

Zielonka, Jan (2007) *Europe as Empire: The Nature of the Enlarged European Union*. Oxford University Press.

Index